Rudolf Hess : The Uninvited Envoy

BY JAMES LEASOR

The Plague and the Fire

Rudolf Hess as a First World War pilot.

JAMES LEASOR

Rudolf Hess

THE UNINVITED ENVOY

Learn, my son, with how
little wisdom the world is governed.
Pope Julius III (1487–1555)

London
GEORGE ALLEN & UNWIN LTD
RUSKIN HOUSE MUSEUM STREET

PRINTED IN GREAT BRITAIN
in 11 on 12 point Ehrhardt type
BY WESTERN PRINTING SERVICES LTD., BRISTOL

ACKNOWLEDGEMENTS

I would like to give grateful acknowledgement to the many people who helped me with the preparation of this book. In particular, I would like to record my debt of gratitude to the following, who were kind enough to make available to me their recollections and impressions of this episode in history.

When several conflicting accounts have been given of some incident, I have endeavoured to strike a mean between them. Any errors are my own.

J.L.

Mr Basil Baird
Mr William Burgess
Mr A. Coles
Mr Richard Collier
Mr William Craig
Dr Henry Victor Dicks
Mr Harry Dinning
Sir Patrick J. Dollan
Dr J. Gibson Graham
Mr A. W. Gittens
Mr J. Harding
Heinz Haushofer
Frau Ilse Hess
Herr Wolf Rudiger Hess
Dr Rainer Hildebrandt
Mr C. Hill
Mr Tom Hyslop
His Grace, The Duke of Hamilton
Dr D. Ellis Jones
Sir Ivone Kirkpatrick

Mr Max McAuslane
Mr David McLean
Mr J. L. McCowen
Mr Matthew Miller
Mr C. H. Mitchell
Mr H. S. Nadin
Mr Douglas Percival
Dr N. R. Phillips
Herr Karlheinz Pintsch
Mr Matthew Plender
Mr J. R. Raine
Dr J. R. Rees
Mr James H. Ronald
Colonel A. Malcolm Scott
Dr Alfred Seidl
Mr J. J. Shephard
Mr John Simpson
Herr Helmut Sündermann
Dr Maurice N. Walsh
Mr Stephen Watts

I am indebted to Mr Richard Wiener for translating many German documents and letters, and to Mrs Joan St George Saunders for undertaking much of the research.

The following is a list of the principal published sources of this story. My thanks are due to The Britons Publishing Company for allowing me to quote from *Prisoner of Peace*.

To Dr J. R. Rees, William Heinemann Limited and David Higham Associates Limited for permission to quote from *The Case of Rudolf Hess*.

To Cassell & Company Limited for permission to quote from *The Second World War* by Sir Winston S. Churchill.

To Mr Willi Frischauer to quote from *The Rise and Fall of Hermann Goering*.

5

ACKNOWLEDGEMENTS

To Sir Ivone Kirkpatrick and David Higham Associates Limited for permission to quote from *Inner Circle*, published by MacMillan.

To Stephen Watts and *The New Yorker* for permission to quote from his article 'The Ageing Parachutist'. It first appeared in *The New Yorker* on February 16, 1957.

I am also indebted to Her Majesty's Stationery Office for permission to publish certain papers which first appeared in *Documents on German Foreign Policy, 1918–1945*, Series D, Vol. XI, *The War Years*, September 1, 1940–January 31, 1941, published by H.M.S.O.

Jack Fishman, *The Seven Men of Spandau* (Rinehart & Co. Inc., New York).

Winston S. Churchill, *The Grand Alliance* (Cassell & Co. Ltd).

The Ribbentrop Memoirs. Introduction by Alan Bullock (Weidenfeld and Nicolson).

Ilse Hess, *Gefangener des Friedens* (Druffel-Verlag).

Hans Baur, *Hitler's Pilot* (Frederick Muller Ltd).

Otto Dietrich, *The Hitler I Knew*. Translated by Richard and Clara Winston (Methuen & Co. Ltd).

Carl Haensel, *Das Gericht vertagt sich* (Claasen Verlag).

Dr Alfred Seidl, *Die Beziehungen Zwischen Deutschland und der Sowjetunion. 1939–1941* (H. Lapp' sche Buchhandlung/Tubingen).

Alan Bullock, *Hitler. A Study in Tyranny* (Odhams Press Ltd).

Richard Collier, *The City that Wouldn't Die* (Collins).

Dr Rütger Essen, *Sven Hedin* (Druffel-Verlag, Germany).

Documents on German Foreign Policy, 1918–1945, Series D, vols. I–IV (H.M.S.O., London, 1949–1951).

Documents on British Foreign Policy 1919–1939, 3rd Series, vols. I–IV (H.M.S.O., London, 1949–1950).

Ciano's Diplomatic Papers, edited by Malcolm Muggeridge (Odhams, London, 1948).

Documents and Materials Relating to the Eve of the Second World War, Vol. I, *November, 1937–1938*; Vol. II, *The Dirksen Papers, 1938–1939* (Foreign Languages Publishing House, Moscow, 1948).

Documents on the Events preceding the Outbreak of War. The Second German White Book (German Library of Information, New York, 1940).

Dino Alfieri, *Deux Dictateurs Face a Face, Rome–Berlin 1939–1943* (Cheval Aile, Geneva, 1948).

Ciano's Diary, 1937–1938 (Methuen, London, 1952).

Ciano's Diary, 1939–1943 (Heinemann, London, 1947).

Herbert von Dirksen, *Moskau–Tokio–London* (Kohlhammer Verlag, Stuttgart, 1949).

The Goebbels Diaries, edited by Louis P. Lochner (Hamish Hamilton, London, 1949).

General Franz Halder, *Hitler as Warlord* (Putnam, London, 1950).

ACKNOWLEDGEMENTS

Sir Nevile Henderson, *Failure of a Mission* (Hodder and Stoughton, London, 1940).

Peter Kleist, *Zwischen Hitler und Stalin, 1939–1945* (Athenaum-Verlag, Bonn, 1950).

Benito Mussolini, *Memoirs, 1942–1943*, edited by R. Klibanksy (Weidenfeld and Nicolson, London, 1949).

G. Ward Price, *I Know These Dictators* (Harrap, London, 1937).

Otto Remer, *20 Juli, 1944* (Verlag Deutsche Opposition, Hamburg, 1951).

Paul Schmidt, *Statist auf diplomatischer Buhne 1923–1945* (Athenaum-Verlag, Bonn, 1949).

Joachim Schultz, *Die Letzten 30 Tage—Aus dem Kriegstagebuch des O.K.W.* (Steingruben Verlag, Stuttgart, 1951).

William Shirer, *A Berlin Diary* (Hamish Hamilton, London, 1941).

General Hans Speidel, *We Defended Normandy* (Herbert Jenkins, London, 1951).

Jean Francois, *L'Affaire Rohm-Hitler*, second edition (Gallimard, Paris, 1939).

Lindley Fraser, *Germany Between Two Wars* (Oxford University Press, 1944).

Arthur Rosenberg, *History of the German Republic* (Methuen, London, 1936).

Heinz A. Heinz, *Germany's Hitler* (Hurst and Blackett, London, 1934).

Willi Frischauer, *The Rise and Fall of Hermann Goering* (Odhams, London, 1951).

My New Order (Hitler's Speeches, 1922–1943), edited by Gordon W. Prange (American Council of Foreign Affairs, Washington, 1944).

CONTENTS

ILLUSTRATIONS

CHAPTER ONE

A Plane Crash in Scotland

'One A/C, no IF,' announced the WAAF radar operator to the plotting room in Inverness, reporting the passage overhead of one unidentified aircraft, as the single plane flew in from the east through the late evening mist above the North Sea. As it crossed the Scottish coast, near Berwick-upon-Tweed, men of the Observer Corps in their sand-bagged look-out posts reached first for night glasses and binoculars, and then for the telephone.

'A ME 110, flying at 180 miles an hour, due west,' they said, recognizing its two engines, the blunt wing-tips, the distinctive rudders at the tail.

'Take more water with it,' retorted the RAF officer sceptically at the other end of the line. He knew that no ordinary aeroplane of this type could fly so far from Germany and carry enough fuel to return. But this was no ordinary aeroplane; and it never would return.

It flew like a dark arrow on its strange and secret mission. Beneath the black crosses on its silver wings the coastline lay as quiet and peaceful as the waveless sea, in sharp contrast to the inferno raging around London, 350 miles to the south. There, throughout that Saturday night of May 10, 1941, bombs burned away 700 acres within hours—one and a half times as much as the Great Fire of London had taken weeks to destroy 275 years earlier. It was easily the war's worst raid on the capital. Despite this, within a decade the damage would be almost forgotten, yet the controversy surrounding this lonely aeroplane and the dedicated man who flew it would still burn on as fiercely as the flames that licked London on that summer night.

In its cockpit, cold and cramped after five hours' flying, despite his fur-lined leather overalls, the pilot flew with plans of peace; plans that could not only change the world but also mould the future of nations and millions yet unborn.

He was Rudolf Hess, Germany's Deputy Führer, Leader of the

Nazi Party, Reichsminister without Portfolio, a member of Germany's Secret Cabinet Council, and of the Ministerial Council for his country's defence.

This man, above all others, had stood closest to Hitler for more than twenty years; frequently he voiced his leader's secret thoughts, always he knew his master's mind.

In the First World War, he had flown flimsy biplanes, raced light-weight aircraft in the years since then—even prepared to make a solo Atlantic flight after Lindbergh. Now he flew alone in an unarmed aeroplane, through a night of fire and ruin, on the most dangerous flight of his life.

He brought plans to end the war—and yet to extend it. His proposal was a riddle, an enigma that has ever since puzzled and perplexed the handful who knew of it; a conundrum with a fearful answer. Should his mission succeed, Russia would become a nation subject to Germany. Krushchev would have stayed unknown as a world statesman. He would be regarded as a competent fitter at the engineering plants and coal mines of Donbas; a Communist worker of local standing and reputation, a one-time locksmith who never found the key to world prestige. Mao Tse-Tung would have remained a Chinese officer who, according to his superiors, 'fought well' against the Japanese.

The Iron Curtain, as it now is, would not exist. Nor would many new nations which have found release from imperial rule or associations through the direct or indirect help and pressure of the Communists. The dreams of Nehru, Nkrumah, Soekarno, and a dozen others of becoming world statesmen and leaders of republics would still have been but dreams and nothing more.

Germany, instead of being split in two, would have become so swollen with power that no other nation in the world could face her on equal terms. In many countries Nazi gauleiters and German ambassadors and business men would wield political, economic and military jurisdiction. Britain might still control a vast Empire seemingly untouched by time and uncorroded by nationalism, but that would only be the outward view. The cancer of corruption would have eaten away the sinews of Britain's Imperial glory. Her apparent power would be dependent on Nazi favour.

But despite this, many in Britain on that Saturday night so long ago would still have welcomed the peace that Hess believed he could bring them as his silver aeroplane flew in from the sea across the patchwork fields. It would have meant an end to war; and to many at that time, rationed, bombed and alone, this seemed enough to ask. The future could look after itself.

Cold and stiff, the dim roar of the engines filtering through his leather flying-helmet, Hess glanced down at his dashboard compass. He had to turn sharply to the west from Holy Island lighthouse to maintain his route. Two compasses strapped to his thighs were evidence of his determination not to veer off course.

But still he stayed firmly on his line. Not bad for a man of forty-eight, he thought with pride. Still, accuracy in such a matter was only to be expected; it was what he demanded from others. As probably the second most powerful man in the world, he did not tolerate fools or errors; his life and Hitler's had touched at too many points for too long.

Hess was probably the only Nazi who called Hitler by the intimate 'du' instead of the formal, more respectful 'sie'; they had been friends for more than twenty years. When they had been imprisoned together in Landsberg fortress, in the early nineteen twenties, for instance, Hitler typed out *Mein Kampf* slowly with two fingers on the prison governor's machine; Hess had added his views and corrected both the Führer's proofs and his spelling. In the years since then Hess had seen his personal star and that of the Nazi party soar to heights of power unimaginable at that time.

Behind him as he flew, the historic capitals of Europe—Berlin, Paris, Prague, Vienna, Oslo—lay in eclipse under German domination. Of all the proud and ancient states of Europe, only Switzerland, Sweden and Portugal stood neutral and uncommitted. Armies, nations, empires had fallen before the unprecedented, apparently unconquerable might of Germany, until now only one small, proud island kingdom remained.

Through his cockpit windshield, Hess could see the white waves beating along an empty coast that looked as rocky and uncompromising as its people.

Of course, Britain *would* be beaten; surely Churchill must realize this despite his brave words? But if only these stubborn creatures in their grey little island, even now drawing their blackout curtains in their pygmy semi-detached villas—if only *they* could also be made to see the obvious! Why, Britain and Germany had more in common with each other than any other two countries; even the British Royal Family had kept their German surname until 1917.

Further fighting was clearly without need or reason, and peace could at once be theirs—for a price. To persuade the British to pay

13

this price was Hess's firm intention and the object of his journey. Was it possible for Hess to persuade Churchill and the War Cabinet that he came in faith and friendship? Could he persuade Churchill, the last antagonist, to come to terms—Germany's terms, Hitler's terms?

These thoughts hammered in his head; his face, naturally serious and saturnine, with deep-set eyes under heavy black brows, was now etched with lines of concentration.

Of course, he was really too old to make such a flight alone; there were so many instruments to watch, so many controls to know. Actions that had been half automatic when one was young became more difficult to remember in middle life. And it would be unthinkable now to miss his way and come down in the sea out of fuel after all his plans and months of careful preparations.

In addition to his three compasses, Hess had strapped a map of his course in a cellophane-covered case to his right thigh; radio guidance signals were also helping him. One was a Luftwaffe direction signal from Paris; the other, dance music being specially transmitted as an interval signal from Kalundborg, a Danish radio station under German control. By maintaining both these signals at a consistent strength throughout his flight, Hess could keep his plane on course and make allowances for drift and wind.

With these aids, plus the view of the British coast, along which he flew so closely that when he descended he could see waves breaking on deserted beaches littered with anti-invasion blocks of concrete, coils of wire and rusting wrecks of cars, Hess felt confident he would reach his destination.

As a final check, he had received a weather report from Goering's Air Ministry in Berlin earlier during the day. This report now caused him some anxiety, for it did not seem to be accurate. Hess feathered his propellers, and looked down at the desolate emptiness of sky and sea. A few small clouds far below him looked like thin strips of ice, remote and ethereal. Instead of this, he had expected to find what the weather report called 'a dense carpet of cloud at about 500 metres'.

For a moment he thought of turning back, for it seemed impossible that with so little cloud cover he could escape the fighter patrols almost certainly prowling on the alert for German aircraft. It was easy to imagine the bristling muzzles of unseen anti-aircraft guns, taking his range. But if he flew back, he reasoned, even if he saved himself, his aeroplane would probably be damaged beyond repair in his attempt at an unexpected night landing. Then, nothing would be secret, and if his mission were to have any hope of success, it must be conducted with speed and absolute secrecy.

It was for these imperative reasons that he was not using less hazardous ways of contacting the British Government, through technically neutral contacts in Geneva or Lisbon. Such negotiations had already been tried and proved fruitless. Also their nature made them slow and the risk of discovery considerable. Further, Hess had already made two attempts to reach Britain to present terms for peace and on each occasion had been forced back; once with engine trouble and the second time when his elevators refused to give him height. This time, he had to reach his objective.

Suddenly Hess saw that a thick veil of white mist draped a section of the coast ahead, reflecting the last rays of the sun so that it became opaque. Clearly, if he could not see the land through it, then no one on the ground could see him, although they might hear his engines. He dived on full throttle into the mist from a height of 2,000 metres, to within several hundred metres of the sea.

This action probably saved his life; at least, he has always maintained that it did. For behind him and quite without his knowledge a Spitfire on coastal patrol had given chase. Such was the power and speed of the Messerschmitt with its two engines, that as Hess says himself, 'I had outdistanced it before I was aware of its presence. I could not look behind; I was too enclosed in my cabin and too dazzled by the reflections. Had I not been tempted to dive for cover, but remained in the clear air at the pace I had been going, he could easily have shot me down.'[1]

Below the white belt of cloud, Hess could see a village with stone and granite houses, some empty streets and people like ants going in and out of doors. It was Belford, a small town about five miles from the coast and roughly ninety miles from his destination.

The lighthouse now lay behind him; he was well past Holy Island. Hess glanced at the gold wristwatch which he wore on his left wrist balanced by a fine gold identity disc and bracelet on his right. He had his wife's Leica camera hanging by a leather strap round his neck; he had left a note for her explaining that he was borrowing her camera because it was loaded and he had no film for his own.

The time was shortly before 10 o'clock. The sun was setting ahead of him, but still, inexplicably to Hess, it was not yet dark. He could see the country beneath him as clearly as if it had been a coloured and raised map. This puzzled him, for by his calculations

[1] In a letter to his wife.

he should now be flying in darkness. He had planned to arrive at his destination, about ten miles on the west side of Glasgow, just after dark, when the German markings on his plane would be difficult to see and the plane itself hard to recognize.

No British lookouts would be expecting a Messerschmitt 110 over Scotland, for it was well known that no standard Messerschmitt 110 could carry enough fuel to fly so far and return to base. He gambled on any report of such a plane being treated with ridicule; and in this he was quite correct.

But one point that Hess had neglected in his calculations was that while Germany enjoyed one hour of summer time, clocks in Britain were set back two hours for double summer time. Hess was thus flying an hour ahead of his schedule; it would still be daylight when he landed.

In his surprise at the lightness of the evening, and still not quite accustomed to the speed of his plane, he came down lower than he intended and roared above the sleepy streets of Wooler with his 2,000 horse-power engines on full throttle. Over their slate roofs and the fields that ringed them in, criss-crossed by hedges like some gigantic quilt of greens, yellow and gold, Hess swept on.

'At this level the visibility was surprisingly good,' he wrote later to his wife. 'I could see for several miles, but must have been invisible to my pursuer.

'I took care not to rise too high, but flew on at not more than sixteen feet from the ground—even less at times, skimming over men, trees, beasts and houses; what English airmen call "hedge hopping".'

Despite the strain of the lonely journey and the fearful consequence of failure, he was genuinely enjoying himself. He was doing something difficult and dangerous, and doing it well; such a combination of circumstances always gave him pleasure. Hitler's personal pilot, 'Father' Hans Baur, had often told him laughingly that the flying Hess liked best of all was skimming through barn doors, taking risks, revelling in the sensation of speed and power and flight.

Suddenly, beneath him, in the misty evening, the houses fell away and the ground rose to meet him; he had reached the foothills of the Cheviot range.

'This was my guiding point, as previously determined, and keeping within a few yards of the ground I literally climbed up the slope,' he recalled afterwards. 'Never before had I ascended a mountain so rapidly. The variometer told me I was ascending. Suddenly I was over my point of orientation—a little dam in a narrow range of hills. Here my course bent to the left.

'I had no need to bother with a map; all the details of the course, points, distances, were already stored in my memory.'

They should have been because, for nearly a year, Hess had prepared for this flight, rehearsing every move, memorizing every landmark he would see. Night after night he had lain awake in his bedroom in his home in Harthauser Strasse, a wide, grey, cobbled road in the most expensive residential suburb of Munich. On the wall at the foot of his bed he had pinned a giant map of his journey. For hours he would lie, propped up with pillows, a single reading light directed like a spot-lamp on this map, the rest of the room in darkness, while he soaked all the details in his mind, and worked out allowances for possible head, side or tail winds.

Each night, when he finished memorizing the visual landmarks of his journey, he would shut his eyes and repeat aloud the distances, the course, the time at which he would have to veer to the left or the right, according to his speed. Then he would pull a loose-leaf notebook to his side on a bedside table, direct the reading lamp on its pages, and within minutes reproduce a rough sketch of the map with its main bearings and degrees.

Since he did this several times every week and often made a number of copies when he discovered errors in comparing this hastily pencilled map with the original, he lived in some fear lest a servant, or his wife, should discover them and draw the wrong conclusions: that he was planning to desert his Führer and betray his country. For this reason Hess purposely drew only vague outlines of the British and Dutch coasts which he would cross, and marked his point of departure with an 'X' and his destination with 'Y'. And, as a further safeguard, instead of writing *Nordsee* for the North Sea, he wrote *Ostsee* for the Baltic.

He could not imagine that his wife would actually discover one of these carefully disguised sketches and read into it an entirely different conclusion: that he would fly not North or East, but South to see his old friend Marshal Petain with a view to improving the relationship between France and Germany.

Hess flew on over Coldstream, Peebles and Lanark. By half-past ten, he was over the stone mansion, Dungavel House, the Scottish home of the Duke of Hamilton, Premier Duke of Scotland, whom Hess called 'my quite unconscious future host'.

Hess now felt certain that he was right on target, for he had studied the largest map of the area available in Germany, and Dungavel was the only house of this size to be marked. There should be a level field or small landing ground on one side, according to his information, for the Duke was a distinguished aviator and, with a companion, had piloted the first aeroplane to fly over Everest eight years earlier, in 1933.

The moon was rising now, and Hess could plainly see a cone-shaped hill which he took to be Dungavel Hill; at once he remembered that it was 458 metres high. But partly because he had come so far without any hitch, and also because of the importance of his mission, he was suddenly seized with doubt; what if this were *not* the house? What if he had somehow flown off course, if he had miscalculated the wind drift as obviously he had miscalculated the time of his arrival?

On a sudden impulse, Hess decided not to circle round the mansion, but to fly on out over the west coast—only a few minutes away —to take his bearings and then, reassured, to return. The sea soon lay beneath him again, calm and cold as a mirror, lit by the rising moon like a lake of glass, and seemingly without a wave. Off the mainland a huge reddish rock, about 122 metres high, stood like a sentinel, pale in the early moonlight. Hess suddenly felt as though he was flying beyond the confines of time in some strange twilight world of dreams; he might be the last man alive.

'Never shall I forget this picture,' Hess said afterwards. He throttled back his engines, flew down the coast for a few miles, searching for a small spit of land like a mole, which he knew from his map should be there if his readings were accurate. Soon the expected thumb of earth appeared beneath him; he *was* right.

For his 850-mile flight from Augsburg, near Munich, in South Germany, Messerschmitt technicians had fitted the aeroplane with a cigar-shaped auxiliary petrol tank which could be jettisoned when it was empty. Hess saw from the green-lit gauge on the dashboard that the fuel this tank contained had already been consumed. He moved a lever by his seat which released it. The tank fell lightly away behind him into the sea, like some strange silver balloon. On the following day a British drifter recovered it from the Clyde.

Thus unencumbered, Hess banked and turned to fly back to Dungavel House and to land. His journey was nearly over; now the hard part and purpose of the flight would begin.

He did not know, as he flew back over the coast, picking up the railway lines that glittered like two silver snakes in the moonlight, watching for a lake south of Dungavel as a further landmark, that he was following the daily routine flight of British RAF pilots under instruction: they would leave Irvine air-base near Prestwick, fly north to Renfrew, then south-east to Dungavel and, using the hill as a landmark, turn south-west again for their base.

Although Hess believed that a landing strip or at least a wide lawn where he could land quite safely lay near Dungavel House, he intended to parachute. His plane was still on the secret list in Germany; it was, in fact, a prototype, immensely more powerful, more manœuvrable, and swifter than any Messerschmitt in service with the Luftwaffe. To let such a machine fall into British hands, regardless of the importance of his mission, would be folly. His aim was to parachute, and let the plane crash and burn itself out.

After his negotiations, whether they succeeded or whether they failed, he would seek the use of a British aeroplane to return him to Germany, or at least to some neutral city from where he could make his own arrangements to reach home.

This would be his first parachute jump, and perhaps his last; and forty-eight was old to begin such exercises.

He came in low over the little village of Eaglesham that straggled on either side of a deserted grey ribbon of road, finishing in a curve above Dungavel, and then climbed steeply until his altimeter showed a height of 2000 metres—about 6500 feet. This was the minimum height from which he dared to jump; it would allow him little time to correct any error in his fall, but, inexpert as he was, he should be able to judge his point of landing.

Now Hess worked with a speed remarkable for so heavily built a man. He switched off the two tumbler switches which cut the ignition of his engines, and set the propeller feathering device to zero so that the wind would not be able to spin the propellers now that the engines had stopped. He feared that if the propellers were still turning, their blades might become entangled with his parachute or its line.

Then, despite his caution and the number of times he had rehearsed this moment in his mind, things began to go wrong. After such a long and unaccustomed flight on full throttle, his two engines, new and barely run in, were nearly red hot. One stopped obediently as he switched off the ignition, but the other obstinately kept on running; the intense heat of the cylinders was still igniting the petrol vapour.

Hess throttled it back furiously, and suddenly it died. But this threw his plans out of sequence; and at his low height and speed, even a second of delay could become dangerous. Now that the engines were silent, only the scream of the wind filled his cockpit.

He reached up with both hands and slid back the cabin roof. Then he stood up to climb out. To his astonishment and horror he found that the tremendous air pressure thrust him back into his seat again with the blunt force of a hammer blow on his head.

'It pressed me up against the back partition as if I was glued to it,' he recalled later. 'In spite of the great care I had taken to find out about *everything* from my good friends at Messerschmitt's, there was just *one* thing I had overlooked. I had never asked about how to jump; I thought it was too simple!'

In the urgency and agony of the moment, Hess did not think to lower the undercarriage of the aeroplane, which would have slowed it down considerably. Instead, he struggled, bracing his feet against the thin metal floor of the cockpit, trying to force his head and shoulders through the opening. It was still impossible: he was trapped in a diving cockpit that within seconds could become his coffin.

As Dungavel Hill raced up towards him with the desperate clarity of the inevitable, Hess suddenly remembered the advice of an old friend and fellow aviator, General Ritter von Greim—who in the last days of the war was promoted Luftwaffe C-in-C in place of Goering. Greim had once explained that the easiest way to escape from a crashing aircraft was to turn the plane upside-down and to drop out. But although Hess had made many flights in this plane, he had never rolled it on its back. Now, when he should have moved the control column to the right, some instinct made him pull it back.

As he came over, the centrifugal force of the turning plane still held him in his seat. This undoubtedly saved his life, as he has admitted. Had Hess fallen at that moment, the strength of the wind would have broken both his neck and his back. As it was, the blood drained from his head with the speed of his flight, and lights and stars flashed in front of his eyes.

One thought hammered on his brain before he lost consciousness: 'I am only just above the ground and flying straight down: soon the crash *must* come. *Is this the end?*'

Then the stars faded and Hess lost consciousness. The deputy leader of the most powerful military nation in the world flew on upside-down in a dead faint, fifty feet above his country's most desperate enemy, held in his place only by the centrifugal force of his looping manoeuvre.

Gradually, mistily, as though from a great distance, Hess again became aware of his surroundings. Within inches of his eyes were the altimeter and air-speed indicator. Both white pointers swung to zero. It was the end of the journey: the flight was over. Years of training, of strict personal discipline, hundreds of hours of solo flight, hammered their frantic message into his fuddled brain; he had to jump now or die.

Somehow, he bunched his legs under him and kicked himself into the air. As he fell, he pulled the rip-cord of his parachute; the cold air whipping his face revived him.

His pilot's training from nearly twenty-five years earlier had made him do mechanically while unconscious what he should have done in the beginning: he had brought his plane out of its semi-looping curve so that it stood almost perpendicularly on its tail. For a second the Messerschmitt hung motionless as it lost the impetus of its climb. This threw Hess back on his seat so that the blood rushed to his brain; as he struggled out of his fainting fit, a fearful awareness of imminent danger consumed him.

He jumped.

As he swung to and fro from his parachute like a giant puppet on strings, he sucked in great lungfuls of air and his head cleared. The plane zoomed away over the fields and crashed in a shower of sparks. As the dark tops of the trees came up gently to Hess, little tapers of flame grew like yellow flowers from the wreckage. Well, it had served its purpose; now to the task ahead.

The pale mists of an early summer night rose from the fields, diffusing the light from the moon. Houses showed blank windows like closed eyes; there were no lights and no movements; nothing lived or breathed. He might be falling into a dead world of silence. The sense of strangeness he had felt above the sea minutes earlier returned with greater strength. Because of this and the mist, and the dizziness that still gripped him, Hess was unprepared for the ground when it came rushing up to him.

His flying-boots suddenly hit the grass and he fell forward grunting for breath, mechanically fumbling with his parachute harness to loosen it in case the wind dragged him along. The unexpected check on his speed, plus the force and shock of landing, caused a second blackout, so that he stumbled senselessly about on his hands and knees in the corner of a field like a drunken man.

As consciousness swam back to him he clawed himself up and stood, spattered with earth, the sweat cold on his forehead, his ears singing with a strange silence after the roar of his engines and the wind. Then, through his thick leather flying-helmet he began to hear faint shouts of alarm from people he could not see.

Hess had no idea where he was, what had happened to him, or why he was there: momentarily he could not even remember his own name.

'Only gradually did it become clear to me that I had reached my goal—or rather a new beginning,' he admitted later. 'Alas, it was more of a beginning than I dreamed!'

CHAPTER TWO

The Mysterious Hauptmann Horn

Ten miles away, along the Eaglesham road, Lieutenant Tom Hyslop, a burly, good-natured officer in the Renfrewshire Constabulary, was driving home from Dumbarton in his black Wolseley police car, with his daughter, Nan. She was a Leading Aircraftwoman, in the WAAF, home on week-end leave.

Hyslop had been visiting the Dumbarton remand home about a difficult case, and his daughter had gone with him for company and because, at that time of strict petrol rationing, a journey by car was to most people sufficiently rare to be something of an outing. As he drove, Hyslop kept his official radio switched on for police messages about air-raids and unexploded bombs.

Shortly after ten o'clock a metallic, impersonal voice came through the static: 'A single enemy plane has crossed the Clyde and is flying inland towards Glasgow. It is difficult to identify, but is definitely hostile and may be in difficulties. All police are to watch in case it lands. Message ends.'

'Why, that's quite near us,' said Nan Hyslop in surprise.

'It sounds *too* near us,' replied her father. 'Let's see if we can hear it.'

He dimmed his masked headlights, pulled the car into the side of the road and switched off the engine. The sky hung clear and empty above them; mist rolled eerily across the darkened fields. Somewhere an owl hooted, and in the distance, an infinity away, a slow goods train chugged along to the docks.

At that moment they both heard an unfamiliar roar of engines in the sky. A plane crossed the moon like a swift dark arrow, racing down towards the ground. As it fell a figure dropped from it and a parachute billowed like a giant puff ball in the sky. Then they heard a crunch of breaking metal. A cow mooed plaintively and began to tear at the cropped grass.

'Come on! Into the car again, Nan!' cried Hyslop. 'That must be the German!'

23

They jumped in and raced on up the road. The plane had apparently crashed somewhere to the left of the Eaglesham road. The nearest approach to it would thus be a lane that joined the Eaglesham road a mile or two away. This was Floors Road, a narrow tarmac lane leading to the farm from which it takes its name, and to two other houses a little farther on. Hyslop gauged that most probably the plane had crashed beyond Floors Farm, about a mile up on the right of the road.

He stopped the car again and wound down his window, listening for any strange sounds that might give him a clue. He thought he heard faint shouts from the direction of the farm, but the wind sang so loudly in the telephone wires alongside the stone wall bordering the lane that he could not be sure. In any case, this was the only way to reach the scene of the crash; he restarted his engine, and set off up the narrow road.

Floors Farm is built around an open space with buildings on three sides. The house stands at right angles to the road, and is approached by a straight tarmac drive from the road. To the left, across a yard, are outbuildings and maroon-painted metal sheds for storing hay and farm implements. Beyond them stands a small, single-storey house with whitewashed walls and a tiny kitchen garden full of fruit and vegetables and flowers. In 1941, this was the home of the farm's head ploughman, David McLean, a bachelor in his mid-forties, and his mother and sister. McLean had emigrated to Auckland some years before the war, but had returned when his mother grew older, to look after her. He was—and is—a stocky, wiry man with a dry edge to his tongue.

At exactly a quarter-to-eleven by the alarm clock, on a night clear with that strange ambience about the air only found on this coast of Scotland, David McLean was preparing for sleep in his small whitewashed bedroom. His mother and sister were already in bed in the next room, and he was on the point of turning out his light and removing the blackout curtain from his window to let in the cool summer air, when he heard an aeroplane flying just above the house.

At first the plane came over with a great roar, the thunder of its engines making the little china ornaments on his mantelpiece tremble and dance with resonance. The noise faded as Hess turned his plane; then it grew louder and suddenly stopped as he switched off both engines. McLean heard only the whining of the wind screaming past the wings. Clearly, something had gone wrong; the plane was crashing.

Was it a bomber likely to explode when it hit the ground?

McLean subconsciously braced himself, holding his breath for the shock of an explosion: but nothing happened. McLean switched off the light and pulled aside the blackout curtains over the window. Then, hands cupped on either side of his eyes, he peered out through the glass across the stone wall at the bottom of his garden and over the empty fields.

At first he could see nothing but grass, silver in the moonlight, and the smooth breasts of the hills in the distance dotted with clusters of trees. Then he made out something white in the sky, like a falling, billowing cloud; a descending parachute.

McLean groped for his boots and his trousers in the darkness, tucked his nightshirt into the waistband, and beat on the wall to waken his mother.

'It's a pilot come down just outside!' he called. 'I think he's a German! Get up! I'm going out after him!'

Then he was off through the front door. He turned right past the raspberry canes, alongside the barns and out through a small wicket gate into the field. He felt sure that the parachutist must be a German, because, after months of hearing English aeroplanes of all kinds and sizes flying overhead from Irvine to Prestwick and back again, McLean was accustomed to the particular drone of their engines. The noise of the two Messerschmitt engines was entirely different from anything he had heard before. Therefore, in his reasoning, if it was alien, it must be an enemy.

By the time McLean was through the gate, the parachutist had landed, but the wind was still billowing in his parachute and dragging him across the thick grass, already damp with evening dew. McLean ran after him, shouting, his bare feet slithering in his boots. He caught up with Hess, who was on hands and knees, and struggling to undo the straps of his harness. As McLean reached him, Hess managed to slip the catches, and the parachute blew away for a few yards, and then fell slowly as the wind left it. Hess crawled away painfully.

'Who are you?' shouted McLean, his voice high in his excitement. 'Are you a German?'

Hess struggled to stand, but he had damaged his right ankle in his inexpert landing and it was too painful to bear his weight. He stumbled, and, instinctively, stretched out his hands to McLean to support him. McLean stood firm, feet wide apart, and slowly the pilot drew himself up to his full height; he was probably a foot taller than the ploughman, and of infinitely heavier build.

25

'Yes,' Hess replied, speaking slowly in the unfamiliar language. 'I am German. I am Hauptmann Alfred Horn. I want to go to Dungavel House. I have an important message for the Duke of Hamilton.'

As he spoke, there came, almost as though on cue, a muffled rumble from the plane which had crashed several fields away. A sheet of flame shot up from it, silhouetting the hedges, the trees, the electric pylons. Both men looked towards the flash.

'Are there any more in the plane, bar you?' asked McLean.

Hess shook his head.

'No. I have no companions. I flew alone.'

'Are you armed?'

McLean patted his pockets with the palms of his hands; he could feel no weapon.

Hess stood on one leg to keep his weight from his painful ankle and patiently raised both hands above his head.

'I am unarmed,' he said. 'I have no revolver.'

By now shouts were coming from the direction of the farmhouse and another man ran towards them, a tall thin figure in the moonlight. This was William Craig, then sixty-eight, and today still a very spry figure at eighty-seven. He had been the first child to be born in the farmhouse, had lived there all his life, and used to say that when he walked to school down the road as a child, he had to peer over the wall to see the little saplings that had just been planted. Now these trees were eighty feet high.

'What's happened?' he shouted. 'Who's out there?'

'A German's here,' replied McLean. 'Go and get some soldiers.'

Across the lane, in Eaglesham House, were billeted a detachment of the Royal Signals. They were technically a searchlight unit but their main preoccupation was radar. Naturally no one locally knew this, for the existence of radar was one of Britain's best-kept secrets at that time. Although some locals felt that these soldiers appeared more studious than martial—most were extremely well qualified in radio and electronics—they wore uniform, and McLean thought that they could deal with a capital enemy pilot better than he could on his own. He had not worn uniform since the days he had been a private in the Cameron Highlanders during the First World War.

In the meantime McLean decided to march his captive out of the field into some place where they could have light; he had only the man's word for the fact that he was unarmed, and, injured as he was, he looked too strong to take on in single combat. The pilot, however, showed no disposition to fight or to escape.

With one arm around McLean's shoulder Hess began to limp towards the little wooden gate. After he had gone a few paces he stopped and looked back across the empty moonlit field. McLean followed his gaze. He was looking at the parachute still trembling slightly in the mist, as huge and ghostly as a gigantic jellyfish.

'I can't leave that,' he said.

'Why not?' asked McLean.

'Well, I owe my life to it,' explained Hess with a small smile.

Was this a trick, a ruse to get McLean out of the way so that he could escape? Was he *really* injured in the leg? Both these thoughts flashed through the ploughman's mind as they stood together in the moonlight, the tall and the short, the captive and his captor, on the edge of the field.

'I'll get it for you,' said McLean suddenly. 'Don't move, though, will you?'

Hess smiled, his teeth white in the moonlight.

'I promise I won't,' he said.

McLean ran over the grass and pulled in the parachute, which was much larger than he imagined, and heavier because it was damp. He compressed it into a huge ball, and held it under one arm. Then, with the Deputy Führer of Germany leaning on his shoulder, the Scots ploughman came into the little hall of his house.

By now Mrs McLean was downstairs with an old dressing-gown over her nightdress and her feet in slippers.

'Shut the door, so I can put on the light,' she said in a matter-of-fact way.

McLean did so, for in the excitement of the moment he had forgotten all about the blackout regulations. His mother's hand groped for the switch; the little bulb glowed in its shade above their heads. Rudolf Hess clicked his heels together and bowed to the short, wizened woman who stared up at him with an expression in which incredulity mingled with curiosity.

He was probably the first foreigner she had seen face to face and certainly the first German; as such, this enemy deserved the closest scrutiny. Everything about him seemed strange and unfamiliar; his field grey uniform, his soft leather flying-boots with the fur showing at the top, his continental courtesy, his stiff way of standing. He was as alien as sauerkraut.

'Are you German?' she asked, drawing her dressing-gown more tightly about her.

'Yes, I am German,' replied Hess, bowing to her again.

She gave a little sniff.

'Ma Gawd!' she announced with feeling. 'What a life!'

This summed up fairly adequately the feelings of them all. McLean was conscious that as captor, or host, he owed obligations to his uninvited and unexpected guest, for nowhere else in the world is the tradition of hospitality—under all circumstances—more strong than in Scotland. He jerked his head a little awkwardly in the direction of the living-room.

'We'd better go in there,' he said gruffly, and pushed open the door.

In the harsh light of the single electric bulb that hung from the ceiling in a china shade, everything shone with cleanliness and polish; the tang of furniture cream was sharp on the air.

McLean indicated the best chair in the room, a big leather armchair with an enormously deep cushion and wide arms. It was the chair reserved for the head of the house, or for the most distinguished visitor; it was easily the most expensive single article of furniture in the whole cottage.

'You sit there,' he told Hess, pointing towards it, speaking slowly and loudly as though by this means he could rise above the barrier of language. Hess sank down into the unexpected depth of the chair, his head back, his arms outstretched.

'I'll get a cup of tea,' announced Mrs McLean and shuffled off to the kitchen. They heard the sound of running water and the bang of a kettle on the hob of the stove.

'Well?' asked McLean, still standing and staring at his guest, and feeling that he should say something.

Hess said nothing for a moment, and then repeated the remark he had made out in the field.

'I have an urgent message for the Duke of Hamilton. Please take me to him at once.'

The Duke of Hamilton indeed! Now who did this fellow think he was, asking for the Duke, as bold as brass, and at this time of night?

'The soldiers will be here,' McLean assured him. 'They will deal with all that. His place isn't far away, anyhow. Probably not more than twelve miles as the crow flies.'

'They'll see to all that. I'm only a civilian, though I wasn't a civvy in the last war. I was in the Highlanders. In Arras.'

Hess appeared interested.

'I was in the Battle of Arras,' he explained.

'Aye,' agreed McLean dourly. 'On the other side.'

Silence hung uneasily between them; David McLean had never imagined himself capturing a German single-handed, and now that the impossible had occurred, the moment held a strange theatrical unreality, made all the more incongruous by the familiar homely surroundings of his own living-room.

Hess looked down at the scrubbed stone floor, at the white walls with their two pictures. One showed a cavalry charge, titled in picturesque scroll, 'The Battle before Belfort'; the other was of a mare and foal in a field, 'Mother and Son'.

Mrs McLean returned with a tray on which were three cups and saucers, which David recognized as their best china, and a big brown earthenware teapot, a jug of milk and a bowl of sugar.

'Will you have a cup of tea?' she asked Hess.

It struck neither of them as odd that the pilot should not be speaking in German but seemed to understand them perfectly; it was all a part of this fantastic, unbelievable evening. Hess had stood up when Mrs McLean entered the room, and he shook his head at her offer.

'Thank you, no,' he said. 'It is too early for me to drink tea, but I would like a glass of water if you have one.'

Annie McLean went out over the stone flags again and came back with a glass of water from the tap. Hess drank greedily and thanked her, and handed it back. They all sat down and the tension eased, and still no one came from outside to their aid or to arrest Hess.

What they had forgotten was that in the blackout, with no window or door showing any light all around the farm, neither Tom Hyslop nor the Signallers brought from Eaglesham House by William Craig, had any clear idea where the pilot had gone. They were blundering about with sticks and rakes among the bales of hay and oil-drums in the barns, expecting at any moment to be attacked by some assailant; for in the darkness every grunt or snort from a cow or a horse in the byre seemed like an advance from armed enemies.

Back in the little house, Hess pulled out a wallet from an inside pocket and extracted a photograph. It showed a small boy about three or four standing in a garden. He handed it up to David McLean, who passed it on to his mother.

'My son,' Hess explained. 'I saw him this morning. But I don't know when I'll see him again.'

Mrs McLean handed back the picture in silence. There seemed nothing she could say, but the natural gesture only emphasized the strangeness of their meeting.

McLean looked at Hess quizzically. He certainly seemed old—possibly not far off fifty—to be flying a plane. His eyebrows were dark and bushy and overhung his eyes like tufts of black gorse on the side of a hill. He sat peacefully and apparently at ease in his chair, and although he was a prisoner, there remained about him an air of authority, of being used to command. His uniform too was of a fine soft cloth, of a quality that McLean, earning barely £3 a week, had never seen before. These were not the same rough shoddy-looking clothes which he had heard that other German pilots wore.

Hess also had a slim expensive gold wristwatch on one wrist and on the other a thin gold chain with a small identity disc. There was no need to tell an old soldier like David McLean that these were not regulation issue.

But what captured McLean's fancy most of all were his magnificent flying-boots lined with fur. Their leather was as soft and supple as a pair of hand-made gloves. Never before had McLean seen boots to compare with these: they are the one point of Hess's equipment that still stays most vividly in his mind.

As he stood watching Hess, the total of all these unexpectedly expensive and luxurious things, plus the pilot's request to see the Duke of Hamilton, made as calmly as though he were paying him a social call, forced him inescapably to the conclusion that this para-chutist was clearly no ordinary run-of-the-mill Luftwaffe pilot. Such men had baled out over Scotland in numbers during the previous few months. All that their ill-fitting uniforms and undistinguished leather boots had in common with this pilot's accoutrement was the basic fact that they were both uniforms in the same service. This German was clearly, in McLean's opinion and vernacular, 'a pot'.

'Who did you say you were again?' he asked him.

'Hauptmann Horn. Alfred Horn,' Hess replied. 'Hauptmann is the equivalent of your "Captain".'

At that moment there came a banging on the front door. McLean looked out. Excited Scottish voices were heard. Two Signallers in battledress with the blue-and-white flashes of the Royal Signal Corps on their sleeves burst into the room.

'I hear there's a prisoner,' one began and then, seeing Hess, stopped in mid-sentence. They stared at him for a moment, interest in seeing their first German in uniform draining their minds of words. So this was the enemy: tall, rather imperious, sitting in the best armchair, legs stretched out. This wasn't at all what they had expected.

'Are you going to take him off?' asked McLean, rather surprised by the fact that they had no rifles. What the dickens was the Army coming to, soldiers coming to seize a German prisoner without rifles?

The soldiers looked at each other; they had apparently not considered that they would have to remove the prisoner once they found him. Clearly they must now consider this point.

As the three Scotsmen stood looking at each other, and Hess sat looking at them, his face imperturbable, as much at ease as if he was sitting by his own fireside, there came a thunder of knocking on the front door. Again those inside heard a confused chatter of voices; two more men crowded into the tiny living-room.

One of them wore civilian clothes and a steel helmet marked with white letters, 'Police'. The other was dressed in civilian trousers with a Home Guard battledress blouse in khaki with the words 'Home Guard' sewn on each shoulder. He had a khaki steel helmet, with the elastic strap under his chin. In his right hand he held an enormous Webley revolver of a type issued to officers in the First World War.

'Hands up!' he cried dramatically. Such was the power of his command that everyone jumped and started to raise their arms; then, realizing their mistake they lowered them sheepishly.

These two late arrivals took charge of the situation. The civilian was Robert Williamson, a local engineer, who was also a special constable, a part-time policeman, on duty at evenings and week-ends. The Home Guard, Mr Clark, was his next-door neighbour.

Both had been off-duty on that particular Saturday, and at home, when they had heard the roar of the aeroplane. Williamson rushed out into his garden and to his horror saw a parachute descending. He felt certain that this must be a land mine, but when no explosion occurred after it had reached the ground he realized he was wrong.

Both men recognized that this was, in the official jargon of the time, 'an incident'. The Home Guardsman picked up a revolver he had kept for just such an emergency for more than twenty years, broke it, slipped in six cartridges preserved from that other, earlier war, and snapped it shut again. Then, grabbing their steel helmets, they set off in Williamson's car.

As they drove together along the Eaglesham Road they saw flames from the crashed plane, flickering against the sky to the right. They turned off along Floors Road and on to Floors Farm; the farmer might have news about who or what had landed. In the moonlight they saw men threshing around the yard with sticks. Someone directed them to McLean's house and they burst into the living-room.

'We were both very excited, and Clark's pistol was waving about dangerously,' Williamson said later. 'Hess was sitting on one side of the fire when we went into the cottage, with old Mrs McLean on the other. He was very calm—rather an impressive figure, with a sort of sardonic smile on his face and a twinkle in his very deep-set eyes.

'We had no idea who he was, but he looked important. My first thought was that he was very different from the youngsters I had always imagined bombing us—much older. Honestly, we didn't know what to do.'[1]

'Are you armed?' asked Williamson.

Hess shook his head.

'No. I am not.'

'Anyone else with you?'

'No. I flew alone.'

'Is your plane likely to explode? I mean, have you some sort of time-bomb in it to go off?'

'No, there's nothing like that in it.'

Seven people—six men and Mrs McLean—now stood in the tiny room, so close together they were almost physically touching. One thought was in all their minds: what was going to happen to their prisoner? Always when German airmen had baled out previously, other units, other men had been on duty. Now they had to make the decision. Hess might escape if they marched him away anywhere, and where indeed could they march him to? Yet clearly he could not remain indefinitely in the McLeans' living-room.

Finally McLean asked Williamson point-blank, 'What are you going to do with him? Are you taking him to the Police Station?'

'No,' replied Williamson. 'That's no good. The local bobby's only got a small house. He's no cell or anything there.'

'What about *your* place?' asked McLean, nodding to the soldiers.

They shook their heads. It would be impossible to take a German prisoner, clearly an officer of rank and consequence, to an establishment where even the British troops were under heavy responsibility not to disclose the true nature of their activities. This was not a reason they could give, however, and so they said nothing.

'I'll tell you what we'll do,' said the Home Guardsman. 'We'll take him down to the Home Guard hut at Busby.'

Everyone brightened perceptibly at this suggestion, partly because

[1] 'The Ageing Parachutist', by Stephen Watts, published in *The New Yorker*, February 16, 1957.

the responsibility would then be someone else's, partly because it was so obviously a sound idea.

Up and down Britain during that summer, disused huts, garages, stables and barns were manned every week-end and throughout most nights by Home Guardsmen. Most of these men had military experience from the First World War, but either because of their age, their health or the nature of their work, they could take no active part in the Second. Since the first invasion scare of 1940, after France capitulated, they had drilled regularly with pikes, rakes, garden forks, shot-guns, elephant guns, antiquated pistols, even muzzle-loaders, for want of more modern weapons. By the time Hess arrived, most were reasonably equipped with Army surplus Lee-Enfield rifles, Vickers machine-guns on tripods and other arms only a generation out of date. But what they might lack in modern armaments, however, they more than made up for with their enormous enthusiasm. To introduce to these keen warriors a living, breathing German from the skies would be an enormous fillip to their morale and interest; they would guard him with such tenacity that he would have no chance of escape.

'You had better come with us,' said Williamson, and nodded towards the door.

Hess stood up. The others backed out into the little corridor of a hall to give him room to leave. He turned first to Mrs McLean and bowed, and then to her son.

'Thank you both,' he said gravely.

Williamson went out first, then Hess, with Clark pressing his huge revolver in the small of his back, then the soldiers.

Describing this later in a letter to his wife, Hess admits that he was not very happy about being thus led out into the Scottish darkness, although his account has no relation to the facts.

'What happened next was much less encouraging,' he wrote, recalling the arrival of Clark and Williamson and his departure with them. 'A civil official appeared at the head of a troop of soldiers—a man who had quite evidently, judging by the smell, been celebrating Saturday with good Scottish spirits, probably having taken an extra shot when he heard that a German parachutist had come down.

'At any rate, he staggered about in a cloud of alcoholic vapour, marching me off and prodding me all the while in the back, with a large revolver, his finger never leaving the trigger.

'As I listened to his incessant belching and stumbling, I felt there

C   33

must have been the finger of God intervening between his shaking hand and the impending shot.'

They climbed into Williamson's car; Hess in front, and Clark behind, and drove off down Floors Road.

Hyslop, racing up past them, had no reason for stopping the car. He arrived in the courtyard of Floors Farm to find he had missed the German pilot by minutes.

With the natural wish of a professional policeman to see as much of the scene of the incident as possible, he left his daughter sitting in his car and went to inspect the plane. The flames were out, but smoke was still rising from the engines; the silver paint of the fuse-lage was blistered and blackened. Some other policemen had arrived with gas-masks over their shoulders, dressed incongruously in uniform jackets and civilian trousers. Hyslop instructed them to keep everyone else away from the wreckage for it was by no means certain that fire might not break out again. Also, the plane might contain some booby-trap which could kill or maim villagers, who, in their eagerness for an authentic German souvenir were already trying to tear pieces from the wings and rudder.

Hyslop shone his shielded torch into the cockpit and round the engines. Then he saw something that surprised him. The muzzles of the machine-guns poking out of the leading edges of the wings like stubby black fingers were packed tight with grease. Not only had they never been used, but they were not intended to be used.

Clearly, the man who had piloted this plane had not come from Germany on a mission of war; he had flown to Britain on a mission of peace.

CHAPTER THREE

Hess, Haushofer and Hitler

Clark, Hess and Williamson sat in uneasy proximity hunched up in the little English car that was so different from the magnificent Mercedes in which Hess had set out on his journey. They drove in silence through Waterfoot, past the smithy and into the shuttered suburban outskirts of Busby. Both Scots were considerably impressed by their passenger's uniform, and felt they should make some kind of conversation, but neither could think of anything to say that would not seem incongruous in the circumstances. Thus they drove in silence until they reached their destination, the Home Guard headquarters. This was a brick Scout hall built shortly before the war.

'We get out here,' Williamson announced as the car stopped.

Hess stood much taller than either of his two companions, and even as a captive there remained about him an air of dignity and authority. He had the bearing of a man accustomed to command, who was suddenly and quite unexpectedly being forced to parley with minor and unimportant officials. Doubtless, someone of authority equal to his own would soon arrive and then these petty frustrations and annoyances would end.

'Come on,' said Williamson, and led the way up a narrow concrete path towards the hall. Clark marched behind Hess with his revolver muzzle pressed into the small of the German's back.

'I was more scared of Clark's revolver than anything else,' Williamson admitted later. 'And probably Hess was, too.'[1]

All the windows in the Scout hall were naturally in darkness, because of the blackout, but the three men could hear voices and movement behind the green-painted door.

Williamson rapped on one of the panels. The talking and the laughter stopped. Men shuffled about on the other side of the woodwork, and then a voice called out uncertainly: 'Who's there?'

[1] 'The Ageing Parachutist.'

35

'The Police and the Home Guard,' replied Williamson importantly. 'Open up! We've got a German prisoner!'

The lock was turned, the bolt pulled back and the door opened.

'Come on in quickly then,' said a corporal, his uniform blouse unbuttoned, a striped collarless civilian shirt visible beneath it. 'We'll be on a peg having this door open in the blackout if you don't.'

Inside the hut twenty or thirty Home Guardsmen off duty were preparing for the night. From nails driven into the walls hung their gas-masks and leather belts and bayonets in black leather frogs. They made a singularly unmilitary spectacle as they stood, in varying stages of undress, by their blankets spread out on the floor. Old men with bare knobby toes and wearing long woollen pants and sleeved vests stared open-mouthed in amazement at Hess. Others were finishing their suppers—fish and chips eaten out of newspapers.

This whole tableau of disorder and unpreparedness so irritated Clark that on the impulse he shouted: 'Turn out the Guard!'

Immediately the standing figures came to life, but owing to the unexpectedness of the order, and their surprise at suddenly seeing a German officer in their midst, some grabbed the wrong boots and equipment. In the middle of this confusion, Williamson glanced sideways at Hess, standing motionless in the doorway; the trace of a smile played about his mouth.

'He was thinking that this couldn't happen in Germany,' said Williamson later. 'I was ashamed, although nobody was really to blame.'

Surprisingly quickly, the Home Guardsmen were dressed in their uniforms, equipment buckled on, bayonets fixed. They ran out of the main door and lined up outside on the concrete, to keep away any inquisitive visitors—and also to prevent any attempt Hess might make to escape.

To one side of the hall was an ante-room with a cardboard notice —'Guard Room'—fastened on the door with drawing pins.

'In there,' said Clark, jerking his thumb towards this room.

The smile faded from Hess's face. He drew himself up to his full height.

'I am a German officer,' he explained stiffly.

Clark raised his revolver and pushed it into Hess's stomach.

'You'll get in there when you're told,' he retorted sharply.

Williamson held open the door and Hess walked into a completely bare room with a whitewashed wall and stained floorboards. A thin fibreboard sheet braced with laths of wood covered the small window.

Out-of-date notices about Scout camps and woodcraft proficiency tests were still pinned on the walls. There were no chairs, no table, not even a box on which he could sit.

Hess looked around this bleak cubicle—and then lay down on the floor. He stretched out to his full length on the gritty boards, and stared up silently and impassively at the single yellowish, misty bulb that lit the room.

Home Guards, peeking around the open door, thought that he was in a coma or that he had fainted. Doctors and psychiatrists who examined him later on, even his gaolers at Nuremberg and Spandau, were to be equally mystified by this type of behaviour. They did not realize that Hess was deliberately adopting a Yoga posture of relaxation. As a boy, brought up in Alexandria where his father was a merchant of some consequence, Hess had frequently watched Arabs when they prepared for arduous camel journeys across the desert. They would lie down on the warm sand with their muscles relaxed and minds cleared of all thought. Within minutes they would arise, refreshed.

Hess learned from them the secret of this gift. Years later, at Nazi rallies, when he would deputize for Hitler because of his commanding presence, his strictly Aryan good looks and his histrionic ability, Hess would often ask for the use of an empty room an hour before the meeting was due to begin. There he would stretch out, just as he stretched out on the floor of the Scout hut in Busby, and as he had lain on his bedroom floor in Munich earlier the same day.

One kind-hearted Home Guard, not realizing the reason behind the posture, felt sorry for this German officer lying full length on the bare floorboards. On the impulse, he picked up a bottle of milk which he should have used for the tea of his platoon, pulled out the cardboard top, and handed the bottle to Hess to drink. The Deputy Führer was much touched; afterwards he described this unknown soldier to his wife as 'a really nice little Tommy'.

At this moment, Hyslop arrived and Hess stood up and bowed gravely to him, and to some other Army and RAF officers who came with him. Hess held up his arms obediently while they searched his pockets. Someone carried a small table into the Guard Room and each article they found on him was placed on it, like exhibits in a police court.

There was an envelope addressed to the Duke of Hamilton, a small hypodermic syringe and a flat box, the size of a tin of fifty cigarettes, which contained an assortment of homeopathic drugs. One was an elixir, which Hess explained had come from a Tibetan Lamasery; it was supposed to be a cure for gall-bladder complaints. With this preparation were various vitamin concoctions, some glucose tablets and sedative drugs.[1]

Apart from his clothes the only other possessions he had were his watch, a camera, and several photographs of himself and his four-year-old son, Wolf Rüdiger. One of these showed the boy with his mother, Ilse Hess. He also had two visiting cards, one in the name of Professor Karl Haushofer, the other engraved with the name of his son, Albrecht. This second card was sewn inside his uniform jacket.

'What is *your* name?' asked one of the interrogating officers.

'Alfred Horn,' replied Hess.

'Age?'

'Forty-seven.'

Later, a physician who interviewed him wrote: 'He appeared to think the assumption of the name Alfred Horn and the year's difference in age between Hess and Horn a master-stroke of cunning.'[2]

This was not strictly accurate. Hess borrowed the name Alfred from his younger brother; he took the name Horn from his mother-in-law's second husband, an artist of some note in Germany. The important thing in selecting a pseudonym was that it should begin with the same initial letter as his real name, in case some of his belongings should bear this letter 'H'.

Hess gave a false age, one year younger than he really was, not as a whim, but for a very sound reason; in the German forces, no one over forty-seven could hold the rank of Hauptmann. Had he admitted that he was forty-eight, a shrewd British Intelligence Officer

---

[1] A report made on this pharmaceutical collection by the Medical Research Council about a fortnight afterwards noted: 'It seems quite clear from the remarkable collection of drugs, that Captain Horn was intent on protecting himself against all assault of the devil so far as his flesh was concerned, and, if he knew the action of all the drugs he carried, he had obviously missed his vocation and ought to have made a very handy practitioner.

'He seems to have protected himself (1) against the pains of injury by opium alkaloids: (2) against the discomfort of headaches by aspirin, etc., (3) against the pains of colic by atropin: (4) against the fatigue of flying by pervitin: (5) against the sleeplessness following pervitin by barbiturates: (6) against constipation by a saline mixture, and against every other ailment to which flesh is heir by mixtures of unknown products made up along homeopathic lines, i.e., so dilute that it is impossible to say what they are.

'This reliance upon allopathy for real bodily ailments and his further belief in homeopathy for other discomforts seem to represent a curious outlook on medical science.'
The Case of Rudolf Hess, edited by Dr J. R. Rees., Heinemann.
[2] *Ibid.*

might have asked him how he equated his age with his rank. He did not choose a higher rank because this was the most senior rank he had reached in the First World War.

Soon an Army truck arrived, and with several officers as escort Hess was driven to Maryhill Barracks, Glasgow.

He complained that his right ankle was causing him great pain. It was impossible for anybody to discover whether the bone was fractured or the ankle simply sprained without making a detailed examination, so from the barracks he was moved to the Military Hospital, in Buchanan Castle, Drymen, 18 miles outside Glasgow. And all this time he kept insisting that he must see the Duke of Hamilton; this was far more important to him than any medical treatment. It was imperative that he should see the Duke.

Back in the Scout Hall at Busby, reaction after the unexpected excitement now gripped the Home Guards, and the various Police and Army and RAF officers who had gathered there. One of these, pondering over the vaguely familiar face of Hauptmann Horn, suddenly turned to an RAF Wing-Commander.

'You know, sir,' he began diffidently, 'I believe this man is Rudolf Hess, Hitler's Deputy. I've seen him in Germany, and the more I think of it the more I'm *sure* he's Hess.'

The Wing-Commander snorted his contempt. 'Don't be a fool,' he said shortly.

*　　　*　　　*

What sort of a man was Hess—why did he suddenly arrive as an envoy uninvited and unannounced, on that Saturday night?

The most generally accepted portrait of Hess at that time was of Hitler's loyal Man Friday. He was like a devoted spaniel who could be relied on never to query his master's judgement or his acts; who could write a speech or deputize for him or conduct a particularly unpleasant inquiry at short notice, and with no question or complaint.

Both as a person and a personality, Hess was popular in Germany, for he seemed to embody so many Bavarian qualities. He was brave, physically strong, he loved his home and his son; also he was of unquestioning loyalty to the Führer, and he could drink beer with the best. More important, he was also one of Hitler's oldest friends, one of the original Party members; his Party Number was 16, while Hitler was No. 7, but they stood on much more intimate terms than this might suggest.

Like Rosenberg and Hitler, Hess was born outside Germany. He was born in Egypt, and studied at the German school in Alexandria for six years. When he was twelve his parents sent him to board at the Evangelisches Paedagogium in Godeberg-am-Rhein. His father wanted to send him to Oxford, but the outbreak of the First World War prevented this. Hess volunteered and served with Hitler in the 1st Company of the 16th Bavarian Reserve Infantry, although they did not meet until after the war. Hitler was a despatch runner, and was gassed; Hess was shot in one lung, and later became an officer with the Imperial Flying Corps.

After the war he still wore his old service uniform when he studied at Munich University; he could not afford to buy a civilian suit. At the University he came under the influence of Professor Karl Haushofer, of whom more later; and wrote an essay on 'The Man Who Will Save Our Country'. At that time of ruin and inflation in Germany, such a leader needed qualities not immediately evident among Hess's contemporaries and friends, although Hess felt he would recognize them in a stranger.

In 1921 he heard Hitler speak, and realized that he had discovered the man he had imagined in his essay. 'This man will restore Germany to a great place among the nations,' he declared, and decided to help him in this historic task.

Apart from a fierce unshakeable loyalty to Hitler from that time on, Hess had an almost equally strong obsession against the Russians. This had its roots in 1919, when Hess, as a member of a small anti-Bolshevik society in Munich, was out in the streets distributing anti-Jewish and anti-Communist pamphlets. As he returned to the shabby headquarters of his society he saw a Red Guard lorry leaving with his confederates. Hess stood back in the shadows until it had gone. All his comrades were later shot.

Hess was also present when the first serious attempt was made to break up a Hitler meeting in a Munich brewery in November 1921. More than a hundred intruders, mostly Communists, were thrown through doors and windows into the streets by about fifty Nazi members. According to Hitler, two men especially distinguished themselves. One was Emile Maurice, who later became his chauffeur; the other was Rudolf Hess, who took a blow on the head from a beer mug aimed at Hitler. Hess still carries the scar.

This day was also notable because it saw the beginning of the Storm Troopers, the *Sturm Abteilung*. Their first function was to protect such rallies and to serve as party police. Soon they became

Hitler's praetorian guard, the real political soldiers of the Nazis.

Hitler always remembered this incident, and he recalled it in *Mein Kampf*.

'Our meeting had hardly begun,' he wrote, 'when my Storm Troopers—for so they became from that day forth—attacked. Like wolves they flung themselves in packs of eight and ten. How many of those men I never really knew until that day—at their head was gallant Rudolf, my present secretary, Hess.'

Thereafter Hess was Hitler's personal adjutant and secretary until 1933; he wrote much of the propaganda during this time and enjoyed the complete confidence of his leader. His strength and influence increased until German Universities, schools, even some religious organizations, came under his overall control.

In 1934 he played a notable part in removing Captain Roehm, once a colleague, latterly a rival to Hitler; some said he was among the executioners. In the following year he signed the anti-Jewish legislation that was to play such a large and horrifying part in the Nazi regime during the last years of the war. In this year also Hitler announced that Hess would take part in the legislation of all Government departments, as well as being concerned with purely Party matters. From this date Hess helped with the preparation of all Hitler's decrees.

Three years later, in 1938, Hess became a member of the Secret Cabinet Council, then engaged in planning the aggression that ended in war. When the war began Hess was further honoured by joining the Ministerial Council for the Defence of the Reich. This contained six members; in these men, under Hitler, was concentrated the ultimate legislative and executive authority of all Germany.

Hess was loyal to Hitler to the point of blindness; even after landing in Scotland he always lowered his voice respectfully when he referred to the Führer.

But nevertheless he could also show surprising gentleness; Professor Haushofer's wife was partly Jewish. Hess shielded her from Nazi criticism and possible persecution. Hess of course had no part in the later atrocities at Buchenwald and Auschwitz and elsewhere; during these horrible years he was in Britain.

Hess was a very superstitious man, and sometimes his superstitions were misinterpreted. When his wife Ilse was preparing for the birth of her child, Hess was desperately anxious to father a son. He knew the old German belief that a summer which sees an unusual number of wasps also sees a predominance of male babies. One afternoon during that summer, when he and his wife and secretary took tea in the garden of their house in Harthauser Strasse, a number of wasps became stuck in the mouth of the honey jar. Hess carefully picked each one out with his spoon, washed the honey off, and then put them out in the sun to dry. His secretary interpreted this as evidence of his kind heart; it was nothing of the sort, but a sign of the strength of his superstitions.

Although he delighted in driving his magnificent Mercedes sports car, painted in a distinctive brown shade which made it instantly recognizable, and although he liked flying for pleasure, Hess never indulged in the usual crude excesses of some Nazis suddenly thrust into positions of power. He had no expensive villas, no art treasures 'borrowed' from museums; his private life was quiet and homely.

But these were largely negative virtues; there seemed little positive to his character. He was not particularly bad—but was he particularly good? Publicly he supported everything that Hitler did; and in many public appearances he loaded the Führer with fulsome praise. Once, in Nuremberg shortly before Christmas, he said: 'We cannot celebrate Christmas without thanking with all our hearts the One Above who sent the Germans their Führer in this time of need and so plainly gave His blessing.'

During the first Christmas of the war, too, Hess wrote an open letter to the mother of an illegitimate child whose father had been killed during the Polish campaign. This was published in all German newspapers.

'We are no longer concerned with antiquated man-made traditions and principles of morality,' Hess declared grandiloquently. 'Today Germany needs robust healthy children prepared to take the place of the men we are now losing.

'The birth of a child is the true symbol of Christmas; therefore we extend our protection to all children who may need it . . .

'If a man dies for his country before he is able to found a home and family, his children, the product of true love, will receive every care.

'I myself am willing to become godfather to all illegitimate children whose fathers lose their lives in the war.'

This was a public declaration. Privately, his views on morality were more orthodox. 'If my son Wolf would . . . produce offspring without my knowing it, so to speak behind my back, and not tell me because of pure cowardice, there would be a hell of a lot of trouble,' he wrote to his wife later.

To many Germans in the nineteen-thirties Hess seemed a symbol of what was best in the Nazi Party's rather dubious programme. After war broke out, and Hitler became naturally much less concerned with issues of domestic policy, it was said that Hess's influence and importance diminished within the Nazi Party; that Martin Bormann, his assistant—and later his successor—was meanwhile growing in authority and importance; that Hess only flew to Scotland to offer peace terms because he felt that such a dramatic act could, if successful, increase his waning influence.

Such considerations may have influenced him, but certainly they were not the main reason why he flew.

Hitler had already nominated Goering as his successor, with Hess next in line, but Hess stood closest to the Führer, for he was responsible not to the Party, but to Hitler alone.

Also, Hess controlled the *Verbindungsstab*, a group that reported on the activities of many people holding high office in Germany. In addition to this it directed the operations of overseas agents and others sympathetic to German aims and ambitions. As such it worked in close touch with the AO, or *Auslandorganisation*, with which Professor Haushofer was closely associated. This dealt ostensibly with the problems of Germans living in foreign lands, but was also used as a convenient cover for various intelligence activities in these countries and elsewhere.

Hess was personally in an impregnable position within the Nazi party and the Reich, standing only beneath Hitler in terms of power and popularity. Haushofer, who had lectured at Munich University when Hess was a student there, came to influence him more and more. At the time of Hess's flight he was in his early seventies, white-haired and benign-looking, with a long academic career behind him.

Before the First World War Haushofer was military attaché in the German Embassy in Tokyo. There he had the temerity to contradict Kaiser Wilhelm's warning to the West that Japan was the 'Yellow Peril'. Haushofer advocated an alliance between Japan and Germany which could smash the Anglo-Saxon world hegemony. This suggestion was treated at the time as being insolent and absurd. Haushofer lived to see not only his theory of Japan's alliance, but also his entire conception of German foreign affairs accepted as a foundation on which a Nazi-dominated empire could be built.

Haushofer was a man of great foresight and, so some said, second sight. During the First War he was a general, and sometimes, for no obvious cause, he would refuse to travel by a given train with his staff, and would make other arrangements. When pressed for his reasons, he would reply that he had a premonition that the train would be bombed. 'And,' Hess admitted once in admiration, 'he was always right.'

Such 'evidence' of psychic ability impressed Hess enormously. Haushofer also believed, quite reasonably, that geographical position, climate, and even the substance of soils played some part in influencing a country's political relationships and reactions. He was ingenious and diligent enough to elevate this theory to the level of a science. He became Professor of Geopoliticks at Munich University; his younger son Albrecht, a bachelor, a poet of distinction, a musician who delighted in Beethoven's sonatas, and a friend of some members of the English aristocracy, occupied a comparable position as Professor for Political Geography and Geopoliticks at Berlin University. At the time when Hess flew to Britain, Albrecht was thirty-eight, ten years younger than the Deputy Führer who was a frequent visitor to the family estate some miles outside Munich.

Karl Haushofer, according to his surviving son, Dr Heinz Haushofer, was a Bavarian monarchist of the old school. After the German defeat in 1918, however, he realized that the monarchy could never be restored; he compromised by making the most of his position as an elder statesman under the Nazi regime.

Some Western politicians of the time saw him as an *eminence gris*, but that was wishful thinking. He was said to control a staff of two thousand strategists, physicists, meteorologists, engineers and economists who checked the information Hess supplied through spies and other agents for Hitler's 'Strategic Index'. This was just not so. Karl Haushofer ran the Geopolitick Institute with one assistant and a typist.

Haushofer was also the part-time President of the German Academy, but he received no pay for his work apart from his pension as a General. He owed his position of esteem in the Nazi organization partly to his intellectual record over the years and also because several of his policies, including that of *lebensraum*—room to live—and his theory of the 'haves and have nots' were adopted by the Nazis as their own.

He helped, if indirectly, to sow the seeds of Hitler's dream to lead a German-controlled Europe that would stretch from the Atlantic to the Urals; he believed that if Germany could capture this area they would be masters of the world.

Haushofer was against making war with England. He admired the liberal ideals of many Englishmen; he pointed out that both races came from a common Germanic strain. But as a teacher at the Military Academy in Munich after the First War he had experienced the full harshness of the Versailles Treaty. In his opinion, and in the view of the men he taught, this demeaned Germany in the eyes of the world. Thus everyone who tried to improve his country's position had his support; Hitler, Hess and the rest came into this category.

He had travelled widely; to India, where he met Kitchener and wrote a brief biography of him; to the Himalayas, where the magic of the mountains laid their spell on him; to Japan, to France, to many European countries. His travels and his experience and his own inner feelings increased his wish to avert a war with the only other European race with whom the Germans had much in common —the English.

His enormous influence played on Hitler at the time of Munich. Heinz Haushofer goes so far as to say that his father 'forced' this agreement on the Führer. Certainly, his father returned to his farm when the agreement was signed and told his family: 'With this Munich agreement we can make German foreign policy for the next ten years.' He was so sure of this that he actually framed a copy of the front page of the Nazi newspaper, the *Voelkische Beobachter*, that gave details of Hitler's meeting with Chamberlain at Berchtesgaden.

On the day war broke out a year later, his wife wrote across this page: 'Please keep as a memory of a great illusion.'

After Munich, in the autumn of 1938, Haushofer prevailed upon Hess to arrange a private interview for him with Hitler *unter vier Augen*—under four eyes, meaning alone and face to face with no one to overhear them.

Haushofer had just returned from a conference of a learned society, the *Volta Society*, in Rome. The subject under discussion had been Africa. Haushofer had talked with the English and French delegates and received the impression, either rightly or wrongly, that it might be possible for Germany to be given control of some territories within this continent; he had in mind the Cameroons. This belief he reported to Hitler in the Home Office in Munich.

'If we abide by the Munich agreement, I am certain that we will be given something,' he said. 'I suggest that you should pay a special visit to England—after all, Mein Führer, Mr Chamberlain came here to see you. This will be interpreted in Britain as a friendly gesture and will do Germany a great deal of good. But, above all, make no moves in the East, especially with regard to Poland, without discussing them first with the Western Powers.'[1]

At this, Hitler stood up, and, without a word, turned on his heel and walked out of the room. He did not even say goodbye. Haushofer sat alone for a few minutes, thinking that the Führer might return; he did not. This was the last time that Haushofer saw him.

[1] Interview by the author with Dr Heinz Haushofer.

CHAPTER FOUR

Haushofer's Hopes

Despite this unpromising reception, the old man remained convinced that he was right and Hitler was wrong. After the defeat of France, Haushofer used his influence with Hess to try and persuade Hitler to offer peace terms to Britain.

Hitler wanted to attack Russia. Hess, Haushofer and Goering warned him of the deadly danger of fighting on two fronts—about which he had himself written in *Mein Kampf*.

'There will be no war on two fronts,' Hitler replied. 'My Atlantic Wall will protect us while we knock out Russia.'

Goering disagreed with this; events would not be so simple. 'We're fighting against a great world power, the British Empire,' he pointed out. 'I am definitely of the opinion that sooner or later . . . the United States will march against us.

'In the case of a clash with Russia, a third great world power would be thrown into the struggle and we would again stand alone against practically the entire world . . .'[1]

Hitler would still not be convinced, but naturally he was willing to negotiate peace with Britain if he could, for this would leave him with only his Eastern Frontier to consider. He was agreeable to such propositions being fully explored, but of course he could take no part in the early stages of any negotiations. If word of his intentions leaked out prematurely in Germany, the effect of his declamations about all-out effort to crush the enemy would be undermined, possibly nullified.

But this did not mean that he did not want peace with Britain—although naturally on his terms—as Mussolini discovered. In June 1940, after France fell, Mussolini travelled with his son-in-law and Foreign Minister, Ciano, to Munich; he was anxious to take over as much as possible of the French Empire in North Africa, plus Nice, Corsica, French Somaliland, Tunisia and other important concessions.

[1] Quoted in *The Rise and Fall of Hermann Goering*, Willi Frischauer, Odhams.

To his surprise, Hitler refused to make any demands on the French that might encourage them to continue the fight against Germany, either from North Africa or from England.

Ciano asked Ribbentrop bluntly: 'Does Germany at the present moment prefer peace or the prosecution of the war?'[1]

Ribbentrop replied with one word: 'Peace.' Ribbentrop added that Britain had already been informed of this wish through certain contacts in Sweden. To Hitler's surprise these produced no reply.

Then, on June 18, Churchill told the House of Commons that the British Government would fight on, whatever the odds, 'so that, if the British Empire and its Commonwealth last for a thousand years, men will still say: "This was their finest hour." '

Words reached Churchill that a message had been sent from the Vatican, by way of Berne, in neutral Switzerland, on the subject of peace negotiations. On June 28 he sent a minute to Anthony Eden, his Foreign Secretary: 'I hope it will be made clear to the Nuncio that we do not desire to make any inquiries as to terms of peace with Hitler, and that all our agents are strictly forbidden to entertain any such suggestions.'[2]

Five days later, on July 3, the British Navy bombarded the French fleet lying at Oran on the North African coast.

These were the results of Hitler's peace feelers; the answer clearly was 'No'.

Nevertheless, Hitler waited for twelve more days, in the hope that such warlike words and deeds might conceal some peaceful intent. Then he addressed the Reichstag on the matter.

'Mr Churchill ought perhaps, for once, to believe me when I prophesy that a great Empire will be destroyed—an Empire which it was never my intention to destroy or even to harm,' he declared.

'I feel it to be my duty before my own conscience to appeal once more to reason and common sense in Great Britain as elsewhere. I consider myself in a position to make this appeal since I am not the vanquished begging favours, but the victor speaking in the name of reason. I can see no reason why the war must go on . . .'[3]

---

[1] *Ciano's Diplomatic Papers*, edited by Malcolm Muggeridge, pp. 372–5; see also *Hitler, A Study in Tyranny*, by Alan Bullock, Odhams, p. 541.

[2] Quoted in *The Second World War*, Vol. II, *Their Finest Hour*, by Sir Winston Churchill, Cassell.

[3] *My New Order* (Hitler's Speeches 1922–43), edited by Gordon W. Prange, American Council of Foreign Affairs, Washington, 1944.

'Naturally,' wrote Churchill later,[1] 'Hitler would be very glad, after having subjugated Europe to his will, to bring the war to an end by procuring British acceptance of what he had done. It was, in fact, an offer not of peace but of readiness to accept the surrender by Britain of all she had entered the war to maintain.'

In Germany Haushofer still hoped that some peace negotiations could be satisfactorily arranged. On September 3, 1940—exactly one year to the day after the war began—he wrote[2] to his son Albrecht, about a meeting with Hess—to whom he referred as Tomo for reasons of security.

'A meeting with Tomo from 5:00 o'clock in the afternoon until 2:00 o'clock in the morning, which included a 3-hour walk in the Grünwald Forest, at which we conversed a good deal about serious matters. I have really got to tell you about a part of it now.

'As you know, everything is so prepared for a very hard and severe attack on the island in question that the highest ranking person only has to press a button to set it off. But before this decision, which is perhaps inevitable, the thought once more occurs as to whether there is really no way of stopping something which would have such infinitely momentous consequences. There is a line of reasoning in connection with this which I must absolutely pass on to you because it was obviously communicated to me with this intention. Do you, too, see no way in which such possibilities could be discussed at a third place with a middle man, possibly the old Ian Hamilton[3] or the other Hamilton?[4]

'I replied to these suggestions that there would perhaps have been an excellent opportunity for this in Lisbon at the Contennial,[5] if, instead of harmless figureheads, it had been possible to send well-disguised political persons there. In this connection it seems to me a stroke of fate that our old friend, Missis (sic) V.R., evidently, though after long delay, finally found a way of sending a note with cordial and gracious words of good wishes not only for your mother, but also for Heinz[6] and me, and added the address.

[1] The Second World War, Vol. II, ibid.

[2] For a complete translation of these letters, see Appendix.

[3] Sir Ian S. M. Hamilton (1853–1947), British general and author.

[4] On the basis of references later in this correspondence the reference here is to Douglas Douglas-Hamilton, Duke of Hamilton.

[5] On June 2, 1940, Portugal had begun a series of celebrations commemorating the 800th anniverary of the foundation of the state and 300th anniversary of the restoration of national independence.

[6] Dr Heinz Haushofer, brother of Albrecht.

'Address your reply to: Miss V. Roberts, c/o Postbox 506, Lisbon, Portugal.[1] I have the feeling that no good possibility should be overlooked; at least it should be well considered.'

A week later, on September 10, Hess wrote to Karl Haushofer.

'Dear Friend: Albrecht brought me your letter, which, at the beginning, besides containing official information, alluded to our walk together on the last day of August, which I, too, recall with so much pleasure.

'Albrecht will have told you about our conversation, which besides volksdeutsch matters, above all touched upon the other matter, which is so close to the hearts of us both. I reconsidered the latter carefully once more and have arrived at the following conclusion:

'Under no conditions must we disregard the contact or allow it to die aborning. I consider it best that you or Albrecht write to the old lady, who is a friend of your family, suggesting that she try to ask Albrecht's friend whether he would be prepared if necessary to come to the neutral territory in which she resides, or at any rate has an address through which she can be reached, just to talk with Albrecht.

'If he could not do this just now, he might, in any case, send word through her where he expects to be in the near future. Possibly a neutral acquaintance, who had some business to attend to over there anyway, might look him up and make some communication to him, using you or Albrecht as reference.

'This person probably would not care to have to inquire as to his whereabouts only after he got there or to make futile trips. You thought that knowing about his whereabouts had no military significance at all; if necessary you would also pledge yourselves not to make use of it with regard to any quarter which might profit from it. What the neutral would have to transmit would be of such great importance that his having made known his whereabouts would be by comparison insignificant.

'The prerequisite naturally was that the inquiry in question and the reply would not go through official channels, for you would not in any case want to cause your friends over there any trouble.

'It would be best to have the letter to the old lady with whom you are acquainted delivered through a confidential agent of the AO (Ausland Organization) to the address that is known to you. For

[1] This sentence is in English in the original.

50

this purpose Albrecht would have to speak either with Bohle[1] or my brother. At the same time the lady would have to be given the address of this agent in L.—or if the latter does not live there permanently, to which the reply can in turn be delivered.

'As for the neutral I have in mind, I would like to speak to you orally about it some time. There is no hurry about that since, in any case, there would first have to be a reply received here from over there.

'Meanwhile let's both keep our fingers crossed. Should success be the fate of the enterprise, the oracle given to you with regard to the month of August would yet be fulfilled, since the name of the young friend and the old lady friend of your family occurred to you during our quiet walk on the last day of the month.

'With best regards to you and to Martha,

Yours, as ever,

R(UDOLF) H(ESS)

Can be reached by telephone through: Linz-Gallspach A.'

Five days after this, on September 15th, Albrecht Haushofer wrote a memo on his meeting with Hess during the previous week. It was marked *Top Secret* and headed 'Are There Still Possibilities of a German-English Peace?':[2]

'On September 8th I was summoned to Bad G. (Godesberg) to report to the Deputy of the Führer on the subject discussed in this memorandum. The conversation which the two of us had alone lasted 2 hours. I had the opportunity to speak in all frankness.

'I was immediately asked about the possibilities of making known to persons of importance in England Hitler's serious desire for peace. It was quite clear that the continuance of the war was suicidal for the white race. Even with complete success in Europe, Germany was not in a position to take over inheritance of the Empire. The Führer had not wanted to see the Empire destroyed and did not want it even today. Was there not somebody in England who was ready for peace? . . .

'I ought not—precisely because of my long experience in attempting to effect a settlement with England in the past and my numerous English friendships—to make it appear that I seriously believe in the possibility of a settlement between Adolf Hitler and England in the

[1] Ernst Wilhelm Bohle, the Bradford born chief of certain Fifth Column activities. He was nominated to be gauleiter of Great Britain when Germany won the war.

[2] Part of the files of the Haushofer family, seized after the war and now in the World War II, Records Division of the National Archives in Alexandria, Va. See 'Guide to German Records Microfilmed at Alexandria', No. 9, page 11 and the following pages.

present stage of development. I was thereupon asked whether I was not of the opinion that feelers had perhaps not been successful because the right language had not been used. I replied that, to be sure —if certain persons, whom we both knew well, were meant by this statement—then certainly the wrong language had been used. But at the present stage this had little significance. I was then asked directly why all Englishmen were so opposed to Herr v. R(ibbentrop)

'I conceded, that, in the eyes of the English, Herr v. R(ibbentrop) like some other personages, played, to be sure, the same role as did Duff Cooper, Eden, and Churchill in the eyes of the Germans. In the case of Herr v. R., there was also the conviction, precisely in the view of Englishmen who were formerly friendly to Germany that— from completely biased motives—he had informed the Führer wrongly about England and that he personally bore an unusually large share of the responsibility for the outbreak of the war. But I again stressed the fact that the rejection of peace feelers by England was today due not so much to persons as to the fundamental outlook mentioned above.

'Nevertheless, I was asked to name those whom I thought might be reached as possible contacts. I mentioned, among diplomats, Minister O'Malley in Budapest the former head of the Southeastern Department of the Foreign Office, a clever person in the higher echelons of officialdom, but perhaps without influence precisely because of his former friendliness toward Germany; Sir Samuel Hoare, who is half-shelved and half on the watch in Madrid, whom I do not know well personally, but to whom I can at any time open a personal path; as the most promising, the Washington Ambassador Lothian, with whom I have had close personal connections for years, who as a member of the highest aristocracy and at the same time as a person of very independent mind, is perhaps best in a position to undertake a bold step—provided that he could be convinced that even a bad and uncertain peace would be better than the continuance of the war —a conviction at which he will only arrive if he convinces himself in Washington that English hopes of America are not realizable.

'Whether or not this is so could only be judged in Washington itself; from Germany not at all. As the final possibility I then mentioned that of a personal meeting on neutral soil, with the closest of my English friends: the young Duke of Hamilton, who has access at all times to all important persons in London, even to Churchill and the King.

'I stressed in this case the inevitable difficulty of making a contact

and again repeated my conviction of the improbability of its succeeding—whatever approach we took.

'The upshot of the conversation was H.'s statement that he would
consider the whole matter thoroughly once more and send me word
in case I was to take steps. For this extremely ticklish case, and in the
event that I might possibly have to make a trip alone—I asked for
very precise directives from the highest authority. From the whole
conversation I had the strong impression that it was not conducted
without the prior knowledge of the Führer, and that I probably
would not hear any more about the matter unless a new understanding had been reached between him and his Deputy.'

Eight days after this, on September 23rd, Albrecht Haushofer
reported to the Deputy Führer what he had done.

'My dear Herr Hess,' he wrote, 'In accordance with your last
telephone call I got in touch with your brother immediately. Everything went off well, and I can now report that the mission has been
accomplished to the extent that the letter you desired was written
and dispatched this morning. It is to be hoped that it will be more
efficacious than sober judgement would indicate.

Yours, etc.

H(AUSHOFER)'

He sent a copy of this letter to his father by the same post, and
although he had done all that had been asked of him, he was by no
means confident of the result.

'Dear Father,' he wrote, 'I am enclosing the copy of a short letter
of serious contents, which perhaps had better be kept by you than
by me. I have now made it clear enough that in the action involved
I did not take the initiative . . .

'Now to the English matters. I am convinced, as before, that there
is not the slightest prospect of peace; and so I don't have the least
faith in the possibility about which you know. However, I also
believe that I could not have refused my services any longer. You
know that for myself I do not see any possibility of any satisfying
activity in the future . . .'

Albrecht also wrote privately to both his parents.

'The whole thing is a fool's errand,[1] but we cannot do anything
about that. According to our latest reports the treaties of union between the Empire and the United States are about to be signed.'

[1] The preceding part of this sentence is in English in the original.

He enclosed copies of what he called 'important documents'. With these he sent a copy of his letter to Hess. It was marked *Top Secret*.

September 19, 1940.

'My dear Herr Hess. Your letter of the 10th reached me yesterday after a delay caused by the antiquated postal service of Partnach-Alm. I again gave a thorough study to the possibilities discussed therein and request—before taking the steps proposed—that you yourself examine once more the thoughts set forth below.

'I have in the meantime been thinking of the technical route by which a message from me must travel before it can reach the Duke of H(amilton). With your help, delivery to Lisbon can of course be assured without difficulty. About the rest of the route we do not know. Foreign control must be taken into account; the letter must therefore in no case be composed in such a way that it will simply be seized and destroyed or that it will directly endanger the woman transmitting it or the ultimate recipient.

'In view of my close personal relations and intimate acquaintance with Douglas H(amilton) I can write a few lines to him (which should be enclosed with the letter to Mrs R., without any indication of place and without a full name—an A. would suffice for signature) in such a way that he alone will recognize that behind my wish to see him in Lisbon there is something more serious than a personal whim. All the rest, however, seems to be extremely hazardous and detrimental to the success of the letter.

'Let us suppose that the case were reversed: an old lady in Germany receives a letter from an unknown source abroad, with the request to forward a message whose recipient is asked to disclose to an unknown foreigner where he will be staying for a certain period —and this recipient were a high officer in the air force (of course I do not know exactly what position H. holds at the moment; judging from his past I can conceive of only three things: He is an active air force general, or he directs the air defence of an important part of Scotland, or he has a responsible position in the Air Ministry).

'I do not think that you need much imagination to picture to yourself the faces that Canaris or Heydrich would make and the smirk with which they would consider any offer of security or confidence in such a letter if a subordinate should submit such a case to them. They would not merely make faces, you may be certain! The measures would come quite automatically—and neither the old lady nor the air force officer would have an easy time of it! In England it is no different.

'Now another thing. Here, too, I would ask you to picture the situation in reverse. Let us assume that I received such a letter from one of my English friends. I would quite naturally report the matter to the highest German authorities I could contact, as soon as I had realized the import it might have, and would ask for instructions on what I should do myself (at that, I am a civilian and H. is an officer).

'If it should be decided that I was to comply with the wish for a meeting with my friend, I would then be most anxious to get my instructions if not from the Führer himself, at least from a person who receives them directly and at the same time has the gift of transmitting the finest and lightest nuances—an art which has been mastered by you yourself but not by all Reich Ministers.

'In addition, I should very urgently request that my action be fully covered vis-à-vis other high authorities of my own country—un-informed or unfavourable. It is not any different with H. He cannot fly to Lisbon—any more than I can!—unless he is given leave, that is unless at least Air Minister Sinclair and Foreign Minister Halifax know about it. If, however, he receives permission to reply or to go, there is no need of indicating any place in England; if he does not receive it, then any attempt through a neutral mediator would also have little success.

'In this case the technical problem of contacting H. is the least of the difficulties. A neutral who knows England and can move about in England—presumably there would be little sense in entrusting anyone else with such a mission—will be able to find the first peer of Scotland very quickly as long as conditions in the Isle are still half-way in order. (At the time of a successful invasion all the possibilities we are discussing here would be pointless anyway.)

'My proposal is therefore as follows:

'Through the old friend I will write a letter to H.—in a form that will incriminate no one but will be understandable to the recipient—with the proposal for a meeting in Lisbon. If nothing comes of that, it will be possible (if the military situation leaves enough time for it), assuming that a suitable intermediary is available, to make a second attempt through a neutral going to England, who might be given a personal message to take along. With respect to this possibility, I must add, however, that H. is extremely reserved—as many English are toward anyone they do not know personally. Since the entire

Anglo-German problem after all springs from a most profound crisis in mutual confidence, this would not be immaterial.

'Please excuse the length of this letter; I merely wished to explain the situation to you fully.

'I already tried to explain to you not long ago that, for the reasons I gave, the possibilities of successful efforts at a settlement between the Führer and the British upper class seem to me—to my extreme regret—infinitesimally small. Nevertheless I should not want to close this letter without pointing out once more that I still think there would be a somewhat greater chance of success in going through Ambassador Lothian in Washington or Sir Samuel Hoare in Madrid rather than through my friend H. To be sure, they are—politically speaking—more inaccessible.

'Would you send me a line or give me a telephone call with final instructions? If necessary, will you also inform your brother in advance? Presumably I will then have to discuss with him the forwarding of the letter to Lisbon and the arrangement for a cover address for the reply in L(isbon).

'With cordial greetings and best wishes for your health.

Yours, etc.

A(LBRECHT) H(AUSHOFER).'

He attached a draft of another letter to the Duke of Hamilton, headed:

Draft Letter to D.H.

'My dear D . . .,' he wrote, 'Even if this letter has only a slight chance of reaching you—there is a chance and I want to make use of it.

'First of all, to give you a sign of unaltered and unalterable personal attachment. I do hope you have been spared in all this ordeal and I hope the same is true of your brothers. I heard of your father's deliverance from long suffering; and I heard that your brother-in-law Northumberland lost his life near Dunkerque. I need hardly tell you how I feel about all that . . .

'Now there is one thing more. If you remember some of my last communications before the war started you will realize that there is a certain significance in the fact that I am, at present, able to ask you whether there is the slightest chance of our meeting and having a talk somewhere on the outskirts of Europe, perhaps in Portugal. There are some things I could tell you, that might make it worth while for you to try a short trip to Lisbon—if you could make your authorities understand so much that they would give you leave. As

56

to myself—I could reach Lisbon any time (without any kind of difficulty) within a few days after receiving news from you.

'If there is an answer to this letter, please address it to . . .'[1]

The Duke received the final letter from Haushofer; he immediately handed it over to the appropriate authorities. Albrecht Haushofer was wise in being pessimistic; these attempts to make contact with the British were as unsuccessful as the earlier attempts through Berne and the Vatican.

'Haushofer,' said a friend afterwards, 'clearly foresaw that a total defeat of Germany would be followed by so weighty a shifting of power in favour of the Soviet Union that crucial parts of the British Empire would also be endangered by it.'[2]

This fact also worried Hess; he placed enormous value on the advice and opinions of the two Haushofers, father and son, and he shared their alarm at the possibility of Hitler fighting on two fronts. These abortive attempts to contact someone of influence were of course known to Hitler, whose disappointment and truculence increased with their failure.

'Hitler,' so Ciano noted, 'would like an understanding with Great Britain. He knows that war with the British will be hard and bloody, and knows also that people everywhere are averse from bloodshed.'[3]

But week merged into week, and month into month, and still no word came from the British either in secret or openly that they would be prepared to make peace. With each hour that passed the need for this to happen became more urgent, for the date of 'Barbarossa', the code name for the attack on Russia, grew ever more imminent. If Britain could be persuaded to come to terms, perhaps even to help and certainly to condone war against Russia, there could be no doubt as to the outcome of 'Barbarossa'; it would be a certain victory won on a single front. As long as eight years earlier, Leon Trotsky had laid down[4] the ideal conditions for such a German attack on the Soviet Union.

[1] The draft letter is in English in the original. The Duke of Hamilton's report of his interview with Hess on May 11, 1941, is printed in *Trial of the Major War Criminals before the International Military Tribunal* (Nuremberg, 1948), vol. xxxviii, document No. 116-M. This refers to a letter dated September 23, 1940, from Albrecht Haushofer. The excerpt printed here is evidently a draft of that letter. See also Rainer Hildebrandt, *Wir sind die Letzten: Aus dem Leben des Widerstandskampfers Albrecht Haushofer und seiner Freunde* (Neuwied-Berlin, n.d.), p. 110.

[2] *Vierteljahrshefte fuer Zeitgeschichte*, 8 Jahrgang, 1960; Walter Stubbe: *In memoriam Albrecht Haushofer*, p. 236.

[3] *Ciano's Diplomatic Papers*, p. 381.

[4] Article in the *Sunday Chronicle*, September 19, 1933.

'An attack upon the West could only be carried out on condition of a military alliance between Germany and the Soviet,' he declared. This already existed. 'The attack against the East could only take place with the support of one or more powerful States of the West.'

This Hess determined to engineer.

Haushofer had already told him that the Duke of Hamilton was Lord Steward and thought 'a personage like that would probably be dining every night with the King, and would have his private ear. Here was a channel of direct access.'[1]

Moreover, Professor Haushofer had also told Hess that he had experienced three dreams on three separate nights in which he saw Hess piloting an aeroplane to some unknown but important destination. In yet another dream he had seen Hess walking in some great castle with tartan tapestries on its walls. With Hess's own recollection of Haushofer's apparent gift of premonition twenty-four years earlier on the Western Front, these remarks made a great impression on him. Nor was the fact that the Duke of Hamilton was the premier Scottish Duke lost upon Hess.

Later, reviewing his thoughts at this time, Hess recalled that there were acts of war between England and Germany, in the course of which the former suffered more damage than did Germany; so that he felt England could not give way without suffering a severe loss of prestige.

'I then said to myself: "This is the moment when your plan must really be carried out, for if you are over in England this might prove an occasion for England to enter into discussions, without loss of prestige." It was my opinion that, apart from the conditions necessary for an understanding, there was a general mistrust to be overcome.

'I was confronted by a very hard decision. I do not think I could have arrived at my final choice unless I had continually kept before my eyes the vision of an endless line of children's coffins with weeping mother behind them, both English and German; and another line of coffins of mothers with mourning children.'[2]

Haushofer had been on friendly terms with the Duke for some years before the war. Indeed, when Ribbentrop, as German Ambassador to Britain, had antagonized many people in this country by

[1] *The Grand Alliance*, Winston S. Churchill.
[2] Part of a statement by Hess to Sir John Simon on June 9, 1941.

his attitude, and his habit of giving the Nazi salute in public, Haushofer came over to try and smooth matters out and to persuade Ribbentrop to change his ways. On this occasion, he stayed with the Duke of Hamilton in his London house.

But Haushofer's letter of September 23, 1940, written at the height of the Battle of Britain, was never delivered to the Duke. Instead, some months later, in early 1941, when reverses were being endured by British Armies in the North African desert, the Duke received a casual and very informal letter from a senior intelligence officer in the R.A.F., a Group Captain whom he knew slightly.

In this note the Group Captain asked him to 'drop in and see me whenever you are next in London'. The Duke had a short leave due about a fortnight after this letter arrived, and, being in London, called to see the Group Captain at his office in one of the Air Ministry buildings.

The Group Captain motioned him to a seat.

'Now what have you done with the letter Haushofer wrote you?' he began conversationally.

The Duke thought that he referred to a letter that Albrecht Haushofer had sent him just before the war, and which he had shown at that time to the proper authorities.

'No, no, not that one,' said the Intelligence officer. 'The one you've just received. *This* one.' And he handed the Duke of Hamilton a photostat of Haushofer's letter of September 23.

The Duke read it in amazement. This was the first he had heard about a letter from Haushofer. He asked how it came into the possession of the Intelligence officer. The Group Captain explained that the censorship authorities had intercepted it and made that copy for him. In fact, the Duke has still never received the original; it had disappeared and has never been traced.

'Well, we're interested in this proposal,' went on the Group Captain. 'We wondered whether you would go out to Lisbon for us and see what it's all about?'

The Duke of Hamilton did not show much enthusiasm for this proposition. It was quite outside his usual Air Force duties, which were occupying all his time, and he naturally had no wish to go on his own authority, and without the fullest briefing. However, he agreed to see the Director of RAF Intelligence to discuss the matter, and a meeting was arranged. A number of officers concerned with the aspects of Intelligence and Security were also present. It was suggested that the Duke of Hamilton should write to Albrecht

Haushofer and explain that he was willing to fly to Lisbon to meet him; a date, time and place could then be agreed.

Still Hamilton hesitated. Finally, one of the Intelligence men asked him bluntly: 'Are you prepared to do it?'

'I will go if I am ordered to go,' replied the Duke quietly.

The others looked at each other uneasily. 'We don't like to *order* people to do these sort of jobs,' one of them explained. 'We like volunteers. Then we can brief them. So I'm asking you, *will* you do it?'

'If it's an order, I will,' replied the Duke. 'But I would like to make some conditions.' He was asked to name them. He pointed out that for an assignment of this magnitude and responsibility he must be able to have direct access to the British Ambassador in Lisbon, and be free to seek his advice on any points that might emerge from his meeting with Haushofer.

The Intelligence officers promised to consider this. They told the Duke that in the meantime he should treat the matter as being in abeyance until he heard from them further. It would come up before the War Cabinet and then they would be in touch with him again. In fact, they never were in touch, for within weeks Hess arrived precipitately and unexpected—under the impression that Haushofer's attempts to contact the Duke of Hamilton in Lisbon had failed. Actually, they had not properly begun.

Frau Hess believes that a further factor influenced her husband and tended to complicate the issue. In the summer of 1939 an English friend gave Hess a copy of General Sir Ian Hamilton's book, *When I was a Boy*; this dealt warmly with the General's reminiscences of his youth when he lived in Germany. It contained a sentence which made a great influence on Hess before he made his flight. 'In Germany as a young man,' the General wrote, 'I dropped my nationality; as a Hamilton I might be taken for a milord—perhaps the Duke of Hamilton.'

Karl Haushofer had already suggested that either Sir Ian or the Duke of Hamilton should be contacted. Frau Hess believes that her husband felt these two men might be related, for they shared the same name.[1]

And so Hess reached his decision. As he put it, he gradually

[1] General Halder noted in his diary on May 15, 1941, that Hitler had explained to the heads of the Army that Hess was flying to Glasgow as 'the first goal', where he proposed to contact Lord Hamilton, head of the British Legion. Hess was shown this extract at Nuremberg and wrote to his wife: 'This is an error due to confusing the Duke of Hamilton with Sir Ian Hamilton.'

'formed the notion of softening the irreconcilably hostile attitude of the British by some unusual and dramatic act'. In a letter to Albrecht Haushofer, which he left behind him, he wrote that in his views there remained only one possibility: 'To cut the Gordian knot of this unhappy entanglement.'

This time, no letters, no agents, no intermediaries would be used: as an earnest of Germany's good intentions, he would fly to Britain himself, to meet the Duke of Hamilton and ask to be taken before the two men he considered most important in Britain and the Empire—Winston Churchill and King George VI.

* * *

At about half-past eleven on Sunday morning, when Hess lay dozing in his hospital bed in Buchanan Castle, Eric Schofield, the general manager of the Glasgow *Daily Record*, was taking a walk through Eaglesham with his dog. This was his custom on most fine Sunday mornings; he lived at Newton Mearns, only a short distance away.

Usually, Schofield found Eaglesham virtually deserted, apart from families walking home from church, or farm and munition workers and servicemen on leave waiting for the Eglinton Arms to open. On this particular Sunday, however, Schofield noticed that small groups of people stood talking together on the corners of the streets and outside cottage doors. As they talked, some of them pointed towards Floors Farm.

When Schofield reached the smithy in Waterfoot, past Floors Road, with its one petrol pump labelled 'Pool', curiosity overcame him.

'What's everyone talking about?' he asked a man in a raincoat, one of a small group in front of the smithy's closed and padlocked doors.

'It's the plane that crashed last night,' the man replied. 'You've heard about it, surely?'

'Not a thing,' said Schofield. 'What about it?'

The man took a deep breath. Then, like the Ancient Mariner, he seized Schofield's jacket lapel with one hand and pointed dramatically towards Floors Farm with the other.

'It came down there just before eleven o'clock last night,' he said. 'A German fighter. The pilot baled out and was taken to Davie McLean's place. Then the Home Guard took him to their hut. Now I believe he's in Glasgow.'

'Well, what's so strange about a Jerry pilot crashing?'

'Ah, I'm coming to that. This fellow flies here all the way across Scotland in some new type of Messerschmitt plane no one has seen before. A plane that's got no ammunition for its guns! That's the first thing. Next, he couldn't hope to get away again because the boys up at the RAF Camp say a plane of this sort can't carry enough juice to take it back to Germany. And the pilot's not the usual sort of Jerry airman, either. He's old, nearly fifty. And then he's not wearing the usual sort of uniform. It's made of special cloth. McLean was telling us that he'd never seen the like of it. Also, he's got a gold watch, and a gold bracelet, and boots that McLean says are as soft as a leather glove. He's a pot all right, a proper pot.'

The man paused before going on to what he regarded as being the most interesting piece of information, and which he had deliberately kept to the last.

'And another thing,' he said with relish, measuring out his words slowly, enjoying every one. 'He was asking for the Duke of Hamilton.'

'Was he now? And what did he want him for?' The man shrugged. 'I don't know,' he admitted. 'But that's who he wanted. Said he had to see him urgently. He seemed proper put out when they told him the Duke wasn't at Dungavel any more. Said he'd come specially from Munich to see him.'

'I wonder who he was?' asked Schofield innocently.

'Ah, that's what we *all* want to know. Who was he? He could speak English, too, *and* he knew exactly the man he wanted to see. Makes you think, doesn't it?'

'It does indeed,' agreed Schofield, and whistled for his dog.

As he walked home through the empty lanes he pondered on what the man had told him. Clearly, there must be something remarkable in the incident, or it would not have caused so much speculation among these usually dour people. It was certainly not uncommon for a German plane to be shot down during that summer, and although such unfortunate pilots occasionally aroused local hostility and were met with pitchforks, they were just as likely to be met with cups of tea until the police or troops arrived.

But none of them had aroused much local interest; certainly nothing like this. Schofield decided to telephone his office and suggest that they followed up the story and find who this strange airman could be.

* * *

1 Youth rally at Nuremberg, 1938. Hess, Hitler and von Schirach.

Rudolf Hess in Tripoli, 1937; a photograph taken by his wife.

A picture of Rudolf Hess's house in Munich before it was bombed in 1944.

10. Mai 1941   11ʰ

x stärkere mehrschichtige Bewölkung, etwas Niederschlag.
Untere Bewölkung an den Süd- und Ostseiten der Gebirge
aufgelockert.

z Bewölkung in mehreren Schichten, im Norden tief
herabreichend und geschlossen, etwas Niederschlag,
untere Bewölkung nach Süden hin auflockernd.

y wolkig, Norden bedeckt und etwas Niederschlag.

2 Photostat of the weather report Hess received before making his flight on May 10, 1941.

A drawing Hess made for his son, Wolf Rüdiger, soon after he landed in Scotland on May 10, 1941. His wife and friends thought it contained some clues of message as to his whereabouts; it did not.

Sunday morning in a newspaper office is a flat, bleak time, the aftermath of Saturday night. Bored, disinterested reporters light cigarettes they do not want, and envy friends and neighbours who have their Sundays free.

On this particular Sunday morning, the *Daily Record* office was deserted except for one or two messenger boys trying their skill on reporters' typewriters, and the duty reporter Max McAuslane, a young man awaiting his call-up into the RAF. He was deputizing for the news editor, who was on holiday.

McAuslane had just read without much enthusiasm a note left by the news editor of the *Sunday Mail*, their companion Sunday paper, concerning a German plane that had crashed at Eaglesham on Saturday too late for their edition to print the news. McAuslane screwed up the note into a ball and threw it on the floor; such events were a commonplace. He began to read the Sunday newspapers, marking with a pencil any item his staff could follow up, when his telephone rang. He picked it up.

'News desk,' he said crisply.

'Schofield here,' replied the general manager. 'I've just been for a walk through Eaglesham. A Nazi plane came down there last night. Everyone's talking about it.'

'Yes, I know, sir. I've got a note here about it.'

'There's something strange about it, in my view. Apparently it's a Messerschmitt fighter, and an awful long way from home. I'm told a Messerschmitt can't carry enough petrol to reach here from Munich—where the pilot says he came from—and get back. Also, he was wearing some kind of fancy uniform. And he says he wanted to see the Duke of Hamilton! There's something odd here, McAuslane. Get a man out to interview everybody he can, and take some pictures of the plane, too. They may be useful.'

As McAuslane replaced the telephone, John Simpson, the chief reporter on the *Record*, came into the office, hung up his raincoat and crossed the big room towards him.

'Anything doing?' he asked.

'No, nothing at all, except that a German plane's come down at Eaglesham. Mr Schofield has just been on to say the locals think there's something fishy in it.'

He repeated Schofield's message.

'You'd better get out there, John,' McAuslane told him. 'There should be no difficulty about finding the site. Take a photographer and give me a ring if it makes anything.'

63

The photographer was reluctant to go on this assignment. 'It's just a waste of time going out there,' he declared. 'Planes are dropping like flies all over the place. What's so special about this one?'

However, he finally agreed to go; but stubbornly he refused to photograph either McLean or his mother. He insisted that his instructions were only to take pictures of the aeroplane, no less and certainly no more.

The editor, Clem Livingstone, was spending that week-end in Callander, thirty-six miles from Glasgow. McAuslane telephoned him about the matter and he decided to return immediately. Although this could simply be the story of a crashed German fighter miles off course, somehow the story seemed to possess enough sufficiently unusual features to merit a full investigation. So by late afternoon, Livingstone was back in his office reading Simpson's story and examining the photographs.

The German pilot was inaccessible, and the local police, with whom Simpson was on good terms, were unexpectedly reluctant to discuss the matter. The most Simpson could discover was that Horn was in an unnamed hospital 'somewhere in Scotland'.

McAuslane assembled the sparse facts at his command. He had no idea whatever of the pilot's identity but suggested that his uniform could only belong to an officer of high social position. The highest foreign title he could think of was a Count.

During the war every newspaper story that contained any mention of military matters had first to be submitted to the local Censor. If he could not give a direction on whether it should be published, he had to seek guidance from his head office in London. The Censor's office in Glasgow was on the second floor of a building in Bothwell Street. This building also contained the War Room for the Glasgow area which dealt with the Civil Defence, the Security Police, and the constant checks kept on people arriving and departing in vessels up and down the Clyde.

McAuslane decided to take the typescript of the story to the Censor himself, instead of sending it by messenger; he had a hunch that the Censor's attitude towards the story might supply a clue as to its importance.

He climbed up the uncarpeted stairs with their walls plastered by notices warning against careless talk, about the collection of emergency ration cards and the location of air-raid shelters, and handed his typed story across the desk to the Censor, a pleasant-faced man of middle-age. He sat down on one of the hard-backed wooden chairs in the cheerless little office and awaited the verdict.

McAuslane was the only newspaperman there; Sunday afternoon, even in war, was not a time of great journalistic activity. Idly, he looked at the clock above the Censor's desk and checked it with his watch: it was half-past four. He kicked his heels against the crossbar of the chair, wondering what the Censor would say to this seemingly innocent story.

The Censor read it through and then took it out of the room to show a colleague; when he returned each sheet bore an oval-shaped blue rubber-stamp: 'Held—C.' This meant that it should not be published; more, that it was unlikely that permission would ever be given for its publication.

'What's the matter with it, then?' asked McAuslane innocently. 'There's nothing objectionable in it, surely?'

'Nothing objectionable,' agreed the Censor primly, smoothing some sheets of paper on his desk with the palm of his hand. 'Nothing objectionable at all. It's just rubbish, that's all.'

'But surely we can publish rubbish if we want to?' pursued McAuslane.

'You'll not be publishing that rubbish,' retorted the Censor quickly.

It was then that McAuslane knew what he had previously only suspected: there must indeed be more in this apparently simple story of a German plane crashing on a Saturday night than had at first appeared.

CHAPTER FIVE

Hess borrows a Messerschmitt

At that same moment, 850 miles south-south-east from Glasgow lunch was ending in Hitler's home, the Berghof at Berchtesgaden. This house stood at the heart of a huge artificial park built in the mountains 100 miles from Munich. It was guarded constantly, and surrounded by several cordons of barbed wire, with electric alarms. It was the home with which Hitler had the warmest and the closest associations.

In his early days as a politician, he would frequently visit the Bechstein family—the piano manufacturers—at their villa on the mountain of Obersalzberg, near Berchtesgaden. Three hundred feet above their house stood a small wooden chalet, the 'Haus Wachenfeld', built before the First War by a Hamburg merchant. Hitler liked this so much that he rented it, and then when royalties from *Mein Kampf* began to multiply, he bought it outright. In those early days, when his income derived mainly from newspaper articles, he would frequently retire here and write or dictate them to Hess, or to his niece, Geli, a girl of seventeen. Her mother, his widowed half-sister, acted as his housekeeper.

As Hitler's power grew after 1933 he enlarged the house and made various improvements, and changed its name to 'Berghof'—literally, the mountain court. As the years passed, what had been a delightful and unspoilt part of Germany became riddled with concrete roads, leading to barracks for guards; to underground air-raid shelters, to garages and guest houses for distinguished visitors.

Here Hitler received Neville Chamberlain, the British Prime Minister when he flew out in 1938 to avert a war over Czechoslovakia. Berchtesgaden was so remote from England then that the flight took seven hours. Later, this was reduced, but one of the attractions of the place for Hitler was its comparative inaccessibility. Here he would retire for short periods during the war, keeping in touch with his commanders in the field by direct lines running through his private exchange. This was fitted with an ingenious device to prevent any operator overhearing any call, even though the call might not be 'scrambled'.

Here, too, Hitler maintained his own strange and private court throughout the war years with its peculiar Wagnerian protocol. Each day had its own ritual beginning late and ending with the dawn, for Hitler was a poor sleeper and hated to be alone. After dinner at night he would sit with whatever guests or secretaries were with him at the open fireplace in the great hall. He would talk and they would listen; for hour after hour his voice droned on, as his captive audience concealed their weariness as best they could. Only at two or three on the following morning would he leave, and they could then creep away, cold and cramped and exhausted, to their own bedrooms.

Usually lunch in the Berghof began at three o'clock in the afternoon, when Hitler had finally finished what he called his 'morning conferences'. But on this particular Sunday lunch was early: later in the afternoon a special reception was being arranged for Admiral Darlan.

On one wall of the dining-room, panelled in light wood, was a gilded clock with imitation rays of light stretching out from each figure. As lunch ended they pointed to 3.30 p.m. Germany had added only one hour for summer time, whereas in Britain, double summer time was in force.

The meal was simple. Hitler, who lived almost entirely on vegetables, for even bread and butter gave him indigestion, had eaten dishes of tomato ketchup, mushrooms, curds and yoghurt prepared by his Viennese dietetic cook. The others at his table—Eva Braun, his mistress; Martin Bormann, the Party Chancellor; Ribbentrop, his Foreign Minister; Air General Ernst Udet and Captain Karlheinz Pintsch, Rudolf Hess's adjutant—had been served with soup, then their single main course of meat, which guests were allowed during the war years, and a dessert of fruit.

Hitler took a final drink of the mineral water he favoured—for alcohol was repugnant to him—and stood up. He bent to kiss Eva Braun's hands, the signal that lunch was formally over, and the other guests pushed back their chairs on the polished wood floor. Pintsch felt the unreality of the occasion. A few hours earlier he had arrived from Munich with the news that Hess had flown to Scotland and a sealed letter for the Führer.

He had no idea how Hitler would receive this information; now, among the familiar faces, he felt he could relax. After all, he had lunched with Hitler, and not at one of the small round tables reserved for adjutants and other guests of low degree, but at the Führer's own table. He was entitled to feel that the news he brought came as no surprise; he was grateful that Hitler had not stormed or raged at him as he so frequently did when bad news was brought to him. He glanced around the table, wondering at the thoughts behind the impassive pudgy mask of Hitler's face. What would happen after lunch?

Usually after lunch on Sundays, as he knew very well, Hitler went out into the yard and fed his police dog and took a brief walk to a small tea pavilion, about fifteen minutes away. After then he liked to retire to his sitting-room on the first floor of the Berghof, which had a balcony and a bedroom adjoining it. There he would remain until half-past eight in the evening, when the same house-guests would assemble for dinner, but always sit down in a different order. There were two exceptions to this last rule; Eva Braun always sat at Hitler's right, and next to her sat Bormann.

On this Sunday, however, Hitler had more important things on his mind than feeding his dog. He walked around the table and then paused behind Pintsch's chair.

Pintsch, an officer in his late twenties, who had seen active service in France before his promotion to be adjutant to the Deputy Führer, looked uneasily into Hitler's sallow, rather greasy face, not knowing whether to rise or to remain seated. On one side of him Bormann stood up and backed away. He wanted no part of any discussion between them; he was too shrewd an ingratiator to give an opinion even if this were sought. And he was particularly anxious not to become involved over this business of Hess flying to Scotland.

This was Bormann's dilemma; if Hess were successful in his mission of peace—then Pintsch could be useful to him. More likely, however, Hess would not succeed. In this case, Pintsch was expendable. Since no one would know for some hours yet which of these situations obtained, the most prudent course was to appear neutral for as long as possible.

But Bormann could not escape so easily. The Führer touched him on the shoulder and gave an almost imperceptible nod towards the door. Bormann understood. Keeping his eyes carefully away from Pintsch's face he left the room. Within a moment he was back accompanied by two young captains of Hitler's personal guard, wearing revolvers at their belts. They marched across the room and stood behind Pintsch's chair. He tried to read some message of hope, some sign of friendship in their faces, but they were as bland and expressionless as death masks.

Bormann cleared his throat. 'Karlheinz Pintsch,' he said in his rasping voice. 'You are under arrest. You will be held under house arrest at Obersalzberg until a Court of Inquiry can be held into your part in the events of today. Heil, Hitler!'

Pintsch stood up; although not a small man, his guards were a head taller than he was. Almost imperceptibly they moved closer to his side. He bowed slightly to the Führer and to the rest of the company, clicked his heels and marched across the room between them, all in step. The other guests watched him go; the room was so silent that Pintsch heard the squeaking of his new leather boots as they walked. He hoped that they could not also hear the thumping of his heart.

The door shut behind him, and in silence the three men walked side by side down the wide marble staircase to the ground floor. As they walked Pintsch permitted himself a wry smile; his departure was so very different from his arrival in Hess's private railway coach a few hours earlier!

He did not know that this was the last day on which he would be a free man for the next three years, or perhaps he would not have smiled at all. In 1944 he was released to serve on the Eastern front—and the Russians captured him within a few weeks.

A soldier in his company, whom he had punished for some trivial regimental offence, told them he had been Hess's adjutant; the Russians were determined to learn the secret of his master's flight. They beat him up, broke all his fingers systematically, one by one, day by day, for ten days; then they starved him and refused him sleep. He kept silent. They were torturing the wrong man; he had already told all he knew.

Eventually, in 1955, after eleven years as their prisoner, and a total of fourteen years in gaol because of his association with Hess, he was free. Only one other man suffered longer for his part in this flight—the man who made it. Hess is still a prisoner.

But all this belonged to the future. On that Sunday afternoon of May 11, 1941, as Pintsch was marched past adjutants, aides and lieutenants whom he knew well, and who looked in astonishment and wonder at him being so obviously under arrest, his mind was not concerned with the future. The present seemed incredible enough.

A small car was waiting for him outside, with its engine running; it was possibly the same one that had come to meet him at the station when he arrived. Pintsch was pushed, not unkindly, into the back seat with a guard on either side and they jerked away down the mountain road, the taste of Hitler's lunch still on his tongue.

Now that they were on their own, with no superior to call them to order, the two captains relaxed perceptibly.

'What's all this about, anyhow, Pintsch?' one of them asked easily. 'I never thought we'd be having *you* in the guard room! Nothing serious, I hope?'

Pintsch shrugged. It could either be very serious or it could be a cause for promotion. As with many great military and political decisions, the difference between success and failure could even be the difference between life and death. Clearly, his guards did not yet know why he was under arrest. They pestered him with questions. Pintsch shook his head and refused to answer.

'It's a long story,' he said. 'Too long to tell here.'

*　　*　　*

It was indeed a long story; the roots went back to the previous autumn, when Hess had first begun to show a deep interest in modern German pursuit planes at Templehof aerodrome in Berlin.

In his search for knowledge about them—and especially how to fly them—he sought the help of Udet, then the Luftwaffe Quartermaster General. But Udet was a cautious, prudent man, and unwilling to let Hess fly without Hitler's permission in writing. He knew that the Führer had forbidden Nazi leaders to pilot their own planes during the war. This was a general order, issued for reasons of safety. It caused little hardship because only Hess could pilot a plane; Goering, a first-war flier with Richthofen's air circus, was too fat to climb into the pilot's seat.

Hess asked specifically that his undertaking should only last for a year, and Hitler immediately agreed to his request. When the twelve months were up in September, 1940, Hitler had apparently forgotten all about the matter; not so Hess. Because nothing was said about renewing this ban, he felt himself free to fly again—and at once began to make arrangements to do so.

Hess was unwilling to approach Hitler for this permission. If he did so it would mean that Hitler would then know officially that he was flying again. And in view of what was planned the Führer could not then deny all knowledge of his intentions if his mission failed or ran into unexpected difficulties.

Udet knew nothing of the reasons behind Hess's wish to fly and since Hitler's express permission was unavailable he declined to help Hess in the matter. Hess therefore sought out Messerschmitt, with whom he had been on friendly terms since the First World War, and his technical director, Theo Croneiss. These two men, knowing Hess's record as a pilot in that earlier war, and of his interest in civil and military aviation since, were naturally willing to help him.

Recalling this later, Hitler's personal pilot, Lieutenant-General Hans Baur, wrote: 'Hess went to Messerschmitt, who, of course, knew all about the prohibition, and declared that he had a special mission about which he was unable to talk. Now, for one thing, Hess was Deputy Führer, and for another he might well have a special mission, so Messerschmitt let him have his way . . .'[1]

He provided an aeroplane for Hess to make short flights from Augsburg; these he described as 'a form of recreation'. Hess was a good empirical engineer; he had suggested improvements to such devices as magnetic mines, largely as a result of close observation and common sense. Messerschmitt was thus interested in his comments on the performance of the modified ME 110.

This new version of a trusted aeroplane which Hess flew to Scotland was intended to carry two men. Hess had it modified for his purpose. To Messerschmitt's displeasure he criticized its range, and persuaded the engineers at Messerschmitt's factory, which had its own airfield at Augsburg, to construct extra fuel tanks of a weight equal to the second man who would normally have accompanied the pilot.

Messerschmitt fitted two tanks, each of 700 litres capacity, into the wings. A radio of unusual sensitivity was also installed. Hess explained that he intended to fly on some of the shorter bombing routes and this was necessary so that he could pick up the directional signals.

Since Hess was the second most important man in the Reich it was not for Messerschmitt to query his requests. He had enough to do in any case, producing war planes at the rate Goering wanted them.

Herr Mortsiepen, a senior Messerschmitt radio technician, reported to the factory's chief test pilot, Flight-Captain Stöhr, that Hess had ordered a special radio set to be fitted in the plane, so adapted that he could use it as he flew. Hess was also showing 'a keen interest' in flying on his instruments and using radio direction beams.

This news the test pilot immediately passed on to Hitler's personal pilot. Four weeks later, Baur met Hess in Hitler's apartments in

[1] *Hitler's Pilot*, Lt. Gen. Hans Baur, Frederick Muller.

Berlin. Later, he wrote,[1] 'He came straight up to me and declared bluntly: "Baur, I want a map of the forbidden air zones."

'I had such a map for my own use, of course, but I dared not let it out of my hands . . . Moreover, that map was clearly marked *Reich Top Secret*, which meant that I was not allowed to let anyone know its contents. This secret map showed those zones over which even German planes were not allowed to fly, or only at certain definite heights; and as the details changed from time to time you couldn't learn them off by heart once and for all. You had to have up-to-date supplements. . . .'

Baur assured him that an aide would always check the map, as a matter of course, before Hess made any flight. 'But this,' Baur wrote afterwards, 'for reasons that were to become very clear to me later, didn't satisfy Hess; he wanted a map of his own.'

Hess told Baur to ask the officer in charge of these secret maps to make one available to him. This officer naturally hesitated to do so, but after some thought he agreed. 'After all, he *is* the Deputy Führer,' he reasoned, 'and I suppose there's such a thing as being over-cautious. I'd better let him have it.'

'With that map, his training on the ME 110, and his industrious studying of instrument and blind flying,' reported Baur later, 'Hess was in a position to fly out of wartime Germany. . . .'

On that Sunday after Hess's flight, while Pintsch was being driven down the mountain side from the Berghof, Goering was already on the telephone to Messerschmitt, wanting to know how Hess had flown away. He told Messerschmitt he must see him the following morning in Munich.

As the aeroplane designer came into his office Goering pointed his Air Marshal's baton at him and shouted: 'As far as you're concerned, I suppose *anybody* can come and fly off with one of your machines?'

Messerschmitt pointed out carefully that Hess was not anybody: he was the Stellvertreter, the Deputy Führer.

'You should have known that this man was crazy,' retorted Goering, following the line Hitler had decided to take.

'How could I be expected to suppose that one so high in the hierarchy of the Third Reich could be crazy?' replied Messerschmitt calmly. 'If that were the case, Herr Marschal, *you* should have procured his resignation!'

At this, Goering unexpectedly burst into peals of laughter, slapping his thick thighs at the hugeness of the joke.

[1] *Ibid.*

'Messerschmitt,' he announced, when his mirth subsided, 'you're quite incurable! Go back to your factory and get on with producing your planes. I'll help you out of the mess, if the Führer tries to make trouble for you.'

It is significant that neither mentioned the matter of Hess being forbidden to fly, and that Goering treated the whole incident with laughter. Altogether Hess had made thirty flights from Augsburg; he made no secret of the fact that he was flying again. Most of his flights lasted for no more than an hour or two, but on one January afternoon, shortly after his private conversation with Haushofer, he arrived with a brief-case, and announced that he would be away for rather longer.

As his plane was being prepared, Hess handed two sealed letters to Pintsch. One was addressed to Hitler personally, and the other to Pintsch.

'Synchronize your watch with mine,' he told his adjutant, and then went on: 'Now, if I'm not back within four hours, open the letter addressed to you. It contains certain instructions. Then take this other letter to the Führer in person. He will want to know where I am.'

They saluted each other, and, within minutes, the aeroplane was a swiftly vanishing speck in the wintry sky.

Pintsch climbed into the back of Hess's official black Mercedes SSK cabriolet to wait his master's return. In the front seat sat his personal driver and detective; they made conversation as the hours crawled by, and afternoon merged into evening and grew bitterly cold. Finally, the four hours of waiting were up. Pintsch added another fifteen minutes for good measure, then opened the letter addressed to him. He read the letter by a shielded torch because it was against blackout regulations to switch on the car's interior light.

'*Mein Gott!*' he gasped in amazement as he read.

'What's wrong?' asked the detective instantly, swivelling round in his black leather coat. 'Why, you're sick, Pintsch,' he said. 'You're white, man. Are you all right? Do you feel faint?'

Pintsch's mouth was so dry in astonishment and horror that he could hardly speak. He shook his head and gasped out his story. 'It's this letter,' he explained. 'The Stellvertreter is flying to England to try and make peace.'

'To make *peace*?' repeated the detective in disbelief. 'Here, let me read it.'

He snatched at the letter. The driver turned on the dashlights, and both men read the words aloud, spelling out each syllable slowly. When they had finished the detective turned to Pintsch again. He was about to speak when all three men heard the faint familiar drone of their master's plane. It was coming back. Down it came on the darkened runway, taxied to the end, turned and came slowly to where they were standing. Hess cut out his engines, pulled back the canopy and climbed down wearily. As he crossed to them on that early January night, he saw from their faces that they knew the contents of the letter.

'Well,' he said easily, 'as you see, I'm back a little sooner than I expected.'

None of the three men in the car said a word. They sat watching him suspiciously. The air was heavy with disbelief, and despite the discrepancy of his rank and theirs, beginning to crackle with hostility.

'I would like to explain a few things to you,' Hess told Pintsch. 'Then you can tell the others if you wish.' He turned to the chauffeur. 'Drive me home. We'll not want you again tonight.'

As the car stopped outside his house, Hess motioned Pintsch upstairs. They climbed up the polished wooden steps to the attic used by Hess's secretary. It was a room under the eaves where they could talk without any danger of being disturbed or overheard.

Pintsch sat down heavily, his legs almost giving way under him. That his master, the Deputy Führer—one of the handful of pioneers who had grown up with Hitler, who were determined to lift Germany from the ranks of fifth-rate Powers to become the most feared country in the world—could be anything less than perfect seemed impossible. That he might possibly be a traitor, a go-between, perhaps even a spy, was unbelievable.

Hess realized the confusion in the younger man's mind, and poured out a brandy for Pintsch. The adjutant drank it down eagerly, choking over the neat spirit. As its fire ran within him, he asked the question uppermost in his thoughts.

'Why were you flying to England without telling the Führer?' he asked bluntly. 'I know that you left without his knowledge otherwise you wouldn't have given me this letter to deliver to him personally.'

As he spoke he handed back to Hess the envelope, still unopened, addressed to Hitler. Hess took it and put it in his desk. He rode the question easily; after all, he had a lifetime of experience behind him in avoiding, evading or explaining awkward questions.

'It's true that Hitler does not know I've made this specific attempt tonight, or that it failed. But it is his most urgent and important wish to have the earliest possible peace with England. I have discussed the matter with him many times. I have also discussed it with Professor Haushofer and with Albrecht Haushofer. There have been many attempts to make contact with the other side through Lisbon and elsewhere already, but they have been unfruitful. What the situation needs is a direct approach. Then we can discover how we stand. That is what I am determined to do. If my plane hadn't let me down I'd have been in Britain by now, perhaps even discussing the matter with the people I want to see.'

Hess paused for a moment, and Pintsch sat back in his chair, relieved and intrigued by what he had just heard. 'I see,' he said slowly, feeling rather ashamed of his earlier feelings about Hess.

Also, the two Haushofers were so well-known and so respected that the revelation that they were also concerned immediately made Pintsch feel reassured. Surely the Professor, whose advice on foreign affairs Hitler used so frequently, whose political theories of *leben-sraum* and the 'Haves and have-nots' have already been incorporated into the Nazi creed, would not go against the Führer's wishes?

One thought returned to alarm Pintsch. 'Even so, sir,' he said, 'Hitler didn't know you were leaving on this mission. Why was that?'

Hess sat down in a chair opposite him. 'I'll try and explain,' he said. 'As you know, I am one of the very earliest members of the party. As you also know, there's a good deal of my thinking in *Mein Kampf*. And I'm sure you'll agree that I can read the mind of our Führer more accurately and positively than anyone else around him. This is reasonable, of course, for we have been together for twenty years—maybe longer. Thus, if anyone should know exactly what Hitler wants, I should be that man. Hitler wants a strong England. And he wants peace with England. That's why we didn't invade Britain after Dunkirk. We could have done so easily enough, as you know yourself. That's why we've tried to open negotiations since.

'Our enemy now is not in the West but in the East. That's where the danger is. That's where the Führer's thoughts are gathered.'

'You mean—Russia?' asked Pintsch.

Hess nodded. 'I mean Russia. If we go on fighting Britain as we are, I fear that eventually Germany will be fighting against the rest of the world on her own. America will become involved. America and Britain together may be too strong for us. It's not a question of spirit or determination, Pintsch, it's a question of facts and figures. Combined, they must be stronger and better armed than we are on our own. This will mean that the new Germany the Führer has built up will eventually vanish. We'll have fought to a standstill against the people with whom we really have most in common. Germany and Britain will both be exhausted. I leave America out of our calculations for the time being because she has enormous natural resources, and also she is so very far away.

'Britain will then discover that, so far as she's concerned, this is very much a Pyrrhic victory. She will lose her Empire—America will see to that. Soon Britain will only be a tiny overcrowded island dwelling on the fading glories of the past.

'America will be the immediate victor. She will dictate her will on the world. But America isn't an adult nation. She is too young, too easily swayed, and without much experience of power. She has a hatred for all colonial powers because she was once a colony. The fact that this was nearly two hundred years ago doesn't alter this attitude. There will be talk of freedom and independence, every nation having the right to determine their own destiny, but the real reason will be America's inferiority complex on this matter.

'But who will step into the void that will be left in many countries? Germany won't be able to. Nor will any other European country with experience of colonization, so I'll tell you who will—Russia. Within a decade, Russia will have become the most powerful country in the world. Events will be entirely out of our control by then, Pintsch, if this happens. Thus it is up to us to try and stop this march of events *now*. I know that this is Hitler's wish. It is his dearest dream that this state of affairs shall be prevented. But there's not much time left to prevent it.'

Hess paused for a moment.

'But the risk to you,' said Pintsch slowly, trying to assess it as he spoke. 'Isn't that enormous? What happens if the British don't believe you are sincere when you arrive there? I know nothing about politics, but this seems a very big gamble to take.'

'I agree,' replied Hess at once. 'It is. But let me answer your points as you make them. First of all, any personal risk I run is nothing compared with what I may achieve. One has to risk something to win anything worth while, and the greater the prize the greater the risk involved. In this case I agree I run several personal risks. I may crash into the sea, or I may be shot down. Or might even be killed when I land. But against that, *if* I am successful, the journey will result in saving literally millions of lives—and *our* future.'

The two men sat in silence for a few moments in the small upper room with its sloping ceiling. Somewhere in the house a radio was playing; the sound of music filtered, muted, through the walls.

'But who will you see when you reach England, if you ever do?' asked Pintsch.

'I will see the Duke of Hamilton.'

'Who is he?'

'He has been like me, a pioneer aviator. He shared the honour of being the first man to pilot an aeroplane over Mount Everest eight years ago, in 1933. He is a great sportsman.'

'That may be, but do you know him, sir? Have you ever met him? I am only asking these questions now because I think that if I don't someone else will later on.'

'I appreciate your interest, Pintsch. Yes, I have met the Duke of Hamilton, although only briefly. We were introduced at the Olympic Games in Berlin, five years ago.'

'But, sir, say you do reach England, why should the Duke of Hamilton see you again? All this is very new to me, but I just can't see it happening as you visualize. First, if you fly in uniform, presumably you will be arrested when you land—if you aren't shot down before you have the chance to land. And, if you fly in civilian clothes then you could be shot as a spy. Next, how will you ever get to see the Duke? You can't very well come down on his doorstep. You'll have to land some distance away and then walk. You'll be picked up in no time. I'm sorry to say all this, sir, but since you have taken me so far into your confidence, I must be frank. I just cannot see how you hope to succeed.'

'I appreciate your concern, Pintsch,' replied Hess. 'I'll try to answer your points as you made them. First, we have already gone into the question of risks, so there's no need to bring up that point again. I'll fly in uniform for the obvious reason that you mention. But in assuming that I won't see the Duke of Hamilton, then you are being altogether too young and naïve. You're proving what you have already said, that you know nothing about politics. I *will* see him; he *will* see me. You say that I can't very well land right on his doorstep? Well, I can, and I will! *At his front door!*'

Pintsch looked at Hess, amazed; he was entirely out of his depth. Was the Deputy Führer of the Fatherland, the second most powerful man in the Reich—possibly in the world—going mad? Or was *he* insane in imagining this extraordinary conversation? Something of his bewilderment showed in his face as he dredged unsuccessfully for words.

77

Hess saw his astonishment and was amused by it. He stood up. 'Ah, you think I'm talking in riddles, eh? Hand me down those maps from that shelf, Pintsch, and I will show you just what I mean. It's all really very straightforward, as you'll see for yourself.'

Pintsch took down the first map and unrolled the canvas. It was a large-scale map of the North of England and the South of Scotland. To his surprise he saw that a route was already charted across it, from Holy Island in the East to beyond Glasgow in the West, in blue pencil.

Hess spread out the map on the table and put a book on each corner to hold it down. Then he moved an adjustable reading-lamp over it and switched off the light in the ceiling. The map was now brilliantly lit; the rest of the room was in darkness.

'Now, Pintsch, let's see whether you are wrong and whether I am right,' he began. 'First, we tend to talk about England and England only, when we really mean Britain. You think I'm going to fly to England? Well, I'm not. I'm flying to Scotland, which is a different thing. I will fly up over Germany and Holland, across the North Sea to Holy Island, here, off the East coast of Britain, near the Scottish border.'

Pintsch interrupted him. 'How will you know when you reach Holy Island?' he asked. 'It's only a tiny dot on this map. It'll be dark when you reach there.'

'Exactly, Pintsch, it will be dark, or at least nearly dark. And that's how I'll know when I'm there, because as you see it has a lighthouse. This light is one of the very few that are still lit in Britain at night in spite of the blackout. Several lighthouses are in use because they mark rocks or reefs or sandbanks. This is one of them. I'll know where I am when I see that light, and then I turn west and fly over the Cheviot hills here. When I come over the east of Scotland there's another lighthouse I'll look for, by this place called Troon. When I see that I'll know I've passed my target, so I'll turn back on the same bearing flying as low as I can, until I see the Duke's house from the air.'

'You'll have to be pretty low to see that,' said Pintsch.

Hess shrugged. 'Possibly, but I'll choose a night when the moon is full. That's why I'd hoped to go tonight. Flying conditions and visibility generally are very good. But there will be other nights, have no fear.

'Now to return: I understand that Dungavel is a very large house, and I'll recognize it because a row of trees are growing fairly near.

78

In between those trees and the house I'm told there is some sort of landing-strip, or at least a flat field, where a plane can come down. If need be, I can parachute without much risk of landing on a church spire. So much for that, Pintsch. Now, shall we assume I've landed at his front door, as I promised, and that it is dark? You agree that this should allow me ten minutes before the police or the troops, or whoever sees me come down can come and arrest me?'

'All right, sir, say ten minutes,' said Pintsch. 'If you ever get past the ack-ack guns.'

'That's a chance I just have to take,' replied Hess. 'But I think I'll be lucky. For one thing, I'll be flying very low and very fast. For another, no one will expect an ME to be so far from home because it can't carry enough fuel. So any report that an ME is around will at first be treated with ridicule. By the time they are convinced it *was* an ME, I'll be miles away—I hope. Right, to continue. Assume I have survived the flak and any fighters sent up to look for me. Imagine that I've parachuted down. I'm out of my parachute harness, out of my overalls, and I'm walking up the front steps of the Duke's home, Dungavel House. Now, what do I do next?'

Pintsch shook his head in bewilderment: this was beyond the frontiers of his imagination. 'I just don't know, sir,' he said honestly. 'I've no idea. The whole thing sounds so unreal.'

'Patience, Pintsch, patience. What do *you* do when you call at a stranger's house? You press the bell. So will I. Soon a servant—possibly a butler, I should imagine, or some other trusted retainer, will open the door. I'll tell him that I wish to see the Duke of Hamilton. The butler will ask who I am. I won't tell him, naturally enough, but I'll hand him a card. The butler will take the card to his master. When the Duke sees the name on it, he'll ask to see me.'

'Why should he?' Pintsch asked. 'Whose name is on the card? Yours?'

Hess shook his head impatiently. 'Of course not. What good would my name be? I don't know the Duke of Hamilton well, but Albrecht Haushofer does. When the Duke sees Albrecht's card, he'll naturally suppose that young Haushofer has somehow come to see him, or maybe that he's been shot down. He can think what he likes, but I'm sure that at least he'll ask Haushofer into his home—if only to keep him prisoner while he telephones the military.

'Then,' declared the Deputy Führer triumphantly, 'he'll not see Haushofer but *Hess!* I don't know exactly what will happen after that, but at the very worst I should have time to explain to him why

I'm there, and the object of my journey. I'll ask to see a government representative and the King. *Now* does my plan make any more sense to you ?'

Did it or didn't it ? Pintsch looked away from the brightly lit map and rubbed his eyes. His mind was bemused with what he had just heard. The plan was audacious, of course, but then so many of the most successful plans of the last few years had been outrageously impossible, and had succeeded.

Why, when the Führer had marched on the Rhine barely five years earlier in the teeth of the French and British armies, who would have given a *pfennig* for his chances of success ? But he had succeded: the gamble had proved worthwhile.

Hess's proposal sounded equally incredible when told by one tired man to another in a tiny room above the linden trees, but when translated into action then its success, although perhaps still improbable, was by no means impossible.

Oddly enough, they both ignored one enormous flaw in the plan that had also not occurred to the Haushofers: what would happen if the Duke of Hamilton was not at home ? Hess and Haushofer had taken the Duke's address of Dungavel House from a pre-war edition of *Who's Who*. Had a contemporary war-time edition been available, they would have seen that the Duke was serving in the RAF and so unlikely to be there.

Pintsch lit a cigarette, but its taste seemed stale and harsh in his mouth, and he stubbed it out again after a few puffs.

'Well,' began Hess gently, 'what's worrying you now? Have I confused you, or do you still think I'm a traitor?'

'I never said that, sir,' protested Pintsch.

'I didn't say that you had said it. I said that you thought it.'

'No one knowing your record, your closeness to the Führer, your personal bravery, and even a fraction of what you have just told me, could ever call you a traitor,' said Pintsch heatedly. 'If you succeed, you'll be called the saviour of Europe, maybe even of the world. But I wasn't thinking of what will happen if you succeed, sir. I was wondering what would happen if you fail.'

'I have also wondered, Pintsch,' agreed Hess quietly. 'But I must not sit about thinking of failure. Germany will always have room for initiative, for people willing to take risks, even against great odds. As a nation, we recognize this. Why, we even have a special decoration for such cases—if they're successful. Do you know what a man must do to be awarded the Austrian Order of Maria Theresa?'

Pintsch shook his head. 'I've no idea,' he said.

'Well, let me tell you,' Hess continued. 'Oddly enough, my wife asked me about this order for some reason only the other day and I looked up the regulations. They provided me with an answer to my own worries, my own problems, my own private doubts about this journey. As you know, some of our decorations are only given for acts of bravery carried out on the individual's own personal initiative. In the case of the Maria Theresa Order, however, something much rarer is required. For this reason it is possibly our strangest order of gallantry. For to be awarded it, a man has to act independently on his own responsibility and *in a manner directly contrary to what has been clearly commanded by his superiors*. Then, if his action is successful, gets the Order!'

'And if he's not successful?'

'Then, Pintsch, he gets shot. His act is officially disowned. I think that this answers your question?'

*   *   *

Hess made a second attempt to fly to Britain, but bad weather forced him back to Augsburg.

The first attempt in January had failed because a fault developed in one of the ailerons, and the aeroplane could not make enough height to cross the mountains.

And then, on the second Saturday in May, Hess discovered that the weather forecasts for several days ahead were good. It seems perfect for his flight and also he was in Munich and so near Augsburg. He felt that he had delayed long enough, and if he did not take this opportunity, he might have to wait weeks for another. So he decided to make his third attempt to reach Britain.

And this time he would not turn back.

CHAPTER SIX

Consternation at the Berghof

Hess and his adjutant Pintsch lived in houses about half a mile apart on the same side of Harthauser Strasse, a wide, grey, cobbled road a few miles out of Munich.

Early on Saturday, May 10, the telephone rang in Pintsch's home. He rubbed the sleep from his eyes, pulled on a woollen dressing-gown, and went downstairs to answer it.

His young son and daughter were already awake; he could hear their chatter from the nursery as he passed the door. He picked up the telephone, knowing before he heard the familiar voice, who would be calling him and why.

'Good morning, Pintsch,' said Hess. 'I'm sure that this is the day we've been waiting for. If it keeps like this it should be perfect for a long flight. Give me the weather information I need as soon as you can, and I'll see you here this afternoon, about half-past two. I've got Rosenberg coming to lunch at twelve, so I won't be free till then. If all goes well, I intend to leave about six.'

'Very good, sir,' replied Pintsch, and replaced the receiver. For a moment, until his breath clouded the glass, he stood looking out of the window, imprinting on his mind the familiar scene of linden trees, a milk-cart coming by, the horse's head obscuring the blue-and-white name-plate of the road. He could not guess that this was the last time he would see these ordinary, unexciting, familiar things for fourteen years, or that this was the last telephone call Hess would ever make to him.

Further up the road, Hess, equally unaware of the future, was dressing in his bedroom overlooking the long lawns and swimming-pool of his home. He put on a light grey civilian suit, for technically he was off duty, and although he regularly appeared in the Nazi uniform he preferred casual clothes at home. Often on summer days he wore the *lederhosen*, the short leather trousers of the Tyrol and Bavaria.

Next to his room was a small study with a desk and chair, and a large Siemens radio in a black bakelite case, kept permanently tuned to the Danish radio station of Kalundborg, which was under German control. Ostensibly, this station put out ordinary radio programmes, music, talks, plays, news bulletins; in fact, the hours of dance music and Wagner that were played every evening also served as a signal to help German bomber-pilots plot their course for England and then for home again. Early morning dance music was now playing, filling the white-walled room with its soft, meaningless sentimentality.

Hess smoothed down his hair in the mirror for the last time. He was tall, well-built, with a rather heavy serious face and deep-set eyes. His brows were so dark and bushy that they overemphasized this feature of his face so that he appeared morose, as though perpetually considering some grave question of State.

Downstairs, he heard the usual early-morning sounds of a household stirring. Outside, in the back garden, the security guards in their black-leather mackintoshes were chatting together. The house was separated from the road by a high hedge and closely planted trees, so that it was difficult for passers-by to see inside. In one corner of the grounds the sunshine was glittering on the surface of the swimming pool.

For a moment Hess stood by the open window, breathing deeply, and then, on the impulse, he threw himself flat on the floor. He lay relaxed for a few moments in his familiar Yoga posture, and then stood up, and walked down the few steps to his wife's room.

Ilse Hess's bedroom opened on to a balcony that ran the whole south side of the house, with a magnificent view over birch trees, now silver with leaves, a wooden pergola clustered with clematis and roses, to an old stone sundial and a shield of trees behind it. The bedroom had a sloping ceiling which was built high up under a narrow gable faced with spruce and pinewood tiles. From the outside, No. 48 looked like a house in a Hans Andersen fairy tale.

Ilse Hess was a pleasant-faced blonde-haired woman whom Hess had married fourteen years previously. They had first met in the early nineteen-twenties; shortly afterwards, Hess and Hitler had been gaoled in Landsberg Prison for eighteen months for attempting to overthrow the Government of Bavaria. They were released after serving seven and a half months in which Hitler wrote *Mein Kampf* and Hess helped him to correct the proofs and added some views of his own.

All three had been very close in those days. Indeed, when Hitler

83

and Hess were released from Landsberg, Ilse was one of the Party faithfuls who went to meet them. They clubbed together with their marks and hired the best car they could afford to make this something of an occasion; it was an ancient Mercedes-Benz with horsehair stuffing coming out of the cracked leather seats. But when Hitler and his Deputy walked out of the gaol in their familiar belted raincoats, hats with snap brims pulled down over their eyes, they were so ashamed of this shabby vehicle that they ignored it and walked smartly down the street and up a side alley. There they waited until it came rattling and steaming after them. Then they climbed in unobserved and drove away.

Indeed they were such close friends that had it not been for Hitler, Hess might never have married Ilse. One night, all three were sitting in the Osteria-Bavaria restaurant—now renamed the Osteria-Italiana—in Schelling Strasse, a restaurant much liked by students, painters, writers and artists. Ilse had just resigned from her job in a local antiquarian bookshop, and she was undecided whether to enrol as a full-time student at Munich University—where she was already taking spare-time English classes—or to spend her savings on a long holiday in Italy.

She explained her dilemma to the two friends. 'There's a third possibility, Ilse,' Hitler said.

'What's that?' she asked.

'My dear girl, has it never occurred to you to marry this man here?' And he pointed at Rudolf Hess.

The idea suddenly seemed so obvious and so excellent that they were married within weeks.

Some Foreign diplomats, advising their Governments on events in Germany as the Nazis came to power, wrongly wrote off Frau Hess as 'a squaw' who lived quietly in Munich with her small son, while Hess took the salute at the big parades, and rode with Hitler through the cheering crowds in the bullet-proof Mercedes. In fact, Hess, a homely, unpretentious man, needed somewhere to retire from the public limelight; Ilse provided this for him. She was an excellent cook, especially of Bavarian dishes.

Ilse Hess was in bed on that Saturday morning, reading propped up against the pillows, when her husband came into her room. She had been unwell for several days, but hoped to be allowed up during the weekend. She laid her book on one side as she saw her husband.

'What are you reading?' he asked. She handed him the book.

He glanced at its spine, and then raised his eyebrows in surprise.

84

It was an English edition of *The Pilot's Book of Everest*, describing the first aeroplane flight over that mountain eight years earlier in a plane piloted by the Duke of Hamilton and Group Captain D. F. McIntyre. English friends on holiday in the Hindelang hills, 130 miles to the south-west of Munich, where the Hesses had sometimes stayed, had given her the book two years before the war. Hess re-read the inscription inside the front cover: 'With all good wishes and the hope that out of personal friendships a real and lasting understanding may grow between our two countries.'

He handed it back in silence, but open at a photograph of the Duke of Hamilton.

'He's very good looking,' he said, to draw his wife's attention to this.

Ilse nodded, a little puzzled, unable to understand the reason for this remark. 'I agree,' she replied, making conversation. 'I wonder if he is as charming as he is good looking?'

'Of course,' retorted her husband. 'He's handsome and he's also a very brave man. Remember, he flew over Everest in a tiny plane and with no possible hope of rescue if anything went wrong.'

'You would have done the same,' said his wife quickly and loyally.[1]

'That's beside the point,' replied Hess tartly.

Ilse thought he appeared to be unreasonably irritated because she seemed to underestimate the importance of the Duke of Hamilton. Hess even went on to suggest that had there been more men in both countries as upright and courageous as the Duke, then Germany and England might not be at war. At the time, Ilse thought his vehemence unnecessary; only afterwards did she realize the thought behind it, and the reasons that prompted it.

Presently, the talk turned to more domestic matters. 'Rosenberg's coming to lunch,' said Hess. 'I've nothing much to do before then, and there's no need for you to bother to get dressed and come down to lunch with us. I'll have it alone with Rosenberg, and then I'll come up and see you afterwards.'

That morning, Hess played with his small son, Wolf Rüdiger, then four years old; his family nickname was Buz. Every morning for the previous few weeks father and son had gone off solemnly to walk hand-in-hand along the Isar River; their garden backed on to

---

[1] After the first West to East Atlantic flight by Lindbergh, Hess had been anxious to attempt the solo flight from Germany to America. But after preparations had gone on for more than a year, the plan was shelved and Kuhn Fitzmaurice Hunefold made this pioneering flight instead of Hess.

it with a special gate opening to a path along the river bank. They would walk as far as the Hellabrun Zoo, often with their wolfhound, Hasso, and his three half-grown puppies, Nurmi, Hedda and Nickl.

The picture of the Deputy Führer holding the hand of his small son was one that did him no harm in the eyes of his neighbours. Hess never took a detective with him; always he and his son walked alone together. Sometimes passers-by would salute him or bow respectfully. At other times he went unrecognized in the weekend crowds of strollers.

Hess came into his wife's bedroom for a second time at about eleven o'clock. 'Look,' he said. 'If you feel well enough, Ilse, please get up and have lunch with us after all.'

Ilse was surprised at his change of mind; she was even more surprised, when, half an hour later, he returned again, shaking his head and waving her back to bed.

'Don't bother getting up,' he said. 'It's really not necessary, for you probably still don't feel very well. I'll lunch alone with Rosenberg, after all. We've much to discuss and time is short.'

'But he's not due until twelve o'clock,' protested Ilse, opening the cupboard for a new dress. 'I've got almost an hour.'

'You don't understand,' replied Hess. 'I was referring to something else.'

So Ilse returned thankfully to bed and her book.

Hess went down into the dining-room that looked out across the lawn, through the french doors with white shutters that opened on to a stone terrace. It was a relatively small room, about eighteen feet square, with a round table large enough to seat four people comfortably, and twice that number when an extra leaf was fitted.

At twelve o'clock the guards opened the iron gates at the end of the drive, and in drove Alfred Rosenberg. He was Hitler's chief adviser on all matters concerned with the ideology of National Socialism, a clean-shaven, powerfully-built man with a quiet, deliberate manner of speaking that echoed the self-confidence which was the dominating trait in his personality. He had been born of German parents in Reval in the Baltic, studied as an architect in Moscow, and moved to Germany to escape the 1917 Revolution.

With Hess, Goering, Roehm and Eckart, Rosenberg had been one of the early stalwarts of the Nazi Party. He succeeded Eckart in 1923 as editor of the *Völkischer Beobachter*, 'the people's newspaper'. Hitler also found him useful because of his contacts with other refugees from Russia who shared his anti-Communist and anti-

Jewish outlook. Rosenberg impressed Hitler on a personal level because of his architectural training, brief though this had been; Hitler liked to consider himself as a potential artist or an architect whose career had been cut short by his need to engage in politics.

As Rosenberg arrived, Hess's butler, George Ferdinand Myer,[1] opened the heavy front door and bowed to him. Myer was used to these private lunches and had laid out a salad, with slices of cold meat and German sausage on the sideboard; the two men could serve themselves. He announced Herr Alfred Rosenberg to Hess, and then withdrew, leaving the two men together.

At about two o'clock Ilse Hess heard their voices filtering up the staircase to her bedroom; doors opened and closed, the tyres of Rosenberg's official car crunched on the gravel chips outside, and the metal garden gates shut behind him with a clang. Apart from the servants, she and her husband were alone in the house.

She dozed a little and awoke to see Hess standing by her bedside, looking down at her as she slept. 'Why, you've changed,' she said with surprise, struggling into wakefulness. Instead of his comfortable grey suit, her husband now wore a light blue air-force shirt with a dark blue tie, bluish grey breeches and airmen's fur-lined boots.

'Yes, I thought I'd give you a surprise,' he explained with a smile.

'But why the blue shirt?' she persisted. Hess preferred to wear a white shirt with his uniform, although his wife considered he looked best in blue; the colour suited his eyes. Every Christmas she would buy him a new blue shirt with a dark blue tie to match it, in the hope of converting him; but on every Boxing Day he would put away these presents in his cupboard and never wear them.

'I'm wearing it to please you,' he told her. She smiled and then saw with more surprise that her husband was wearing flying-boots.

She sat up in bed and pointed towards them. 'But why the boots? What's up? Is there anything wrong?'

He shook his head, and, reaching out for her hands, held them in his. 'Nothing at all,' he explained. 'I've just had a call from Berlin, and I've got to go there. As I'm driving, I thought I'd call in at Augsburg on the way. I can put in an hour or two flying while the weather is good.'

---

[1] In 1945, the British arrested Myer. Drawing himself up to his full 5 ft. 6 in., he addressed the senior officer in English. 'Sir,' he said coldly, 'I'm surprised to be troubled by you gentlemen. After all, I *have* been a butler in a house where the Prince of Wales was a guest.' He was set free.

The explanation mollified his wife to some extent; but even so, Saturday afternoon was an odd day for such excursions. Also, the works at Augsburg would be closed.

At that moment the butler knocked on the door, and entered with a tray of cups and saucers; they usually took tea together when Hess was home.

They drank in silence, and then Ilse spoke. 'When do you think you'll be back?' she asked her husband.

He looked away for a moment, and gave a shrug of his shoulders. 'I'm not quite certain. Perhaps tomorrow, perhaps not. But anyway, I'll certainly be back by Monday night.'

'I don't believe you,' said Ilse firmly. 'You will be away much longer.'

Afterwards, Hess admitted to her that he went 'hot and cold by turns' when she expressed this disbelief in his early return.

Frau Hess had her own ideas as to her husband's destination. After France had capitulated in the previous June, Hess had on several occasions prepared for journeys that had not materialized. He explained his actions thus: 'I may have to make a long journey some day, Ilse, without any warning.'

Hess had accompanied Hitler to Compiègne, where the French Armistice was signed in 1940, and, partly because of this and the fact that he spoke French well and retained a respect for old Marshal Petain, against whom he fought at Verdun, Ilse thought that he might be referring to some special mission to Petain.[1]

Once Frau Hess answered the telephone in the study when her husband was not at home, and a man she had never heard before, under the impression that he was addressing Hess's secretary, dictated a weather report to her, for two unknown places which he referred to as X and Y.

'Rather astonished, I got down this, to me, quite incomprehensible message,' Frau Hess wrote later. 'But I noticed from the confused manner of the secretary, who had just come in, that this was something I was not supposed to know anything about! However, she must have told my husband; for, from that day onwards, I frequently took down such reports—sometimes by actual request. It was now

[1] 'It is not generally known that it was my husband who, before the signing of the armistice terms in the historic railway coach at Compiègne, urged upon Hitler in a long and earnest discussion the unwisdom of forcing any terms that might offend the honour of a defeated enemy and thus tend to bar the way to a lasting understanding between the two nations,' wrote Ilse Hess in her introduction to *Prisoner of Peace*. 'It was only after assurance on this that he withdrew his original refusal to be present at Compiègne.'

presumed, so I thought, that they had acquired an innocent appearance in my mind.'[1]

The belief that her husband was planning a long journey, which might keep him away from home for some time, was greatly strengthened by the long hours he had spent with his son during the past three weeks. As she sipped her tea she recalled whole mornings passed in Hess's workroom, with models of planes and tanks and trains, as well as their regular walks along the River and to the Zoo.

'What caused me more surprise than almost anything else during those last weeks was the astonishing amount of time—and that in the middle of the war—that my husband spent with our son,' Ilse Hess wrote later. 'This seemed to me inexplicable. How different it was to look back on, knowing the circumstances, and seeing how everything fell into place!'[1]

'Anyhow, come back as soon as you can,' Ilse said. 'Buz will miss you.'

'I'll miss him, too,' agreed Hess, almost speaking to himself. Finally he stood up; it was time to leave. 'Well, I must be off,' he said briefly. 'Goodbye.'

He bent and kissed his wife and walked to the door. As he opened it, he turned and looked back at her as though on the point of saying something more: and then he thought better of it and was gone. Afterwards, he admitted that he had been frightened to stay a moment longer in case she said something that showed she knew more about his plans than she had admitted.

He went down the stairs, took his trench-coat from the peg in the ground-floor cloakroom, and shut the house door behind him for the last time.

A small suitcase had already been placed in the boot of the black supercharged five-and-a-half-litre SSK Mercedes that waited outside the house. It was of a size and power reserved only for the most senior Party officials at such a time of petrol rationing. Three men stood by it. One was Pintsch, his adjutant, who held open the door. Next to him was Hess's personal private detective in a black leather coat; and then his chauffeur.

'Are we all ready?' asked Hess, looking from one to the other.

Pintsch nodded. 'Whenever you are, sir,' he replied briskly.

'You have the report I asked for?' continued Hess.

'In my case here, sir.' Pintsch patted the side of his brown leather brief-case.

[1] *Ibid.*

89

'Then we'll go,' said Hess.

As he stepped into the car, he took one last look at his house: long, low, white-walled, with white shutters, it was the sort of place he had often dreamed of owning when he was out of work, after the First World War.

He climbed inside the car and sank back on the black quilted leather beside the driver; he never rode in the back seat unless travelling with the Führer on some State occasion. The door clicked behind him. Pintsch and the detective climbed into the rear of the car. One of the house-guards opened the big iron gates and saluted as the car drove through.

They turned left, past the Hellabrun Zoo with its green and silver roof-tops. Children were at the turnstiles with their parents for their Saturday afternoon treat to see the giraffes and elephants and lions.

They drove on through Munich, round the squares where the stone statues spouted water, through the streets almost empty of traffic but thick with shoppers. Soon they were out on the deserted autobahn that lay like a wide white ribbon across the red earth of the Fatherland. Hess knew every metre of the way to Augsburg as well as he knew his own back-garden. The view was equally familiar; tall fir trees wearing fresh spring leaves, oxen pulling the ploughs; and, like background music, cattle-bells tinkling faintly in the distance.

The driver cut in the supercharger, and with a soft hiss the huge car seemed to take flight. Hess settled down more comfortably in his coat, looking through the narrow windscreen at the three-pointed star on the radiator. About fifteen kilometres out of Munich, by one of the yellow-and-black signposts, they entered a strip of woodland with crocuses growing at the roadside. Hess turned and touched the driver on the elbow.

'Pull in here for a moment, please,' he ordered.

The big wheels bumped over the grass, off the road. After the hum of the engine and tyres, the unexpected silence sang in their ears. Hess opened the door; Pintsch slid out and stood beside him. Hess looked at his watch.

'We're a bit early yet, according to my timing,' he said. 'Let's take a walk and get some fresh air.'

The two men strolled off under the trees. The wood seemed strangely silent; there were no birds. Now and then, as the wind changed, they heard the familiar soothing tinkle of cow-bells from herds grazing on the lower foothills beyond the trees. The two men walked without speaking for a moment, busy with their thoughts, and then Hess turned to his adjutant.

'Let me see the weather report, please,' he said.

Pintsch handed over a twice-folded sheet of thin paper on which he had typed the latest available news on the weather. Hess walked on, reading it, trying to memorize its contents, and then handed the sheet back without a word.

Both knew what lay ahead; so did the two men who sat in the car. Scotland seemed an infinity away.

'You certainly have a good day for the flight,' said Pintsch with what confidence he could find. 'That's one thing.'

In the deep lonely silence of the woods the cliché sounded more than usual. Hess nodded; he did not reply. There was too much he could have said: what about the adverse factors, the miles of sea, the waiting Spitfires and the anti-aircraft guns?

They walked on for half-a-mile or so and then Hess looked again at his gold wristwatch. 'It's time we were getting back,' he said, but still he seemed restless to leave the peace of the forest. He postponed the moment of departure, walking on alone, hands behind his back, Napoleon fashion, savouring for a last time the sunlight and the trees; the sounds and scenes of Bavaria, among which he had grown up. Finally, he returned to the car. Pintsch held open the door; Hess entered without a word.

The driver pressed the starter-button and the Mercedes turned out on to the autobahn. In a few more kilometres they branched off along another road to the private airfield adjoining the Messerschmitt factory. They slowed down as they passed the works and stopped at the airfield entrance. Two sentries were on guard, rifles slung over their shoulders. They recognized the car, for Hess was a regular visitor to the Messerschmitt concern.

One of them raised the black horizontal boom from the gateway to let them drive through. The road stretched off emptily in the distance behind them; it led to Lagerlechfeld, where Hess had landed in his fighter plane after his final flight in the First World War, twenty-three years ago. It seemed somehow symbolic to Pintsch that now he was taking off from a point so near on a flight of incomparably greater importance.

The driver stopped the Mercedes on the concrete runway near the main hangars. The airfield research manager, Herr Piel, came forward, clicking his heels and bowing. Because it was Saturday, the airfield deserted and the factory closed, Piel and the sentries had opened the hangar doors themselves and manhandled out the silver-grey Messerschmitt. Now it stood, wooden chocks before the wheels, pointing down the runway into the wind. The tips of its wings trembled slightly in the mild afternoon breeze; it seemed very small and fragile for such a long journey.

Hess chatted briefly with Piel and then went round to the rear of the car and opened the boot. Pintsch removed his suitcase for him and carried it into the two-storey administrative building near the hangar. The driver and the detective followed. Piel waited outside. In silence, the four men climbed the concrete stairs with cream-painted walls on either side, past the notices about fire-hydrants and air-raid shelters, until they reached a landing and a small room overlooking the airfield. From this height the plane looked smaller than ever.

Hess took the suitcase from Pintsch and went into an ante-room. The other three men stood about making small talk until he returned, wearing a jacket that matched his blue Luftwaffe trousers. Over this he wore an unfamiliar set of fur-lined flying-overalls. Pintsch asked him what had happened to his own. Hess shrugged.

'Someone seems to have taken them instead of his own,' he explained with a grin, 'so I've taken someone else's! I've left a note for the owner telling him I've only borrowed them—though I don't know when I'll be able to let him have them back!'

Pintsch took the suitcase that now contained Hess's raincoat, and they went downstairs again and out into the early evening. It was just on six o'clock.

Hess shook hands with them all, as was his habit before he left on any flight. He had a map-case strapped to one thigh, a Leica camera slung around his neck. This belonged to his wife; days later, she opened her leather camera-case and found it empty, except for a hastily scribbled note: 'Sorry, mine has no film, so I've taken yours!'

A bulky figure in his borrowed overalls, he lumbered himself up into the plane. Piel stood and watched for his thumbs-up sign as Hess went through the preparations for flight. The right hand to turn on the petrol, the left for the stick, the right for the starter of each engine. Slowly, the black-tipped propellers began to turn, sluggishly, one after the other. The exhausts spluttered and then roared, coughing gouts of pale blue smoke. As Hess warmed up each engine, the plane trembled against the chocks.

At last he nodded to Piel and gave him the thumbs-up sign with both hands for both engines. Piel's homely Bavarian face was creased against the wind from the propellers, one hand turned up to protect his eyes from the blast. He bent down and pulled the rope connected to the chocks.

Slowly the little aeroplane moved forward into the wind, its tail bumping on the oil-stained concrete. Hess opened both throttles, and the tail went up; within seconds he was airborne. He flew to the end of the runway and then turned in a wide left-hand sweep, dipping low over the little group who stood and waved goodbye to him. Then he was gone, over the tops of the fir trees, over the fields and the hills to the north.

'Well,' said Pintsch as brightly as he could. 'That's that. A nice take-off. We've got a long wait on our hands now, I suppose.'

He looked at his watch; the hands showed ten minutes past six. Hess had left on schedule.

'I suppose you're right,' agreed Piel without much enthusiasm. 'I must say I can think of better things to do on a Saturday night than hang around this place. I see it seven days a week as it is. How long do you think he'll be?'

'I don't know,' said Pintsch frankly. 'I've no idea at all.'

As he spoke, he put his hand into his inner jacket pocket and felt the sharp corner of the letter Hess had given him to take to Hitler if he did not return through engine trouble or some other hitch. He was to wait for four hours before he delivered it.

Pintsch did a quick mental calculation. Assuming that Hess did not return within this time, he could reckon on leaving the airfield by half-past ten. Allowing an hour to reach Munich station, he could catch the night train and be in Berchtesgaden early on Sunday morning. By then Hess should have made contact with *someone* on the British side; by that same time on Sunday night the war might be over. So much for dreams; in fact, by six o'clock on Sunday night, both Hess and Pintsch were under guard; one in Scotland and the other in Germany.

The minutes and then the hours ticked by slowly. At first Pintsch talked with the detective and the driver, but soon the secret they all shared dredged their tongues of words. They walked up and down the edge of the airfield, concealing their anxiety from Piel as best they could, listening for the distant beat of a returning aeroplane.

After three hours, Piel, knowing nothing of the plan behind Hess's flight, began to worry because he had not returned. He feared trouble and reprimands and explanations and reports; what could have happened to the Deputy Führer to keep him away for so long? If Hess did not return very shortly, he would find it difficult to bring down the plane safely, for an early evening mist was beginning to cover the ground and already was thick enough to make height difficult to judge. What would be said to him—worse, what would happen to him—should Hess crash? Or if Hess should be injured or—the thought seemed too terrible to consider—if he were killed?

'Herr Pintsch,' he said at last, unable to contain his worries alone any longer. 'As you can see, it is growing very misty here. I think I should telephone Professor Messerschmitt and explain that Herr Hess has still not returned. And if he comes back now I think he will have difficulty in landing. Perhaps the Professor can suggest something. I must say I'm very anxious.

'Not only is Herr Hess the Deputy Führer,' he went on, 'but his plane is still on the secret list, and *anything* could have happened. If we could get another plane up in the air now, or at the latest within an hour, before the light fails, perhaps they might see if he's come down. But if we wait much longer the mist will be too thick here to see anything. Why, man, Herr Hess won't be able to see his own way back! I can't delay any longer, for this place can be bad enough to find in the day sometimes. At night, without any lights and in a mist, he'll never get down again safely. Don't you see that?'

Pintsch nodded. 'I see it quite well,' he agreed, 'but I'm positive there's no need to worry. Of course it's possible that Herr Hess will come down at another airfield, if he can't get back here, of if he's in any difficulties. Anyway, I'm sure he's all right. He's a good flier, you know. Or perhaps you don't think he is?'

Piel shook his head vehemently. 'Oh no, it's not that at all,' he insisted. 'I agree, he's an excellent pilot. But, even to the most expert pilot, things can go wrong—things that have nothing to do with flying. A broken wire, maybe, water in the petrol, a bird flying into a propeller. I tell you, Pintsch, I don't like it.'

'Neither do I,' agreed Pintsch, 'but there's nothing you or I—or anybody else—can do about it now. So don't worry yourself about this. I'll take full responsibility.'

With this, the unhappy manager had to be content.

Shortly after nine o'clock, Pintsch went into an empty office in the administrative building, locked the door behind him, carefully fixed the blackout curtain on to the window, sat down at the desk and picked up the telephone. He asked the operator for an official unlisted number in Berlin, the telephone number of a branch of the Air Ministry where commanders of bomber stations all round

Germany could ring to be given radio direction signals on which to fly.

'Pintsch speaking, adjutant to the Stellvertreter, Herr Rudolf Hess,' he said, cupping his hand around the mouthpiece in case anyone else should hear him, although the building seemed deserted. 'Over to you.' There was a click as he and the offices in Berlin both pressed the switches to 'scramble' the line and make it impossible for anyone to tap the wire and overhear their conversation.

'I'm speaking on behalf of the Deputy Führer,' he went on. 'He has asked me to repeat my request for a radio beam from Augsburg, to a point about fifteen kilometres west of Glasgow, in Scotland, on Dungavel Hill. Can you give him a beam?'

'It's very difficult,' came the metallic unknown voice over the miles of wire, over the pine forests, above the mountains. 'In fact, Herr Adjutant, I think it's impossible. We've got a hell of a big raid going out tonight on Britain. It's our biggest so far—around five hundred planes. They're using all the beams we have.'

'I didn't know that,' said Pintsch, wondering how this would affect Hess's plans, for he had not known it, either.

'It's awkward for me, too, for I've promised Herr Hess a beam, and he's already in the air. I'm at Augsburg—the Messerschmitt works—and I've no means of contacting him. It looks like trouble all round.'

'I'll do what I can, I promise you,' promised the man in the Air Ministry. 'I tell you what, we can give him a beam for one hour until 2200 hours, if that's any use. After that, it's more than I can do. I've got my orders. You'll have to go above me for permission. Sorry.'

'Right. Thanks for that, anyway. Goodbye.'

The line went dead. Pintsch replaced the receiver and sat thinking, head in his hands, wondering where Hess was now; what his thoughts would be in his small cold cockpit far above the fluffy dark clouds. Would he think that Pintsch had let him down?

Pintsch imagined him tuning the radio round the dial for the signals that never came, wondering whether the set was faulty, peering down at his compasses to check his bearings.

A knocking on the door disturbed his thoughts. He opened it; Piel was outside, even more agitated.

'I thought I heard the 'phone,' he explained nervously.

'You did,' replied Pintsch. 'I was speaking on it myself. An official call. Look, I don't think there's any use either of us hanging around here any longer. I think I know Herr Hess better than you, and I expect he has come down somewhere. Maybe he's had engine trouble or something. If so, he'll have it put right and he'll be back here in the morning. The best thing I can do is to run you back home —I've still got his car here—and if you don't hear either from him or from me by the early morning then I suggest you ring your chief. But don't lose any sleep on it. You've only had this for *one* night. I get it all the time!'

Piel appeared considerably cheered by this reasoning. He locked up his office and followed Pintsch to the car. Behind them, the runway stretched away, seemingly without end, running from dusk into darkness like a vast wide road leading nowhere.

The guards lifted up the boom to let the car go through. Pintsch acknowledged their salute as the car turned back on to the autobahn, its masked headlights throwing forward a small silvery pool of light in which midges and night-moths danced briefly and were gone. They all sat in silence until Piel had been dropped at his home, and then Pintsch ordered the driver to pull off the road and put out their lights.

'There may be trouble about what the Stellvertreter's doing,' he explained. 'I just don't know yet. It depends whether he's successful or not. I've got a letter from him to take to the Führer. Now for your plans. This big car is far too conspicuous to use, and also, everyone knows whose it is.

'You two get some supper,' he continued, 'and then put this car into the garage. Pack your kit and take the small DKW out of Munich to Gallspach. We have a friend there. Wait there with him if you can, or at least in the village, if you can't—until you hear how the flight has gone, whether it's been successful or not. I'll do my best to get a message to you as soon as I have some news.'

Without mentioning the man's name, Pintsch was referring to a homeopath whom Hess had frequently consulted in the small Austrian village of Gallspach. The driver and the detective could change into civilian clothes in Gallspach, and no one need suspect that they were anything but two soldiers on a brief leave.

'In the meantime, take me to Munich station. I'll catch the train to Berchtesgaden and we'll say goodbye,' he said. 'Heil Hitler!'

The driver restarted the big car and drove along the deserted roads towards Munich. None of the men spoke; each was busy with his own thoughts. They reached the station, and the driver stopped. He and the detective shook hands with the adjutant.

'Well, good luck,' said Pintsch, his throat a little tight.

3 Hess prepares for his flight to Britain in the machine he used. Pictures taken at Augsburg airfield by his adjutant and staff.

Above Hess gets ready.

Hess's helmet is adjusted.

4 The engine won't start.

Hess takes off.

'Good luck, sir,' chorused the others.

We'll need it, thought Pintsch. He shut the door and stood for a moment among the few taxis parked in the forecourt with their clumsy apparatus on the roof for making gas from wood.

Then smartly, briskly, as the adjutant of the Reich's Deputy Führer should appear, he marched up the steps and into the station-master's office. He explained to a duty clerk that Herr Hess wanted his private railway carriage to be attached to the next train to Berchtesgaden.

'There's no direct train tonight, Herr adjutant,' replied the clerk. 'We'll have to unhitch Herr Hess's carriage at Freilassing.'

Pintsch shrugged irritably; he did not want to be bothered by such administrative details. 'What time will we reach Berchtesgaden in that case?' he asked.

The man consulted a timetable, his thick fingers with their bitten nails fumbling on the edges of the small pages, his eyes poring over the small print. 'You should be there by seven o'clock tomorrow morning, Herr adjutant,' he replied.

'When is the next train out?'

'At 2400 hours,' replied the clerk. 'Where can we reach you when the carriage is ready? Perhaps you may care to wait in it until the train goes?'

'No, thank you. I'll join the train just before it's due to go.'

The man clicked his heels, gave the Heil Hitler salute which Pintsch returned, and went back to his place behind the table.

Pintsch came out of the office and looked at his wristwatch: he had a long wait ahead of him. There was no real need for him to travel in the Deputy Führer's carriage: he could have made the journey just as quickly in an ordinary compartment, but, somehow, for some reason which he still cannot fully understand, it seemed important to use this carriage at the time; perhaps it was because it represented authority and stability, and on that Saturday he needed both.

He walked slowly among the crowds who still thronged the platforms waiting for trains; soldiers, sailors, airmen, girl friends; civil and military policemen; old women in their black clothes and stockings and rubber-soled canvas shoes.

There was very little light in the dim gloomy cavern of the station under its domed glass roof, apart from shaded blue bulbs at the platform entrances and some illumination from the refreshment trolleys and bookstalls. He had a peculiar sensation of walking in a strange twilight world divorced from reality; at about the same time Hess was experiencing the same dream-like unreality of the view above the west coast of Scotland.

The minutes crept by: at five to twelve by the station clock, Pintsch began to look out for the dark green carriage in which he had so often travelled with Hess. Some railway official recognized him, saluted and led him to it.

'Will Herr Hess be travelling tonight?' he asked.

'Not tonight,' said Pintsch.

'Is he away from home?' continued the official, anxious to make conversation with someone so close to high authority.

'Yes,' agreed Pintsch shortly. 'He is away from home.'

He had not admitted this earlier in the station-master's office in case someone who outranked him had refused to hook the coach on to the train.

He took his seat in the blacked-out compartment, a little fusty with the steam heat. The carriage had not been used for weeks to his knowledge, and had probably grown damp in some neglected siding. Whistles blew, doors banged shut, there was some last minute shouting from a crowd of soldiers with kitbags trying to catch the train, and then they began to move. It was exactly midnight.

Pintsch switched off the shaded reading-lamp at his head, rolled up the blackout blind from one window and opened the window. The cool fresh night air blew in. His forehead felt clammy and damp with reaction; only then did he realize how tense he had been, and how tired he was. He put up his feet on the opposite seat and lay back, eyes shut. Within minutes he was asleep.

At some early hour on the following morning he heard shouting and the clanging of levers dimly in his sleep. Through the open window, as he stirred into wakefulness, Pintsch saw railwaymen with shaded oil-lamps working to unhitch his carriage and hook it up behind another train. Then he slept again and did not wake until nearly seven, when they were approaching Berchtesgaden.

Precisely at seven o'clock the train pulled into the small station at Berchtesgaden. Pintsch climbed out. What happened to the carriage now was of no importance to him; all that mattered was how he was received, and how Hitler regarded the letter he carried with him.

He went into the station-master's office and telephoned to Hitler's adjutant, Albert Bormann, Martin Bormann's brother, whom he knew well. Albert Bormann had his quarters next to the Führer's house. He was surprised that Pintsch had arrived so unexpectedly.

'What are *you* doing here?' he asked curiously.

'I've a letter from Herr Hess for the Führer which I must deliver personally,' Pintsch explained. 'I want to see the Führer as soon as I can.'

'You'll have a job,' replied Bormann. 'He's got a full day ahead of him. First, there's Todt seeing him today and then we've got a reception in the afternoon for Admiral Darlan. But I'll do what I can. In the meantime, I'll send a car for you.'

Presently the little grey car arrived. Pintsch climbed in beside the driver and was soon racing up the deserted mountain road with its magnificent view of the Alps; past precipices, over bridges, towards Hitler's house.

'What makes you so anxious to see the Führer this morning?' asked Albert Bormann, who stood waiting for him in the marble-floored entrance hall.

'I'm sorry, but I just can't tell you,' replied Pintsch. 'I don't want to be secretive about it, but you know how these things are. As I explained, I've a sealed letter from my chief for him.'

'How is he these days?' asked Bormann chattily. 'Still keeping up his flying, eh?'

'Yes,' agreed Pintsch noncommittally. 'He's still flying.'

'Well, I'll see what I can do,' said Bormann, and disappeared into his own office. In fact, he did nothing at all; Pintsch was kept waiting for several hours.

A strange atmosphere prevailed at any house where Hitler was working. Secretaries and aides and adjutants padded about trying to look important, carrying sheafs of paper and brief-cases and files, and talking in whispers as though they were in a church or in some other holy place. In a sense many of them believed they were, for Hitler, as well as being a political and military head of the Third Reich, also commanded other loyalties: he was the embodiment of the unconquerable German people, a Wagnerian legend come to life.

Pintsch, who had met Hitler many times with Hess, knew something about his hysterical ravings, his pathological inability to see a point of view other than his own if he did not wish. Now, as he waited, he looked around the hall for some friendly face, and saw Dr Fritz Todt, Hitler's Minister of Armaments and Munitions, the man who had built the Siegfried Line, sitting with what composure he could muster in one of the rococo easy-chairs.

'I understand you have an appointment with the Führer, Dr Todt?' Pintsch began.

'That is so,' agreed the other man cautiously. 'It's down for eleven o'clock but I want to see him sooner if I can.'

'Dr Todt,' said Pintsch, sitting down in a chair beside him. 'I would like to ask you a very great favour. I've just arrived from Munich with a special sealed despatch to the Führer from Herr Hess. It is of the utmost importance that I deliver this at the earliest possible moment. I would not ask this favour normally, but in these circumstances I would be most grateful for your permission to have a brief interview with the Führer, and to hand him this, before you see him.'

'Certainly, Pintsch,' replied Dr Todt easily. 'By all means. I take it that you won't be very long delivering this despatch?'

'I should think not more than a few moments, sir,' replied Pintsch hopefully.

As they spoke, Hitler came down the central staircase. He was wearing a dark grey uniform, and soft leather shoes. His face was expressionless and rather pallid. He had been working in his study since seven that morning; it was then shortly after ten o'clock.

Dr Todt and Karlheinz Pintsch stood up, clicked their heels together and bowed towards their Führer. He acknowledged their presence with a nod.

Pintsch took a pace forward. 'Mein Führer,' he began, 'I have a message here from Herr Hess.'

Hitler held up his hand. 'Wait a minute, Pintsch,' he said. 'Can't you see that Dr Todt is here? He has been wanting to see me for some time. I'll see you afterwards.'

He turned to the Labour Minister, but Pintsch stood his ground. 'Mein Führer,' he persisted, 'I have already spoken with Herr Minister Todt and explained the importance of my letter. He is quite willing that I should present this to you first.'

'Really?' said Hitler. He was now in the hall; he stood looking at Pintsch, eye to eye, a rather small, pudgy figure in his undress uniform. He was so close that Pintsch could see the open pores around his fleshy nose.

'Very well, Pintsch,' he said at last. 'Give me the letter.'

Pintsch put his hand into his inside jacket pocket and pulled out the sealed envelope.

'Come into the study,' said Hitler. An orderly opened the door into a wide room panelled in light wood with a red marble floor. This room was the heart of the house. It had huge windows that could slide away to give the illusion that the breathtaking view of the mountains beyond was actually inside the room, like some magnificent landscape painting come to life.

Hitler worked standing up at his table, with a gigantic globe at one side. On it stood a wide, shaded reading-lamp, a bowl of flowers, a blotter with two glass inkwells. Here he signed his papers, corrected his speeches, drafted memoranda, considered military plans and made the decisions that had changed the face of Europe.

This room, too, had seen some of the greatest events in his career —and more were to come. Here he had received Mussolini, King Carol of Rumania, Neville Chamberlain. Here he had interviewed Schuschnigg and set in motion the machinery that ended the independence of Austria. Here, too, on the last day of 1940, with France, Poland, Czechoslovakia and Austria all his; with Britain seemingly on the edge of defeat and with plans already in progress to invade Russia, he had raised his glass—for once filled with champagne— and toasted the complete victory he was sure the New Year would bring.

The room would also see darker moments. Here he would sit among a group of guests, their faces as pale as his own, while the great German ship *Bismarck* drifted rudderless, and at the mercy of the waves and British guns, after she had sunk the *Hood*. Radio messages from the doomed crew—two thousand Germans locked in a floating iron tomb hundreds of miles away on a bitter sea poured in, and there was nothing whatever their Führer could do to help them, except to listen and to mourn.

Here, too, in this room, Hitler would hear other news as the shadows of his defeats grew longer. At this desk he received first news of a setback at the Baranov bridgehead on the Russian Front, which began the German retreat from the East, and marked the end of a dream that so nearly came true. Here, too, a pale-faced orderly would deliver the message that told him of the Allied invasion of France, news that marked the end of his triumphs.

Now Hitler walked across the thick beige carpet to his desk, and then turned to face Pintsch. He looked at him for a few moments in silence, then took a pair of reading spectacles from his breast pocket and put them on. With the bright spring sunshine from the vast window pouring in over his shoulder, he opened the envelope and began to read.

After the first few lines he looked at Pintsch.

'Where is Hess now?' he asked. Pintsch swallowed. Standing stiffly at attention, thumbs in line with the seams of his breeches, he replied: 'Yesterday evening, Mein Führer, at 18.10 hours, he flew from Augsburg to Scotland to see the Duke of Hamilton.'

'At this particular point in the war that could be a very hazardous escapade,' said Hitler gravely, and picked up the letter again.

As he read on, his brows contracted. He put down the letter and pressed a buzzer. An adjutant appeared.

'Find out where Reichsmarshal Goering and Herr Ribbentrop are,' he told him.

Hitler read the letter through for a second time, before the adjutant reappeared, clicking his heels.

'Reichsmarshal Goering is in Nuremberg, and Herr von Ribbentrop is at home in Fuschl,' he reported.

'Send for them both at once. It is a matter of the highest urgency.'

The adjutant bowed and withdrew. Hitler picked up the letter again, and this time he read it through aloud in a voice little more than a whisper.

'And if this project—which I admit may have only a small chance of success—ends in failure and the Fates decide against me, this can have no detrimental results either for you or for Germany: it will always be possible for you to deny all responsibility. *Simply say that I was crazy . . .*'[1]

Hitler lowered the letter and turned away from Pintsch, looking out over the mountains towards Salzburg. The room seemed very still. Sunshine glittered on the glass covers of the bookshelves on the far wall. The scent of the flowers was very strong.

Another door opened; Eva Braun came in. She was wearing a tweed skirt and woollen jumper, with flat walking shoes. She looked at the two men, and then announced in a small voice: 'Lunch is ready.' Hitler nodded; he could see Dr Todt later on. He folded up the letter, carefully replaced it in the envelope and put it in his right-hand jacket pocket. Pintsch hesitated; he had not been dismissed. Hitler seemed to ignore him. As they walked along the pillared corridor to the dining-room, Martin Bormann came out of a room.

'What's happening?' he asked Pintsch, in a whisper. Like his younger brother, he could not understand why Pintsch was there without his master.

'The Stellvertreter has flown to Scotland,' Pintsch explained.

[1] Memorized and made available to the author by Frau Ilse Hess.

Bormann backed away precipitately, anxious to avoid any contact that might involve him.

'To Scotland?' he repeated incredulously. 'Oh, that's nothing to do with me. I know nothing about that,' he added hastily. 'Now don't try and involve me.'

They reached the dining-room. Todt was already there with Dr Otto Dietrich, Hitler's Press adviser; Hewel, one of Ribbentrop's assistants from the Foreign Office, and General Karl Bodenschatz, from the Air Force.

During lunch Goering arrived in a great hurry, anxious to know the reason for his call. Bodenschatz had been unable and unwilling to say on the telephone why he was wanted.

Hitler explained briefly what had happened. First, Goering's face registered incredulity, then anger. Finally, as he grasped its significance, he became reassuring.

'He'll never reach Scotland, Mein Führer,' he said soothingly. 'If he's flying a ME 110 he hasn't the range for one thing. I tell you, he's down in the German ocean already, and food for the fish.'

'He's had extra petrol tanks fitted to give him range,' Hitler pointed out. 'Anyway, you don't know Hess like I do. He'll get there all right. At this very moment, he's probably sitting down to lunch with the Duke of Hamilton in Scotland . . .'

CHAPTER SEVEN

'The Worm is in the Bud'

This was not quite accurate; at that precise moment Hess was lying in bed in Buchanan Castle at Drymen, a small town outside Glasgow. The castle had been taken over at the outbreak of war as a military hospital.

Two soldiers with fixed bayonets stood guard outside the room of the Deputy Führer. Hess lay, eyes closed, the pallor of his face accentuated by his black hair and the stubble already darkening his chin. It was barely eighteen hours since he had arrived, but so far as he was concerned, he had been there an eternity, for nothing had gone according to his hopes and intentions.

True, he had seen the Duke of Hamilton, but it had not been as he had often pictured the meeting, between equals; Hess was in bed and under guard for the interview. Worse, the Duke, while polite, had been formal—to the point of asking him how he could prove he *was* Hess.

A few hours earlier, when Hess was on his way to the Busby Scout Hall, Air Marshal Sholto Douglas, the Chief of Fighter Command, was on duty in the Fighter Command Ops Room at Bentley Priory, in Stanmore, Middlesex. News reached him that a Messerschmitt 110 was down outside Glasgow; a report that at first he found hard to believe because he knew that such an aircraft could not possibly carry enough fuel from Germany to return.

Then the Commander of No. 34 Group, the Royal Observer Corps, rang him from Glasgow with further information. 'We've got the pilot of that ME 110, sir,' he reported. 'He's in hospital now and wants to see the Duke of Hamilton.'

The Observer Corps who—when they had earlier reported that the Messerschmitt was flying over Glasgow unaccompanied—had been caustically advised to 'take more water with it', were naturally elated at this vindication of their own accuracy in aircraft recognition.

The city's Assistant Group Officer, Graham Donald, had driven out to Eaglesham to examine the wreckage of the plane, and then he followed Hess to the little Scout Hut. He had not spoken to Hess, but something about his dark craggy eyebrows, his stiff military bearing, rang a bell of recognition; this middle-aged pilot with the gold watch and the capsules of medicine was the Deputy Führer of the Third Reich.

For the four nights before Hess landed German aircraft had made dispersed raids in many parts of Scotland. The Duke and his officers had been on duty for most of these nights, and indeed had slept very little all that week. On the afternoon of Saturday, May 10, the Duke flew a Hurricane to Drem fighter station in North Berwick. Over the Firth of Forth he indulged in a practice dog-fight with his second-in-command.

They returned later that afternoon, hoping for an early and undisturbed night.

In the early evening one solitary German aeroplane was reported to have crossed the east coast of Scotland near Holy Island and was flying inland. This news was received with less than enthusiasm at Turnhouse, for they thought that it could possibly be a German weather machine sent out in advance of a big raid to test weather conditions on the spot.

Then news came that this aeroplane had apparently dived from about 18,000 feet, flying on across Scotland at about 50 feet, just above the rooftops. The Observer Corps reported that it was a ME 110. There was an acrimonious discussion between the Observer Corps and the RAF as to how a ME 110 could possibly be so far from home. A fighter from Turnhouse went up after it, but such was the plane's speed that they could not even approach it.

Then came a report that the plane had crashed in flames outside Eaglesham. On top of this came the more important news that a heavy raid had begun on London.

'Thank God,' thought the Duke. 'At least that means a chance of a quiet night here.' He left the Ops room and went to bed.

Hardly had his head touched the pillow than the telephone rang. The Controller spoke to him urgently.

'Will you please come to the Ops room, sir, at once?'

'Why, is there an attack?' asked the Duke.

'No, sir.'

'Are there any Germans about?'

'No, sir.'

'Then why the devil *should* I come back?' demanded the Duke. 'I've only just got into bed.'

'We have some information that I think you should know immediately,' the officer explained guardedly.

Wearily, the Duke of Hamilton rose, dressed and crossed to the Ops Room. He was told that the pilot of the solitary aeroplane had landed by parachute. He gave his name as Hauptmann Alfred Horn and wanted to speak to the Duke personally. Within minutes Fighter Command and possibly even the Prime Minister's office knew that this German, Alfred Horn, had landed and asked specifically to speak to the Duke of Hamilton. But no one knew that he was Hess—and the Duke, who knew no one called Horn, had no idea of his identity.

The Duke rang the interrogating officer. 'When are you going to interview this German who wants to speak to me?' he asked him.

'Tomorrow morning, sir,' replied the officer.

'I'll come with you,' the Duke told him.

Next morning, Sunday, they drove together to Maryhill Barracks, where Hess was under guard in the sick-bay. Before they went into the room, where Hess lay in bed under white sheets and regulation red blankets, the Duke of Hamilton was shown the odd selection of items Hess had brought over; his phials and tubes and capsules of homeopathic remedies, and his photographs of himself and his son.

Hess asked to speak to the Duke alone. As the other officer withdrew and the door shut, the Deputy Führer announced dramatically: 'I am Reichsminister Hess.'

The Duke replied that he could not say whether this was so or not.

'I can give you *proof* of my identity,' insisted Hess, feeling under his pillow for his wallet. Triumphantly, he produced the photographs he had already shown to the McLeans. 'There you are,' he said, holding out a photograph of himself. 'That proves it. This is a picture of me.'

'I can see that indeed,' agreed the Duke. 'But because it is a picture of you it does not mean that it is a picture of Hess.'

The two men looked at each other; the Duke in puzzlement, Hess in disappointment. 'I never thought of that,' replied Hess slowly. 'I never thought of that.'

It was too much. Hess shut his eyes. Reaction from the strain of the long flight was setting in; mingled with this reception it produced an amalgam of despair. He began to mutter about his hopes for negotiating peace between Britain and Germany, his need to meet some senior Government representative.

'I am on a mission of humanity,' he explained. 'The Führer does not want to defeat England. He wants to stop fighting.'

Hess did not speak English very well, and the Duke's German was a little rusty. Hess, however, began to give the reasons for his flight, and to talk of his hopes for making peace between Britain and Germany.

Partly to give himself time to decide what he should do, and partly because of the language difficulty, the Duke interrupted him, and explained that he wished to fetch an interpreter. Then they could discuss the matter further and more fully. Hess nodded agreement.

On his way out of his room the Duke saw the officer in charge of the sick-bay. 'You might have a very important prisoner here,' he told him. 'I think it would be wise to move him out of Glasgow, and keep him somewhere in secret with a double guard.'

Hess was therefore moved to the military hospital in Buchanan Castle, in Drymen, about eighteen miles away.

The Duke put two or three photographs of Horn in his wallet, in case they should prove useful for identification, and then drove back to Turnhouse. He travelled by way of Floors Farm, Eaglesham, where he examined the crashed Messerschmitt. He was quite thankful that the drive took about an hour because, as he says now: 'My mind was burning as to what the next step should be.'

On his return to Turnhouse he telephoned his Air Officer Commanding and asked for immediate leave. He explained that he had something of the highest urgency to communicate to the Foreign Office; something that related to his earlier discussions with the Intelligence people.

'Who will command the station?' asked the AOC, not much concerned with odd communications to the Foreign Office. The Duke named an officer, and leave was granted.

He then telephoned direct to the Foreign Office in London and asked to speak personally to Sir Alexander Cadogan, the Permanent Under Secretary. Finally, after being referred from one department to another, he made contact with Sir Alexander's secretary. The Duke was naturally unwilling to explain the reason for his call on an open line, but insisted that he had something of the highest importance to pass on. The secretary did not appear impressed by this information.

'Sir Alexander is an extremely busy man,' he replied over the miles of wire. 'He might be able to see you in a week or ten days' time. He is very, very busy.'

'But this is a matter of the *utmost* urgency,' persisted the Duke justifiably irritated by this reply, and yet quite unable to give any hint as to what the matter might be.

For some time they argued fruitlessly and fractiously and at cross purposes, and then another voice began to speak, and the secretary withdrew. The newcomer was 'Jock' Colville, Mr Churchill's personal secretary.

'The Prime Minister understands you have something important to tell him?' said Colville briskly.

The Duke of Hamilton agreed that this was so, but he could not go into details on the telephone. 'Look,' he said briefly. 'I'll be at Northolt in one and a half hours from now. Kindly have a car there for me, and I'll explain the whole thing.'

On the tarmac outside his office a Hurricane aircraft stood ready to be delivered to a squadron near London. The Duke decided to fly this down to Northolt and gave orders for it to be fuelled, and checked. Within half an hour he was in the air. He landed at Northolt late in the afternoon and reported to the watch-hut. An officer said that an urgent message awaited him. What was it? he asked. No one was quite sure; the message was sealed, but apparently it contained important instructions.

The Duke opened the envelope. Inside was a short note; he was to fly on to Kidlington airfield, a few miles outside Oxford. This was the airfield nearest to Ditchley Park, where the Prime Minister was spending the weekend.

While he was in the watch-hut some junior pilot climbed into the Hurricane and for reasons of his own had started to 'dope' the engine—priming a hand-pump to the carburettors. When the Duke of Hamilton took the controls again, the engine, new and hot after its long flight from Scotland, found the mixture far too rich, and refused to start. After trying for about twenty minutes, the Duke had to admit defeat. He could not spend any more time on it. He therefore sought out the duty officer, a young flight lieutenant, and told him what had happened.

'You've got to give me a plane,' he explained urgently. 'I don't care what it is, but I must have some sort of aeroplane to fly to Kidlington. It's a matter of the highest priority.'

The flight lieutenant did his best to find an aeroplane, but all seemed in use or under other orders. Eventually, a little Magister training aircraft was discovered in a hangar, and this was wheeled out for the Duke.

Waiting only long enough to check the fuel, he flew on to Kidlington.

On landing he taxied the plane to the the end of runway, cut his engine and climbed out. An enormous black car was waiting for him on the edge of the tarmac; the chauffeur saluted.

'The Duke of Hamilton?' he asked. The Duke nodded. The man held open the rear door of the car for him, and he climbed in thankfully, leaving the aircraft where it stood. He never saw either the Magister or the Hurricane again; and no one has ever asked him what happened to them.

'Where are you taking me?' he asked the driver, as he sank back on the cushions.

'To Ditchley Park, sir. To see the Prime Minister.'

Until then the Duke had no idea why he had been instructed to fly to Kidlington; he had thought vaguely that perhaps Sir Alexander Cadogan must have found time to see him after all. That weekend Churchill was at Ditchley Park, with several of his staff: 'the Prof', Professor Lindemann, later Lord Cherwell, his scientific adviser; General Ismay, now Lord Ismay, his Military Secretary; Brendan Bracken, later the Minister of Information, and some others.

Ditchley Park, an estate of roughly 4,300 acres, is a few miles from Blenheim Palace where Churchill was born. Owned by Mr and Mrs Ronald Tree, old friends of the Prime Minister, it is an eighteenth-century mansion built on the grand scale, with seven reception rooms, twenty-four bedrooms and ten bathrooms, a Dower House and thirty cottages. Sir Walter Scott had made Ditchley famous in 'Woodstock'. Churchill made it even more famous during the war, for this was his secret headquarters on weekends when the moon was full and Chequers presented too obvious a target for German bombers.

In a small wooden cubicle off the hall sat Miss Mary Shearburn, the duty secretary, ready to take any incoming calls. If their importance warranted interrupting the Prime Minister she would type out the message on a slip of paper and carry it in to him.

Throughout that Sunday evening the telephone kept ringing with news of the previous night's gigantic air-raid on London, the worst of the entire war. Streets, squares, whole districts were in ruins and ablaze; the water-pumps ran dry, the casualties were unknown, and at that time unknowable; nothing comparable had occurred to the capital since the Great Fire three centuries earlier. Each new report of the spread of death and devastation was taken in to the Prime Minister; twice he left his seat to ask for further details.

The Duke of Hamilton arrived at Ditchley Park to find Churchill and his guests finishing dinner; they wore dinner-jackets or service uniform. The Duke was, of course, well known to the Prime Minister: they had met many times in the House of Commons in the days when the Duke had been a Member of Parliament, and elsewhere.

'What's all this?' asked the Prime Minister gruffly, as they shook hands.

'Sir, I regret that I cannot possibly tell you in public,' replied the Duke. 'I must see you in private.' Churchill looked at him quizzically for a moment and gave a little grunt.

As the meal finished the guests left the room one by one. Soon Churchill was alone with Sir Archibald Sinclair, the Air Minister, and the Duke of Hamilton. As soon as the door was closed, the Duke explained that a German giving the name of Alfred Horn, but claiming to be Rudolf Hess, had parachuted down in Scotland and had asked to speak to him personally. He had gone to see him; Horn or Hess had announced that he came to offer peace to Britain. The Duke produced the photographs of him; certainly he *looked* like Hess.

For some time after the Duke finished talking no one spoke. 'Churchill,' he says now, 'looked at me as though I was out of my mind.' Indeed, in the improbable surroundings of a great country house, remote from the war, the whole story must have sounded almost unbelievable.

Then Churchill broke the silence. 'Well, never mind Hess for the moment,' he said gruffly. 'I'm going to see the Marx Brothers.'

A projector had been set up in another room, where the other guests sat waiting for the Prime Minister to join them. The Duke was given a comfortable chair, but, exhausted by the events of the day and his lack of sleep on the four previous nights, he immediately fell asleep, and remembers nothing about the film, which was *The Marx Brothers Go West*.

At midnight he awoke. The picture had finished, the lights in the room were being turned up, and Churchill, refreshed and full of energy, was preparing to start work for the second time that day. He put on his magnificent mandarin dressing-gown, embroidered with red and gold dragons, pulled the belt tightly around him and lit a new cigar. Then, until nearly two o'clock in the morning, he cross-examined the Duke on his meeting with Hess, and the events that led up to it.

'He asked me every conceivable question,' says the Duke. 'I made the answers as factual as I could, and then he asked me for my opinions. Did I think that this man really was Hess? I replied that I did. He wouldn't have mentioned Albrecht Haushofer if he had not been Hess.'

Finally Churchill sat back, and as though thinking aloud he said slowly: 'The worm is in the bud.'

But what did Hess *want*? asked the Prime Minister. *Why* was he over here? Was the news of his arrival being broadcast by Germany? Lastly, was this man lying in a Glasgow hospital bed under guard really Rudolf Hess, or was he an impersonator, briefed for some secret mission?[1]

This was feasible, and the only way to discover whether Horn was actually Hess was to confront him with someone who could question him closely about his background, his family, his beliefs. Even though an impersonator would have arrived well briefed as to Hess's background, it was unlikely that his cover-story could stand up to a rigorous cross-examination. But by then the hour was so late that nothing could be done about the matter; everyone therefore went to bed.

By this time Hess had been in British hands for more than twenty-four hours. For all the progress he had made, for all he had achieved since he left Augsburg nearly thirty hours ago, he realized that he might as well have stayed at home.

After breakfast next morning, the Duke of Hamilton motored back to London in a convoy of three cars. Churchill sat in the first, the Duke in the second, and some other officers travelled in the third. They drove at a fantastic speed, through streets virtually emptied of other traffic by petrol rationing. Their drivers crossed red lights, ignored policemen's signals, and swept by on the wrong side of street islands.

Once, in Western Avenue, on the outskirts of Chiswick, a prowling police car accelerated from a side street to try and stop them. The police driver passed the third car, drew level with the Duke in the second, and then came up behind Churchill in the leading vehicle. All the time his gong was booming like a temple bell. Not for one moment did Churchill's chauffeur slacken pace. Instead, he gave reply, sounding an even louder gong with which the Prime Minister's car was fitted. The police, recognizing the occupant, fell away smartly.

---

[1] Doubles were used during the war on several occasions, most notably before D-Day in 1944. Then the British employed an actor, Clifton James, to impersonate General Montgomery. He flew to Gibraltar, stayed with the Governor, then travelled on to North Africa. The intention was to delude the German High Command into believing that an Allied landing was probably to be made from the Mediterranean instead of in Normandy. The manœuvre was successful.

The convoy reached Downing Street by ten o'clock and Churchill at once called Anthony Eden, the Foreign Secretary (now Lord Avon) into his room and told him what had happened.

'If this *is* Hess, it may be that he is fleeing from his country,' Churchill pointed out. 'You must look into this closely.'

The Duke then went to Eden's office and told him in detail of his interview at Maryhill Barracks. By this time it was afternoon. Sir Alexander Cadogan was contacted; he, in turn, telephoned Ivone (now Sir Ivone) Kirkpatrick in his office at the BBC where he was Controller of European Services. Kirkpatrick had been First Secretary in the British Embassy in Berlin from 1933 to 1938, and was acknowledged to be one of the greatest experts on the Nazi Party. He would clearly be able to tell whether Horn was indeed Hess, or a double.

'Tell me,' Sir Alexander asked casually, 'did you see much of Rudolf Hess when you were in Germany?'

'I did,' replied Kirkpatrick.

'Do you think you knew him well enough to be able to identify him *now* with certainty if you saw him again?'

'I'm certain of it. I couldn't fail to recognize him.'

'That's what I thought,' replied Cadogan. 'I don't want to say any more now on this open line, but I think it would be a good idea if you could come round to see me at once in the Foreign Office.'

Rather mystified, Kirkpatrick drove through the grey streets of London, where shop windows sagged open, their splintered glass held by a patchwork of paper strips. Rubble lay piled on the pavements, huge craters contained such unlikely sights as buses upside down, bedsteads, the entire plumbing system of a block of flats. The blackened shells of ruined houses were still smoking after Saturday night's devastation; dust hung thick in the air as demolition gangs and salvage teams toiled to remove the worst of the debris.

Ivone Kirkpatrick showed his pass at the Foreign Office entrance and was immediately escorted to Sir Alexander's office. There the whole situation was explained to him.

'Are you quite sure that you can recognize Hess without any possibility of a mistake?' Cadogan persisted.

'Quite sure,' replied Kirkpatrick, although he admitted later: 'I did have one horrid moment of misgiving at the possibility of being hoaxed by an expert impersonator.'[1]

Sir Alexander then explained what had happened; he added that

---

[1] *The Inner Circle*, Sir Ivone Kirkpatrick, Macmillan.

5 Hess and Karl Haushofer. His son was adviser on British affairs to the German Foreign Office.

Frau Hess and her son, Wolf Rüdiger, today, at the hotel she manages, Die Bergherberg, Hindelang.

6 *Left :* David McLean's cottage at Eaglesham, Scotland, where Hess landed.

Right : The gatepost of Hess's house in Munich as it is today. The house was destroyed in 1944.

Left : Frau Hess's mountain chalet, Die Bergherberg, Hindelang.

Right : Front door of the chalet with their old letter-box with the surname Hess on it.

the Duke of Hamilton had already seen Hess and made a report on his interview. While they discussed the matter, Anthony Eden, the Foreign Secretary, entered the room from a War Cabinet Meeting. His instructions were that Kirkpatrick should first identify Hess beyond all dispute. Once he was positive that Horn was Hess, then he should transmit to the Foreign Office any statement the prisoner cared to make.

Because of the urgency of the matter, a special plane was being prepared at Hendon to fly Kirkpatrick and the Duke of Hamilton to Scotland immediately. This sounded a most efficient arrangement, but was better in the promise than the performance. It was clearly not easy to find a suitable aircraft at once; most aeroplanes capable of carrying two passengers in addition to the pilot were being used for more obviously warlike purposes that week.

Eventually, after some delay, a machine was produced. This was a slow, rather out-moded aeroplane of the type that had carried Churchill with Beaverbrook, Halifax and General Ismay to France eleven months earlier on the Prime Minister's desperate but un-successful attempt to persuade the French not to surrender. The plane took several hours to prepare; but by five o'clock that after-noon Kirkpatrick and the Duke of Hamilton sat back thankfully in the old-fashioned wicker chairs inside its cabin and awaited the take-off.

A strong headwind delayed them, and they were forced to come down near Catterick, the depot of the Brigade of Guards, to refuel at an RAF airfield. No one had seen fit to inform the authorities at Catterick of their arrival or of the need for speed to send them on their way. Worse, the airfield had been heavily bombed during the weekend with severe casualties. The officers concerned thus viewed with some distrust the sudden descent of this unlikely aeroplane in which one passenger claimed to be a Duke, and the other a senior Foreign Office official. There were telephone calls and more delays; finally they were allowed fuel and took off on the last half of their journey.

It was not until twenty to ten that night that the two men finally landed at Turnhouse, hungry, cold and tired. The Duke was told that an urgent telephone call of No. 1 priority awaited him. He rushed to take it; the operator put him through immediately to the Secretary of State for Air.

'What's the result?' asked Sir Archibald Sinclair from London. '*Is* this man Hess?'

'We have only just reached Turnhouse, sir,' replied the Duke. 'We haven't seen him yet.'

'There's just been a report on the German wireless that Hess is missing,' replied Sir Archibald. 'You must see him as soon as you possibly can.'

'It will take a bit of time before we reach him,' explained the Duke. 'He's been moved some miles from here.'

'Never mind,' said Sir Archibald. 'I must have your report as soon as possible.'

Such was the urgency that they did not stay for a meal, or even a wash, but raced on by car to Buchanan Castle. Because of the secrecy of their mission, the Duke asked his adjutant to drive them. Unfortunately, the adjutant was a stranger to the area. All road signs and place-names had been removed throughout Britain some months previously to confuse German troops who might land in any invasion attempt. The job had been done so thoroughly that the lack of any signs or place-names—even removed from advertisement hoardings —certainly confused two tired travellers on this Monday evening. Doors were locked and bolted at dusk; locals were unwilling to help unknown motorists in case they should be spies or enemy agents. Thus, not unexpectedly, they lost their way, and it was after midnight when they finally reached the Castle.

The Commandant was waiting for them in the yard, and led them immediately along ancient stone-flagged corridors, lit by un-shaded electric bulbs, up flights of stairs so cold they could see their breath in front of them, until they reached a small wooden door under the roof. This opened on to a tiny room with a sloping ceiling, in peace-time used by some minor member of the household staff. A light flicked on and the three men looked down at the sleeping figure of Rudolf Hess.

Wearing a pair of grey flannel pyjamas which were the British Army issue to soldiers in hospital, the Deputy Führer lay in an iron bedstead, covered by a brown Army blanket.

'Accustomed as I was to the pomp and splendour in which the Nazi nabobs lived, I surveyed the bare room in silence,' wrote Kirkpatrick later. 'Then we woke up the prisoner and after a moment of dazed uncertainty, he recognized me and gave me a warm welcome.'[1]

An orderly produced two wooden chairs and Hess pulled out from under his pillow a bundle of manuscript notes. Lying in his grotesque pyjamas, unshaven, he propped himself up on one elbow, and began

[1] The Inner Circle.

to talk. On the journey north Kirkpatrick had discussed the Nazis and their faults with the Duke of Hamilton, and had explained how of them all he hated Hitler most. Now, instead of going at once into the object of his visit, Hess launched into a eulogy of Hitler, which lasted for one and a half hours! Kirkpatrick sat stoically and expressionless through all this outpouring. In view of his own earlier observations about Hitler, this torrent of fulsome praise struck the Duke as being rather comical.

The monologue might well have lasted even longer had not another No. 1 priority call brought Kirkpatrick to the telephone. The Foreign Secretary wanted to speak to him from Downing Street.

'Have you interviewed him yet?' Mr Eden asked.

'We have,' replied Kirkpatrick, 'and we can definitely say that he is Hess.'

'Well, why has he come here?'

'We don't know yet. He's spoken for one and a half hours so far, and he hasn't yet reached the point of explaining why he's here!'

As these three men sat in such unlikely proximity in a bare attic room under the eaves of this ancient castle, a handful of men in a Glasgow newspaper office a few miles away were preparing to publish news of Hess's arrival in Scotland, regardless of censorship restrictions. They had reached this decision not out of bravado or for any political motives, but simply because they felt it was such 'a good story', and they were all such enthusiastic journalists that they could no longer keep it to themselves.

When the censor told Max McAuslane on the previous afternoon that the account he had written of Hess's parachute descent could not be published, McAuslane returned to the office and his story was put on the spike. Even so, his editor, Clem Livingstone, was not disposed to let matters rest there. He made a telephone call to a private radio monitoring service, run by Polish refugees in Scotland, and maintained by the owners of the *Daily Record*.

He asked to be informed directly they picked up any news broadcast from Germany that seemed to them to be in any way unusual. This was indeed a very wide brief.

Early on Monday evening, when the Duke of Hamilton and Ivone Kirkpatrick were still battling north in their aeroplane against a headwind, this enterprise was rewarded. A messenger-boy brought John Simpson a brief note from the monitoring station: 'Berlin Radio announces Rudolf Hess missing.'

Hess, the Deputy Führer, the confidant of Hitler, the second most dangerous man in the enemy camp! At once the expensive uniform of Hauptman Horn, his hand-made boots, his air of authority, the quiet dignity he had maintained through all his humiliations, fitted perfectly into a mosaic of identity. Simpson walked into Livingstone's little office, separated from his own by a frosted glass screen, and laid the flimsy piece of typing paper on the editor's desk.

'That's our boy friend,' he announced with a grin. Livingstone read the message and nodded.

The two men looked at each other, the same thought in both their minds; they had achieved the scoop of a lifetime, a story that would be told and retold around the world wherever journalists met, but— would they ever be allowed to print it?

On the assumption that a way around the censorship might somehow be found, Livingstone decided to prepare an edition announcing Hess's landing. But first he wanted one further proof that Horn was Hess. He told Simpson to collect a folder of photographs of men with dark hair and prominent eyebrows from the newspaper's photographic library and take them out to David McLean, to see whether he could easily identify his visitor from among them.

Simpson collected pictures of Tyrone Power, Cary Grant, various local and national sports personalities, and one of Hess. Then, while the office Austin was brought round to the front of the building, he and Livingstone worked out a simple code to use when telephoning back the result of this test, in case any rival newspaper should overhear the call.

If one of the McLeans agreed that Hess was their visitor, then Simpson would simply say: 'Thumbs up, once.' If two identified Hess, then he would say: 'Thumbs up—twice.' And if McLean, his mother and his sister all identified Hess, he would say: 'Thumbs up —three times.' This would mean that there could be no possible doubt as to his identity; the onus of deciding how or whether the *Daily Record* could print this sensational news would then rest with Clem Livingstone.

While Simpson drove out to Eaglesham, the editor and his staff prepared a special edition using all the pictures and facts they could discover about Hess and his career.

Meanwhile, in the McLean's whitewashed cottage at Floors Farm, Simpson laid a photograph of Cary Grant on the kitchen table.

'Is that the man?' he asked.

McLean shook his head. 'That's no the fellow,' he said at once.

'Is this the man, then?' Simpson produced a picture of a famous international footballer.

'No, no, the man who was here on Saturday was a bigger fellow altogether and much older. He wasn't the sort of man I'd like to meet on a dark night!'

Gradually all but one were eliminated. Then Simpson laid the photograph of Rudolf Hess on the table. He kept his hand over the face of another man in the picture—Adolf Hitler.

'That's the man!' cried McLean instantly. 'I'd recognize him anywhere.'

'What do *you* say?' Simpson asked Mrs McLean.

'I agree with David. That's the man who was here on Saturday.'

'Yes, that's him all right,' agreed Miss McLean.

They stood looking at each other in the little homely kitchen with the oil-cloth fixed by drawing-pins to the table. At no time had Simpson mentioned the name of Hess, nor did he remove his hand to show that in the photograph Hess was talking to Hitler. None of the McLeans thought to ask more about their visitor; they still thought of him as Horn.

Simpson went out to his car. At the first red-painted telephone booth on the Glasgow Road he stopped, dropped two pennies in the coin box and dialled the *Record* office.

'Thumbs up, three times,' he said triumphantly when Livingstone came on the line.

For Livingstone, in his small stuffy room in the centre of the building, the moment of decision had come. *Could* he publish? *Dare* he publish? Censorship on newspapers in Britain during the war was advisory but not statutory. This meant that editors were technically free to publish at their own risk any news the censors had refused to pass. But by so doing, they laid themselves open to prosecution and very severe penalties. The newspapers concerned could be closed, and the editors imprisoned. They might thus easily ruin themselves professionally by one foolish move. If Livingstone went ahead and published this news, on what grounds could he be charged? He was not helping the enemy, nor, so far as he could see, was he spreading 'alarm or despondency' which, at that time, was almost equally dangerous and undesirable.

Germany had already announced that Hess was missing; McLean had identified Horn as Hess. Thus, if Livingstone published the news that Hess had landed near Glasgow, he was only carrying public knowledge one step further. He did not see how the Germans could possibly put this information to any use against Britain. Like the other journalists involved, Livingstone—who died some years ago—does not appear to have considered the possibility of any serious purpose behind Hess's visit; or whether a premature announcement about his arrival could influence this in any way. It was enough and sufficient that he had arrived; the thought of a world scoop that could scarcely be equalled and never bettered unless Hitler himself flew to Scotland, ousted all other considerations.

So Livingstone made up his mind; he would publish the news and risk the consequences. Nonetheless, he gave instructions to print a first edition of Tuesday's *Daily Record* that contained no reference whatever to Hess. Livingstone feared that if he published his scoop in this early edition, rival newspapers would copy it; within a few hours the story for which he was risking so much could be common property.

Just after midnight, when the Duke of Hamilton and Ivone Kirkpatrick were climbing the stone steps to Hess's room in Buchanan Castle, Livingstone prepared to print his edition with the uncensored story under the heading 'RUDOLF HESS IN GLASGOW'. At that moment, one of the teleprinting machines in the editorial office, which feed in news from news agencies, began to clatter into action.

'Hess One,' the message began. Then followed a few wrong letters and figures jumbled up as the machine sorted out its electronic vocabulary, and finally: 'RUDOLF HESS IN ENGLAND.'[1]

The teleprinter chattered out a statement authorized by Mr Duff Cooper, then Minister of Information, and issued from 10 Downing Street at 11.20 p.m. that night.

'Rudolf Hess, the Deputy Führer of Germany and Party Leader of the National Socialist Party, has landed in Scotland in the following circumstances.

'On the night of Saturday the 10th inst., a Messerschmitt 110 was reported by our patrols to have crossed the coast of Scotland and to be flying in the direction of Glasgow.

'Since an ME 110 would not have the fuel to return to Germany this report was at first disbelieved.

---

[1] 'For perhaps the only time in history, Scottish newspapermen did not pause to object to the inexactitude that normally acts on them as a raw irritant—the use of "England" when "Britain" is meant. This once, they submitted to England's embracing Scotland.' Stephen Watts, in an article published in *The New Yorker*, February 16, 1957.

'However, later on, a ME 110 crashed near Glasgow, with its guns untouched. Shortly afterwards a German officer who had baled out was found with his parachute in the neighbourhood suffering from a broken ankle.

'He was taken to hospital in Glasgow where he at first gave his name as Horn, but later on declared that he was Rudolf Hess. He brought with him various photographs of himself at different ages, apparently in order to establish his identity.

'These photographs were deemed to be photographs of Hess by several people who knew him personally. Accordingly, an officer of the Foreign Office who was closely acquainted with Hess before the war has been sent up by aeroplane to see him in hospital.'

So Livingstone's courage was rewarded; he had his scoop and he had it legally. He added one important word to his headline so that it read 'RUDOLF HESS IN GLASGOW—OFFICIAL', and gave orders to begin printing.

He telephoned to the circulation department with instructions that no copies of editions containing this story were to leave the building until he personally gave permission. In the few hours available before copies went on sale, no other paper could produce anything like so strong a coverage as the *Record*. But some might try, simply by 'lifting' the story and printing it as their own. To deny them this opportunity, Livingstone ordered that all doors leading to the street should be locked so that no one could leave the building. This would prevent a copy of the paper reaching a rival's hands.

Nowadays, such an act might result in union trouble. Then, owing to air-raids, such orders were frequently given in the interests of safety. They simply meant that men coming off the night shift in the early hours of the morning walked down the stone stairs to their underground air-raid shelter where they drank tea, played cards and smoked and chatted, waiting for the all-clear.

Earlier that evening, a bomb had cut the main telephone link between London and Glasgow. Thus Livingstone discovered, not entirely to his distress, that he was unable to pass on his story to his newspaper's group headquarters in the Gray's Inn Road: he had the story to himself.

As he digested this information his telephone rang. The Associated Press, an American news agency, was on the line.

'Where are they speaking from?' asked Livingstone.

'London,' replied his assistant, handing him the instrument.

'How can you be?' Livingstone asked the caller. 'The line's down. It's been bombed. I can't get through to London myself.'

The man ignored this. 'What do you know about Rudolf Hess?' he asked.

'Before I tell you,' replied Livingstone, 'you tell me how the devil you got through to me with the line down between here and London.'

'I rang the Air Ministry and they managed to fix me up somehow with a line to Edinburgh,' the caller explained. 'The Edinburgh exchange connected me up with you. Well, I've answered your question, so now can you answer mine?'

'Before I tell you anything,' said Livingstone, 'will you promise to credit the *Glasgow Daily Record* in your messages?'

'Listen, bud,' retorted the Associated Press man from his desk in London. 'For this kind of story we'll credit the Lord God Almighty, if necessary.'

Livingstone began to speak, and as he spoke, Max McAuslane entered the office. Throughout that week he was working on a late night shift, from 8.30 each evening until four o'clock on the following morning. During air-raids reporters working these hours usually stayed at home until the all-clear sounded, not through any managerial concern for their safety, but simply because travelling became difficult during a raid. Also, they might only reach their offices in time to be sent back home to cover some local bomb-story or incident.

McAuslane, waiting in his flat in Mary Hill for the all-clear, switched on his wireless for the midnight news, and heard that Hess had landed in Scotland. At once he realized its significance. He grabbed a raincoat, and disregarding the air-raid, raced for the office. By the time he arrived, the edition was roaring away.

Livingstone sat him down near a powerful office radio to monitor foreign news bulletins, and make sure their newspaper was mentioned. Most of what McAuslane heard was completely unintelligible, but every now and then he recognized four words that could not readily be translated into Hindusthani, Chinese, Malay, Portuguese or Spanish: 'Rudolf Hess . . . *Daily Record* . . .'

It was enough; they had scooped the world.

All through that night news agencies and newspapers throughout Britain, and from neutral and allied countries, telephoned the *Record* office for further details. McAuslane dealt with most of these calls personally, repeating the details of his interview until his throat was hoarse.

In the early hours the line to London was repaired. One distant reporter used the opportunity to ask what Hess was having for breakfast. This was impossible to answer; they didn't even know where Hess was, let alone what he was eating.

'Oh, tell him chicken and white wine,' said Livingstone wearily. McAuslane passed on this information as a joke; it was printed as fact. Later this formed the basis of questions in the House by MP's who considered it disgraceful that an enemy of Britain should live so luxuriously within these shores at a time of austerity and rationing.

It was nearly midday on Tuesday before McAuslane finally went thankfully down the stairs into the wide front hall and out to catch his bus home after the most hectic night of his life.

A few weeks later he joined the Royal Air Force, and on his first morning in uniform received a letter, forwarded on by his wife. It came from his late employers. They announced that they had 'pleasure in enclosing our cheque for your services rendered in connection with the story of the landing of Rudolf Hess.'

He looked at the cheque which was pinned to the letter. For all his work, for the priceless publicity he had helped to win his newspaper from innumerable other papers, magazines, news agencies and broadcasting stations throughout the world, Max McAuslane was richer by £6—less income-tax.

CHAPTER EIGHT

The Führer's Quandary

While this was going on in Britain, what was happening in Germany? Why did Berlin Radio admit that Rudolf Hess was 'missing'?

Although those closest to Hitler realized that Hess had carried out what the Führer wanted—and with Hitler's knowledge except for the actual time and date of his flight, for this was largely dependent on the weather—they were professional politicians, and as such were anxious to cover themselves in case Hess's mission failed.

Privately they thought that it would; Churchill was not a man to agree to peace on the terms that Hess could offer. But if by some incredible good fortune peace negotiations with Britain were to be opened, then naturally Hess would be acclaimed in Germany as a hero. In that unlikely case, no one, apart from a small group of high Nazis, need realize that there had been any doubts at all about the outcome. Thus Hitler waited with mounting impatience and irritation for news from Britain of his Deputy's arrival, and his subordinates prepared plans for disowning Hess and his mission in the event of failure. Hitler calculated that if Hess's visit was going to be successful he should have some word back about it within hours. If no news arrived after, say, twelve hours, they could be fairly certain that Churchill was not willing to negotiate peace on any terms whatsoever.

'Hess was supposed to send a message on his arrival,' wrote Goering's biographer later.[1] 'Hitler realized that something had gone wrong when there was nothing but silence, tormenting silence, from Britain.'

This unexpected silence made Hitler think that Hess's flight was to be used by the British for propaganda purposes. It certainly contained lethal ammunition for an anti-Nazi broadside. If the situation were reversed and Anthony Eden had suddenly and unexpectedly parachuted on to Berchtesgaden, Germany would certainly exploit that situation to the full. Hitler had no reason to believe that Britain would do otherwise.

[1] *The Rise and Fall of Hermann Goering*, Willi Frischauer.

The way in which the British might do this—and its effect upon opinion in Germany, Italy and Japan, quite apart from the rest of the world—was appalling to consider. The best defence would naturally be to discredit Hess before the British mentioned him, but this was by no means easy to do for Hess was both popular and important in Germany. For twenty years he had been the Führer's friend and confidant. Thus, if it were announced that Hess had suddenly fled without Hitler's knowledge or consent—then *why* had he done so? Why should the second most important man in the Third Reich suddenly desert and fly to the enemy?

If such a flight could be undertaken in the middle of the war by a person of his high authority and position *without* Hitler's consent, then what did Hess fear? Was there disagreement between the two top men in Germany? On the other hand, if it was announced that Hess had flown *with* the Führer's knowledge—of the plan if not of its timing—then what doubts gnawed at Hitler's mind that he should dispatch his Deputy on such a desperate mission?

Clearly, whatever statements or denials were made, the majority of Germans would assume that Hitler had known of his intention, otherwise how could Hess succeed in acquiring a suitable aircraft for his long journey? How could he receive weather reports—as they would guess that he must have done—and fly above all German defences without any question? If ever news leaked out that he had actually asked Hitler's personal pilot—in Hitler's private apartment—for secret maps to help him on his way, the inference would be obvious!

The permutations on these questions were as endless as they were agonizing. The damage they could do in Germany and also in neutral or uncommitted countries would be incalculable. But that was only one part of the worry. What if the British drugged Hess with pentothal or other specifics that would break down the barriers of discipline and reserve, and allow them to uncover Hitler's innermost secrets—and his plans to attack Russia? What if Britain had already warned Russia of his intentions?[1]

Hitler, at his desk in his study, with the largest window in the world overlooking the magnificent hills, worked out a timetable of events so far. Hess had left Augsburg at ten minutes past six on Saturday evening. The distance to Dungavel House was roughly 850 miles. Thus, allowing for a possible head-wind and for the extra

[1] In fact, on April 3, five weeks before Hess arrived, Churchill had warned Stalin that such an attack was possible. Stalin made little use of the information.

hour added to British summer time, Hess should have reached his destination by eleven o'clock that night. On this reckoning, by the time Pintsch delivered Hess's letter to Hitler on Sunday, more than eighteen hours had elapsed since Hess left Germany. Yet no word had been received from Britain about his landing.

Surely such an event as the arrival of the Deputy Führer could not go entirely unremarked, whether or not the British Government had any intention of negotiating with him? Unless he had crashed into the sea his plane must have flown above many cities and large towns in Scotland. Had he been brought down by fighters or anti-aircraft fire? Or had he crashed on the way?

These worries consumed Hitler, for although Hess had given him the key to extricate himself from all knowledge of the plan if it failed —he could simply say that he had gone mad—this he was understandably loth to do until he was quite certain he had no other course left. For one thing, this statement was demonstrably not true. And if it were put out, then surely many Germans would ask why his madness had not been recognized at an earlier stage—and how many more in high office were similarly afflicted.

Hitler sought the advice and opinion of those around him. Goering, in particular, as head of the Luftwaffe, was placed in an awkward situation.

'Can he make it?' Hitler kept on asking him. 'Can he get there on his own. You're an airman—tell me.'

'It's a fifty-fifty chance,' hedged Goering uneasily, using the English expression.

'So! You're speaking English already,' retorted Hitler angrily. 'If Mussolini hears of this he'll think I've been trying to make a separate peace with England.'

General Karl Bodenschatz, who had been Goering's friend since the First World War, when they both flew in Richthofen's famous squadron, noted that 'Hitler's consternation and surprise were supremely played'[1] at the news of Hess's flight.

'If Hess does reach Britain then it will provide the British with a unique propaganda opportunity,' said Goering, pointing out to Hitler what he already knew too well. 'We must issue a communique to come out before they can do anything with it.'

'But perhaps Hess has come down in the sea—as you told me you were sure would happen,' replied Hitler. 'If that is so, then nobody will know . . .'

[1] *The Rise and Fall of Hermann Goering.*

Goering shook his head; a communique should be prepared. Bodenschatz took down the gist of it from Hitler's dictation. Ribbentrop and Goering added amendments. Seven different drafts were made—and all were destroyed.

As Bodenschatz and Goering left the Berghof just before dawn on Monday, Goering winked sympathetically at his old comrade.

'The Führer has really slipped up, hasn't he?' he said with a wry smile.

Describing the incident afterwards, Goering's biographer wrote:

'It was clear to all that Hitler, faithful to his wartime practice of discussing top secrets only with the people immediately concerned, had hatched a plot with Rudolf Hess, his closest associate. If Hess could convince Britain that Germany was about to attack Russia, peace in the West might, after all, be possible. He could bring off the *coup* which Goering had failed to achieve with diplomacy and the Luftwaffe . . .

'Every single surviving member of Goering's entourage . . . (is) convinced that Hitler not only hoped to make peace with the West but to persuade the British Government to join in Germany's attack on Russia. Hitler's bewilderment in Berchtesgaden was due to the fear that his plot had failed . . .'[1]

Finally, on Monday, around noon, Hitler decided that he could wait no longer for the signal from Hess that had still not reached him. He ordered Dr Otto Dietrich, his Press adviser, to draft a deliberately vague communique that would contain references to mental illness—Hess's own suggestion—but it was not to be released until Hitler personally gave the order.

Dietrich, fully aware of the pitfalls of such a course, gave instructions that all broadcasts from Britain should be monitored in the hope that some announcement might be given, either in code or clear, about the arrival of the Deputy Führer. This might help him considerably in drafting his bulletin.

At about the same time, in Glasgow, Livingstone was giving identical instructions for all German broadcasts to be studied in the hope that they might provide a clue as to Horn's identity.

Meanwhile, Goering interviewed Messerschmitt, as we have seen, but he treated the matter with laughter. It was not important; he would help Messerschmitt 'if the Führer tries to make trouble'. Had

[1] *Ibid.*

Hess really flown away without Hitler's knowledge, Messerschmitt, for all his usefulness as an aeroplane manufacturer, would have faced a charge of treason.

* * *

Bormann, Hess's deputy and a man to whom he had been losing some political ground in recent months, thought it unlikely that Churchill would agree to peace with Germany. Bormann therefore calculated that, provided Hess had not disappeared on his journey, he would shortly have to be discredited by Hitler in a monumental way. Only this would silence German speculation as to his motives and authority.

As Hess's chief assistant, Bormann saw this as an unexpected and unprecedented chance to improve his own position. Caution warred with his fierce ambition. He reasoned that while the odds of Hess failing in his mission were overwhelming, there still remained a slender chance that it might succeed. His prudence and his highly developed sense of political survival restrained him from any precipitate act until Monday, when Hitler decided that he could wait no longer before acknowledging that Hess was missing. Bormann shrewdly calculated that the Führer would not do this without good reason; very possibly the time limit for Hess to send his message was long past. Only then did Bormann decide to put into action his plan of discrediting Hess through his wife, Ilse.

* * *

Hitler insisted that the statement about Hess must be worded sufficiently loosely to allow its retraction or alteration. After several drafts, Dietrich struck the right note; accordingly, Munich radio broadcast this announcement on Monday evening:

'It is officially announced by the National Socialist Party that Party Member Rudolf Hess, who, as he was suffering from an illness of some years' standing, had been strictly forbidden to embark on any further flying activity, was able, contrary to this command, again to come into possession of an aeroplane.

'On Saturday, May 10, Rudolf Hess again set out on a flight from Augsburg, from which he has not so far returned.

'A letter which he left behind unfortunately shows by its distractedness traces of a mental disorder, and it is feared that he was a victim of hallucinations.

'The Führer at once ordered the arrest of the adjutants of Party

Member Hess, who alone had any cognisance of these flights, and did not, contrary to the Führer's orders, of which they were fully aware, either prevent or report the flight.

'In these circumstances it must be considered that Party Member Hess either jumped out of his aeroplane or has met with an accident.'

In Rome, Count Ciano, Mussolini's son-in-law and Foreign Minister, heard this strange and vague announcement and was not impressed by it.

'A strange German communique announces the death of Hess in a plane accident,' he wrote in his diary[1] on that day. 'I cannot conceal my scepticism of the truth of this version. I even doubt whether he is dead at all.

'There is something mysterious about it, even though Alfieri (the Italian Ambassador to Germany) confirms the report that it was an accident.'

Hitler also sent Ribbentrop, his Foreign Minister, to Rome, as General Franz Halder, Hitler's Chief of Staff until 1942, noted,[2] 'to inform the Duce of the offer of a separate peace'.

Ciano was still unhappy about the whole episode.

'The Hess affair has a tinge of tabloid news,' he wrote in his own diary on the following day. 'Hitler's substitute, his second-in-command, the man who for fifteen years has had in his grasp the most powerful German organization, has made an aeroplane landing in Scotland. He fled, leaving a letter for Hitler.

'In my opinion it is a very serious matter; the first real victory for the English. In the beginning the Duce believed that Hess had been forced to make a landing while he was on his way to Ireland in order to start a revolt, but he very soon abandoned this thesis, and he now shares my impression of the exceptional importance of this event.

'Von Ribbentrop unexpectedly arrives in Rome. He is discouraged and nervous. He wants to confer with the Duce and me for various reasons, but there is only one real reason; he wants to inform us about the Hess affair, which is now in the hands of the press all over the world.

'The official version is that Hess, sick in body and mind, was a victim of his pacifist hallucinations, and went to England in the hope of facilitating the beginning of peace negotiations. Hence, he

---

[1] *Ciano's Diplomatic Papers.*
[2] General Halder's *Diaries.*

is not a traitor; hence he will not talk; hence, whatever is said or printed in his name is false.

'His conversation is a beautiful job of patching things up. The Germans want to cover themselves before Hess speaks and reveals things that might make a great impression in Italy.

'Mussolini comforted von Ribbentrop, but afterwards told me that he considers the Hess affair a tremendous blow to the Nazi regime. He added that he was glad of it because this will have the effect of bringing down German stock, even with the Italians.

'Dinner at home with von Ribbentrop and his associates.

'The tone of the Germans is one of depression . . .'

Ribbentrop spent only one day in Rome. After he left, Ciano wrote:

'Contrary to expectations, the speculation of Anglo-American propaganda on the Hess case is quite moderate. The only documents that are really harmful are the German dispatches, confused and reticent. Alfieri writes that confusion in Berlin is at its height in all circles . . .'

Then, on the Friday following Hess's arrival in Scotland, Ciano noted:

'a lull of expectancy in the Hess case. Even the British press mentions a mysterious peace mission, going so far as to imply a pre-arranged agreement between Hitler and Hess. This is in contrast to Ribbentrop's declarations, and also to German agitation, which isn't decreasing . . .'

Ilse Hess, on the Monday after her husband's departure, still knew nothing of the turmoil he had caused. She had not altogether believed his half promise that he would be back by Monday, but his movements were so erratic and so unpredictable that his unexpected departure had not alarmed her. She was almost recovered from the indisposition which had kept her in bed on the Saturday, and on Monday afternoon she decided to give a film show for the staff in what the family called her husband's 'great working room'.

This working room, generally used for entertaining official guests because it was the largest room in the house, had a brick fireplace at one end. On one side of the chimney-piece hung a huge oil painting of dark forests with green fields beyond; a view from the Black Forest over the Rhine looking towards the French hills. This canvas concealed an opening in the wall to a small room beyond. The chains that supported the painting passed over weighted pulleys; a touch on the frame of this picture was sufficient to slide it up the wall and expose an aperture a foot square.

Through this a conversation could be recorded; inside it, something of value could be concealed. On this particular afternoon, it contained the lens of a film projector. At the other end of the room a screen was set up, and, with Ilse Hess sitting with her dressing-gown wrapped round her, the film show began.

Half-way through it, one of her husband's aides appeared in the darkened room searching for her. He was the brother of one of Ilse's closest friends, and so called her by her first name. He was blundering about in the dark, falling over chairs, peering at faces in his anxiety to discover where she sat, repeating her name in a loud whisper: 'Ilse! Ilse!'

Finally he found her, and sat down on an empty chair by her side.

'What's wrong?' she asked sharply, rather annoyed at the commotion. 'What's happened?'

At the sound of her voice, the operator switched off the projector and the sound died in the loudspeaker. One by one lights came on round the room, and Ilse saw the familiar faces looking around at her, blinking in the sudden unexpected glare. The aide, the youngest on Hess's staff, and barely out of his teens, dredged for words.

'Something awful has happened to the *Brotherr*,'[1] he said in a strained voice.

'*What* has happened?' asked Ilse.

'He's dead. He's crashed into the sea in his plane.'

At the words a gasp of astonishment and pity came from everyone in the room. There was a scraping of chairs on the polished wooden floor as they stood up, all eyes on Frau Hess, wanting to give her what comfort they could, and not knowing what to say.

'Into the sea?' she repeated incredulously. 'What sea? Where was he? What was he doing? What happened? Who told you this, anyway?'

The young fellow could only swallow nervously, his mouth dry with fear and foreboding. 'I can't say,' he replied wretchedly. 'I've told you all I know. I heard something on the radio, just the last few words of some statement about it.'

---

[1] *Brotherr* means literally the 'bread man' or the breadwinner. It is also a familiar way of referring to the head of a family or a business; a warmer, friendlier equivalent of 'boss'.

Ilse Hess stared at him in amazement and disbelief; before the direct gaze of her blue eyes he flinched and looked away.

'You'd better go and put some proper clothes on,' he said nodding towards her dressing-gown. 'People will be coming here to see you about this. It won't look well for you to be questioned like this.'

'Questioned? By whom? Why should I be questioned? And what about?'

No one replied. Her mind was a turmoil of confused thoughts, but one took precedence. If her husband, the Führer's Deputy, had met with such an accident, then surely Hitler must know more about it. She and her husband had known him intimately from his earliest days as a political figure. Why, Hitler had even suggested that Rudolf and Ilse should marry. How odd, then, that he had not already been in touch with her about this accident! The thought jarred, but then she immediately dismissed it. After all, Hitler was so enormously busy, directing the course of the war, he probably had not been able to spare time to do so. Perhaps he did not even know about it himself.

'I must speak to the Führer immediately,' she said. 'Please put me through by telephone. He's at Berchtesgaden.'

'That's impossible,' said the aide with a sudden, uncharacteristic sharpness.

'Don't talk rubbish,' Ilse retorted. 'I'll get the number myself.'

The others stood aside to let her out of the room. As soon as the door closed behind her she heard their buzz of excited conversation and conjecture. She walked into her husband's study, carefully closed the door behind her and sat down at his desk. Only then, as she waited for her telephone call to Berchtesgaden—the only call she ever made on 'State Priority', the top priority in wartime Germany —did she begin to feel any personal reaction from the news.

Could it be that Rudolf really was dead? Or was something far worse, far more dangerous being concealed from her? Her whole world, so pleasant, so secure until that Saturday barely forty-eight hours ago, seemed suddenly to be crumbling and about to disintegrate around her. She felt almost physically ill with foreboding and dread.

The telephone bell interrupted her thoughts; she picked up the instrument and gave her name to the operator in the Berghof. She expected that this would be sufficient for her to be put through to Hitler immediately; but it was not. She was told that she could not speak to him; he was engaged and on no account was to be disturbed. Would she care to speak to anyone else?

With some reluctance she asked to speak to Martin Bormann.

Although no friend of hers, or of her husband, Bormann was her husband's deputy; if anyone knew what had happened or what was happening, he should be the man.

Martin Bormann and Ilse Hess had several reasons for not being on good terms. For one thing, she distrusted him and felt (quite correctly) that he was anxious to oust her husband to take his job himself. Next, she had once advised his younger brother Albert to go against Martin's wishes. Albert had wanted to marry one of Ilse's friends, the daughter of a Bremen physician, who had been on Hess's personal staff before the war. Martin did not like the girl, but Ilse encouraged the marriage. For this Martin Bormann never forgave her; they had not talked to each other for some months after the wedding. Indeed, this telephone conversation was the first time they had spoken to each other for more than a year; it was also the last until nearly the end of the war when Bormann, seeing the inevitability of defeat ahead, and anxious for any friendly spirits, suddenly telephoned the woman he had deliberately humiliated and asked if she could help him in his hour of ruin.

'I know nothing, Frau Hess,' Bormann told her now, determined not to be helpful. 'You'll have to wait until we can get some further news. In the meantime I am sending my assistant, Dr Hansen, to see you. I want you to co-operate with him. Goodbye.'

The line went dead. As Ilse replaced the receiver she saw the young aide standing on the other side of the desk; he had come into the room so silently that she was unaware of his entry.

'How do you *know* my husband is dead?' she asked him. 'Who says so?'

'It was on the wireless. I told you,' he explained.

'Nonsense,' retorted Frau Hess with spirit.

'Not for one second did I believe anything really tragic had happened,' she wrote later. 'In moments of extreme tension there comes to us, from regions outside the fields of reason, a knowledge that will not let us be deceived.'[1]

She walked back to the working room. Her staff were still there, talking in undertones, little groups of people clustered together, wondering fearfully what the future held for them. No one had any interest in continuing the film show; the screen was rolled up and put away, the projector dismantled, the painting of the Black Forest lowered over the hole in the wall.

Ilse telephoned her husband's brother in Berlin. Hess had used

[1] *Prisoner of Peace*, Introduction by Ilse Hess.

his first name—Alfred—when he called himself Alfred Horn. Alfred Hess was equally mystified at the pronouncement of Rudolf's death; he also thought it unlikely to be true.

Ilse Hess sat and waited for Dr Hansen to arrive. There was nothing else to do, no one else to telephone. Hansen was a senior Nazi Party official, and did not arrive until after midnight, a cold-faced, correct man, hoping desperately beneath his bland appearance that he was not going to be personally implicated.

Frau Hess now discovered with some surprise that instead of being able to help her with information, Hansen wanted her to help him. He appeared incapable of accepting her assurance that she knew nothing about her husband's disappearance except the fact that he had said goodbye to her on Saturday afternoon and gone off with his adjutant to Augsburg, wearing a pair of flying-trousers and flying-boots. She pointed out to Dr Hansen that surely all members of her husband's staff—of whom he was one—knew their chief well enough to be quite sure that he would never discuss state secrets with his wife.

'The term "state secrets" produced a powerful reaction,' she wrote later. 'Up to this point the emissary had been somewhat confused, but, if a little pale, he remained polite and not unfriendly; but now he turned to me and informed me that if a single word of what I (supposedly) knew should leak out I would be arrested. He then turned on his heel and left the room.'[1]

Clearly Hansen's intention had been to discover whether Frau Hess knew that Hitler was implicated; there was just a faint chance that Hess might have been unwise enough to tell his wife. On Tuesday morning Professor Karl Haushofer came to see Ilse Hess. He well knew the reason that lay behind her husband's flight, for he had taken an active part in the earlier attempts to make contact with the British.

'Since these feelers were without a doubt extended with the knowledge of Hitler,' Frau Hess noted, 'Haushofer—contrary to my own conviction—persisted in the view, right up to the day of the trials in Nuremberg when his evidence was taken, that Hitler had "despatched" my husband, or as he maliciously put it "sacrificed him".'[2]

After Haushofer left Ilse Hess, she felt exhausted by frustration

---

[1] *Prisoner of Peace.*

[2] Colonel Otto Skorzeny, who rescued Mussolini from captivity on Hitler's orders after Italy sued for peace on September 8, 1943, noted that the attempt would be disowned by Hitler if it was unsuccessful, in the same way that Hitler disowned Hess when his mission failed. (Serial of his life, *Daily Express*, April 15, 1952.)

and doubt. She took her little son in her arms, and, overcome by weariness, fell asleep in an armchair holding him closely. Suddenly she was shaken awake by an excited secretary. There was news of the *brotherr*. They had just heard a news flash on Munich radio that had first been broadcast by the BBC. Her husband was alive and had landed in Scotland.

CHAPTER NINE

Conversations in a Castle

In Buchanan Castle, Hess, very much alive, was pouring out his mind to Ivone Kirkpatrick and the Duke of Hamilton.

He produced a bundle of notes. Then, referring to these from time to time, he embarked on a long account of British and German relations over the past forty years, and 'sought to prove that Germany's legitimate aspirations had always been thwarted by the treacherous brutality of British policy'.[1]

In the middle of this long and tedious monologue, carried out in the small hours in a tiny room up under the eaves of the ancient castle, the Duke of Hamilton, exhausted after the journey and this long, fruitless diatribe, was nearly asleep. Hess, having slept for two hours or more, was fresh and anxious to continue. But he had so much to say that by three o'clock on Tuesday morning he had still not reached the point of importance: why had he arrived uninvited as an envoy on his own in this strange, dramatic manner?

Kirkpatrick, knowing the type of man with whom he was dealing, held up his hand to stop this Niagara of repetition, and insisted that before Hess went any further, he should explain why he had come to Britain and what he hoped to do now that he had arrived.

Hess replied that he had come personally to try and convince Mr Churchill and the Government that Britain had no hope of winning the war. In these circumstances it would only be common sense to negotiate peace. The British army had been expelled from Europe almost exactly a year before, and had neither the strength nor the ability to return there. German bombing raids on Britain would increase in frequency and severity, and gradually, with more food convoys being sunk, Britain would first be starved out of resistance, then possibly even out of existence. Finally, the British Government would be forced to make peace if only because they could not continue to make war. This future, as Hess described it, was indeed bleak, with little hope or light to relieve the gloom.

[1] *Inner Circle*, Sir Ivone Kirkpatrick.

Hess paused to let the gravity of his words sink in; his listeners preserved calm faces.

'Is Hitler going to invade Britain?' Kirkpatrick asked him.

Hess 'looked rather sheepish, and said he really did not know'.[1] He felt that it was more likely that Britain would gradually be isolated from her Allies and driven to a position of desperation and despair.

'He could claim to be in the Führer's closest confidence,' wrote Kirkpatrick later.[2] 'He was therefore in a position to speak with complete authority, and he could assure me that the Führer, who had always entertained a high regard for Britain and its Empire, would be prepared to conclude a magnanimous peace on the following terms: Germany hegemony on the continent of Europe and the return of the former German colonies; British hegemony in the overseas Empire, which would remain intact and be guaranteed by Germany.'

Of course, Hitler could not attempt any negotiations with Mr Churchill, and so some other Prime Minister should be appointed with whom Hitler felt he could begin talks. In the meantime Hess asked for a certain German prisoner-of-war to be released, so that this man could act as his personal secretary and aide during what he optimistically called 'the forthcoming peace conference'.

It was four o'clock in the morning when Hess finished speaking: pale streaks of dawn were already in the sky. Weary, stiff, cramped and cold, the Duke of Hamilton and Mr Kirkpatrick took their leave of him and climbed down the stone stairs. A night sister—for Hess was still under medical supervision—made them some scrambled eggs, which they ate gratefully. It was six o'clock before they were back at Turnhouse airfield; Hess by then was fast asleep again.

At half-past eight Kirkpatrick telephoned the Foreign Office and gave a brief account of the discussion.

'I was told that the Government was embarrassed by the whole affair, and did not know exactly how to handle it.'[3] In the meantime they said that they would be grateful for any details about the prisoner's appearance, what he was eating, how he looked, and so forth. This would help them to satisfy the insistent curiosity of the newspapers. Kirkpatrick dictated a full report of his interview and this was flown to London by special plane.

[1] *Inner Circle.*
[2] *Ibid.*
[3] *Ibid.*

He had received no reply by the following morning, and so decided to accompany the Duke of Hamilton on a brief visit to HMS *Victorious*, an aircraft carrier which had only recently been commissioned. As he reached the ferry across the Firth of Forth a messenger raced up to him bearing a further communication from the Foreign Secretary: he was to continue his interviews with Hess.

Kirkpatrick decided to telephone the Foreign Office.

The Air Marshal in local command, anxious to be helpful, explained that he had just had a new 'scrambled' telephone installed in his office. On this it would be simple for Kirkpatrick to speak with safety and confidence, for no one else could possibly tap the line.

This was quite true. As soon as they picked up the telephone it gave vent to such a mass of wailings and cracklings that it was impossible to hear the speaker's voice. Finally, he abandoned attempts to use the scrambler, and got through to London *en clair*.

Kirkpatrick asked the Foreign Office what he should talk to Hess about; he had carried out all his instructions and felt sure that Hess had told him all he had to say.

The reply was diplomatic. 'What you choose to discuss must be left to your own discretion,' he was told.

Kirkpatrick therefore returned to Buchanan Castle, and without great enthusiasm once more climbed up the long stone flights of stairs to the attic. Hess was pleased to see him but obviously depressed and disappointed by the fact that nothing seemed to have been done at once about his proposal.

He had expected instant action. For this reason, and a rather naïve belief that he would be back in Germany within a matter of hours, he had brought no clothes apart from what he wore, and no articles of toilet; not even a toothbrush. He pointed out rather petulantly that peace was 'very serious', and 'Hitler was not a man with whom it was safe to toy.'

On a more personal level, Hess admitted that he was not at all impressed by the arrangements to accommodate him. After all, he was a Minister of the Reich, the Deputy Führer, and yet soldiers on guard outside his room wore hobnailed boots and stamped about in a way he felt sure had been ordered simply to annoy him. For another thing, he considered that the electric light in his room was too bright: it definitely hurt his eyes. And when a doctor had asked him to lie on a sofa so that he could be examined thoroughly in case he had injured himself elsewhere, in addition to his ankle, when making his parachute jump, Hess had been horrified to see that a fresh sheet had not been spread out beneath him. He pointed out that he felt it was quite likely for him to have contracted some skin disease from this sofa, which must have been used by many other people.

Rudolf Hess's obsession with his health was no new thing. For years the Deputy Führer had refused to eat any fruit or vegetables that had been fertilized with artificial manure. He did not eat eggs or any dried food, because he did not consider them 'pure'.

Dr Felix Kersten, the Finnish physiotherapist who had exercised tremendous influence over Himmler, first treated Hess—at Himmler's request—in the previous summer. Once Dr Kersten found him in bed under a huge magnet swinging above him from the ceiling. 'There are twelve equally large magnets under my bed,' Hess explained. Apparently a man from Lubeck had assured him that these would draw harmful substances out of his body and restore his strength; Hess believed him.

Knowing his idiosyncrasies, Kirkpatrick listened to his complaints, and then, on instructions, paid Hess a third visit. During this discussion he asked him for his views on the German-Russian pact. Was there any remote possibility that Hitler might suddenly decide to attack Russia?

'Hess replied that it was quite out of the question. I pressed him again and again, but he assured me that Hitler was a man who stuck scrupulously to his engagements. I got the impression that Hess was so much out of things that he really did not know.'[1]

In fact, he did know. He was aware of the plan and disapproved of it, according to his adjutant, because such an attack involved fighting on two fronts—against which Hitler had fulminated in *Mein Kampf*—in addition to enormous lines of communications. Either of these military circumstances were dangerous, as any old soldier knows; Hess thought that together they could be catastrophic, as indeed events proved.

Preparations for 'Barbarossa,' Hitler's attack on Russia, had been going on for five months—since December 18, 1940—by the time Hess arrived in Scotland. On that December day, Hitler had issued a directive explaining how Russia would be invaded. The core of his argument was that he could crush Russia in 'a quick campaign' before the end of the war against Britain. He felt that Britain must have come to some secret arrangement to receive aid from Russia, for otherwise, by all the rules of war and logic, she should have

[1] *Ibid.*

surrendered long ago. By attacking Russia Hitler also hoped to capture raw materials which he was otherwise forced to pay for under the German-Soviet Agreement.

A month before this directive was issued, Ribbentrop invited Molotov to Berlin, possibly to lull Soviet suspicions regarding a German attack, or maybe to try to divert Russian influence and interest from Europe towards India and Persia, where they could be more harmful to Britain. In the meantime, Hitler's forces in East Germany had nearly trebled. In December 1940 he maintained thirty-four divisions there; by the time Hess landed in Scotland in May, the total had swollen to eighty-seven.

But during his stay in Buchanan Castle, Hess preferred to discuss less weighty matters with Ivone Kirkpatrick. He returned to his complaints; he had no German books to read; he did not like the officer in charge of his guard; he was sure poison was being put into his food.

In London, meanwhile, Churchill had given directions for the treatment of Hess. He addressed a memorandum on this subject to Mr Eden on the Tuesday.

Prime Minister to Foreign Secretary. 13 May, 41.

'1. On the whole it will be more convenient to treat him (Herr Hess) as a prisoner of war, under the War Office and not the Home Office; but also as one against whom grave political charges may be preferred. This man, like other Nazi leaders, is potentially a war criminal, and he and his confederates may well be declared outlaws at the close of the war. In this case his repentance would stand him in good stead.

'2. In the meanwhile he should be strictly isolated in a convenient house, not too far from London, and every endeavour should be made to study his mentality and get anything worth while out of him.

'3. His health and comfort should be ensured, food, books, writing materials, and recreation being provided for him. He should not have any contacts with the outer world or visitors except as prescribed by the Foreign Office. Special guardians should be appointed. He should see no newspapers and hear no wireless. He should be treated with dignity, as if he were an important general who had fallen into our hands.'[1]

On the Friday night, six days after Hess had landed, when Ciano in

[1] Quoted in Sir Winston Churchill's memoirs, *The Second World War*, vol. III; reproduced by permission of H.M.S.O.

Rome was perturbed about what he called 'Hess's mysterious peace mission', the Deputy Führer was brought south to the Tower of London.

A colony of newspaper reporters and photographers were ensconced at the Buchanan Arms Hotel opposite the main entrance of the Castle. To put them off the scent, Hess was driven in an ambulance through a back way and to a railway siding outside Glasgow. The London express stopped for a few moments while an extra carriage was hooked on.

Lieutenant Colonel Gibson Graham, who was in charge of the Medical Division at the hospital, and so had charge of Hess, travelled with him. Guards were posted in the blacked-out corridor of the train, facing inwards towards the compartment.

'Must I have these men staring at me?' Hess asked irritably. 'I can't sleep a wink under all these eyes.'

'I'm sorry,' replied Graham mildly, 'but you will have to.'

Hess grunted. 'I'll remember this after the war,' he said shortly.

Despite the conditions of secrecy, word had somehow sped ahead to Euston; a crowd of sightseers had gathered to jeer him. He accepted their greetings with a smile and raised his right arm in a half-salute.

It was considered by no means beyond the possibility that Hitler would attempt to rescue Hess from Buchanan Castle—as he rescued Mussolini when he was a prisoner later in the war—and although a whole battalion of soldiers had taken up their positions around the Castle against just such a contingency, Hess would obviously be much safer in the Tower. He was driven from Euston in an ambulance with a second vehicle following full of armed soldiers.

Hess did not know where he was, but he soon found out. A young officer on guard duty, anxious to secure his autograph, rather diffidently asked Hess whether he would give him his signature.

'Certainly,' replied Hess, to the young man's surprise. 'But you must let me have a sheet of paper to write it on.'

Much delighted at this, the officer produced the only paper he could find easily—a sheet of notepaper marked 'The Tower of London'. He handed this to Hess with the heading underneath. Hess took it, and turned it over.

'So that's where I am,' he said with a smile, and handed it back unsigned. In fact, Hess was in the room occupied by Sir Roger Casement before his execution in 1916.

Churchill was fully aware of the speculation that Hess's arrival was causing in America, and so sent a long telegram to Roosevelt about the matter.

'Former Naval Person to President Roosevelt. 17 May 41.[1]

'Foreign Office representative has had three interviews with Hess.

'At first interview, on night of May 11–12, Hess was extremely voluble, and made long statement with the aid of notes. First part recapitulated Anglo-German relations during past thirty years or so, and was designed to show that Germany had always been in the right and England in the wrong. Second part emphasized certainty of German victory, due to development in combination of submarine and air weapons, steadiness of German morale and complete unity of German people behind Hitler. Third part outlined proposals for settlement. Hess said that the Führer had never entertained any designs against the British Empire, which would be left intact save for the return of former German colonies, in exchange for a free hand for him, in Europe. But condition was attached that Hitler would not negotiate with present Government in England. This is the old invitation to us to desert all our friends in order to save temporarily the greater part of our skin.

'Foreign Office representative asked him whether when he spoke to Hitler having a free hand in Europe he included Russia in Europe or in Asia. He replied, "In Asia". He added however that Germany had certain demands to make of Russia which would have to be satisfied, but denied rumours that attack on Russia was being planned.

'Impression created by Hess was that he had made up his mind that Germany must win the war, but saw that it would last a long time and involve much loss of life and destruction. He seemed to feel that if he could persuade people in this country that there was a basis for a settlement, that might bring the war to an end and avert unnecessary suffering.

'At second interview, on May 14, Hess made two further points:

(1) In any peace settlement Germany would have to support Rashid Ali and secure eviction of British from Iraq.

(2) U-boat war with air co-operation would be carried on till all

---

[1] Quoted in Sir Winston Churchill's memoirs, *The Second World War*, vol. III; reproduced by permission of H.M.S.O.

supplies to these islands were cut off. Even if these islands capitulated and the Empire continued the fight, the blockade of Britain would continue, even if that meant that the last inhabitant of Britain died of starvation.

'At third interview, on May 15, nothing much emerged save incidentally some rather disparaging remarks about your country and the degree of assistance that you will be able to furnish to us. I am afraid, in particular, he is not sufficiently impressed by what he thinks he knows of your aircraft types and production.

'Hess seems in good health and not excited, and no ordinary signs of insanity can be detected. He declares that this escapade is his own idea and that Hitler was unaware of it beforehand. If he is to be believed, he expected to contact members of a "peace movement" in England, which he would help to oust the present Government. If he is honest and if he is sane this is an encouraging sign of ineptitude of German Intelligence Service. He will not be ill-treated, but it is desirable that the Press should not romanticize him and his adventure. We must not forget that he shares responsibility for all Hitler's crimes and is a potential war criminal whose fate must ultimately depend upon the decision of the Allied Governments.

'Mr President, all the above is for your own information. Here we think it best to let the Press have a good run for a bit and keep the Germans guessing. The German officer prisoners of war here were greatly perturbed by the news, and I cannot doubt that there will be deep misgiving in the German armed forces about what he may say.'

From the Tower, Hess was moved to Mychett Place, near Farnborough. Two detachments, one of Coldstream Guards, and the other of Scots Guards, were detailed to look after him under the command of Lt. Colonel A. Malcolm Scott, of the Scots Guards.

Colonel Scott had barely three days to make the place impervious to any attack, by digging trenches, fixing trip-wires, setting up camouflaged machine gun posts, even making tunnels from one part of the grounds to another. During this time, concealed microphones were also installed up the chimney and under the floorboards, in case Hess should give away any German secrets during conversation or when talking in his sleep. So much had to be done so quickly that the last civilian workman left only a quarter of an hour before the arrival of the ambulance containing Hess, and the escort of two cars.

Later, a young officer, Douglas Percival, joined the detachment. Hess and Percival got on well together. Both were tall men, keen on outdoor sports and especially mountaineering.

'When Germany has won the war I'll give you a castle in Scotland,' Hess announced magnanimously one day. 'Is there any place you'd like?'

'What about Balmoral?' suggested Percival jokingly. Hess agreed that this was a good idea. The next day, when the security officers heard the record of this conversation, they took Percival to one side and warned him against such jokes.

'You mustn't say that sort of thing, Douglas,' they said seriously. 'Someone may think it's true!'

Officially Mytchett Place was 'Z' Camp, and Hess was referred to as 'J' or Jay. Unofficially he speedily became known as 'The Squire of Mytchett Green'. His aeroplane followed him south; it went on exhibition in Trafalgar Square to help to raise War Savings, and was later removed to the Imperial War Museum.

Kirkpatrick also came to London—although he travelled a day after Hess, to help give the impression that Hess was still in Buchanan Castle.

Kirkpatrick saw Churchill and Eden, and to both of them he gave a full personal report of his interviews. At the end of his account, Churchill remarked dryly, 'Well, if Hess had come a year ago and told us what the Germans would do to us we should have been very frightened—and rightly. So why should we be frightened now?'

Kirkpatrick suggested that perhaps Hess might give away more valuable information if he was interviewed by someone more competent to deal with problems of intelligence or briefed on political matters.

'Mr Churchill did not relish this advice,' he wrote later, 'since it involved a meeting with Hess, which might prove embarrassing.'[1]

Churchill was already privately perturbed lest the public in Britain and uncommitted countries might feel that he was considering peace terms with Hess. Speculation in British newspapers had already ranged from allegations that Hess was a schizophrenic to theories that he was fleeing Germany because he felt convinced Hitler would lose the war, and to other suggestions much nearer the mark, that he had come to negotiate a peace.

At that time in Britain, despite what may now be said to the contrary, such a suggestion would have found considerable favour in

[1] *Inner Circle.*

many parts of the country. After twenty months of war Britain had been humiliated in France, in Greece and in North Africa. Many of her greatest and proudest cities, her most ancient buildings, were blackened smoking shells, with summer weeds already sprouting in the ruins.

On that Saturday night, when Hess had been flying north, more than 900 hundred tons of German bombs had rained on London alone within twelve hours. In that single night—only one of many—1,500 Londoners died—roughly as many as had perished in the terrible San Francisco earthquake in 1906. This was the measure of pain being endured night after night in city, town and hamlet.

In addition to such tremendous physical attack and the complete disruption of so many lives, other factors were involved. Food was short and heavily rationed; motorists were allowed five gallons of poor quality pool petrol every month; clothes were on coupons; a fresh egg once a week was a treat, and a shillingsworth of meat was held sufficient for seven days of dining.

Night after night thousands crept down to damp air-raid shelters in their back gardens, to cellars strengthened by railway sleepers, to London Underground stations with tiers of bunks; others cycled to the country, to sleep rough in the open fields rather than endure the horrors of still further bombardment. Worse, the U-boats were causing fearful losses among the convoys of supply ships coming from America: 2,314,000 tons of shipping were sunk between April 10, 1940, and March 17, 1941. In the three months of March, April and May, 179 ships—totalling 545,000 tons were lost.

Against the background of these depressing figures, Hess's claim that Britain could be starved out of further resistance was not impossible. Many people, knowing little of these facts, but sensing the weight of opposition against Britain, thought privately that peace on any terms that did not offer actual humiliation was preferable to taking the brunt of the ferocious German assaults that would presumably grow worse.

In the Dominions and Colonies the state of preparedness was wretched; the defeats at Hong Kong, at Singapore, at Rangoon, were still ahead. Only a handful of people in the Cabinet really knew the extent and weight of arms against Britain. They found little comfort in their knowledge, and as Churchill said, those who knew most, feared most.

Nor was it forgotten that America, while declaring herself to be the arsenal of democracy, took care to see that the weapons this arsenal produced were not all sold to Britain at cut prices. And with British firms working almost wholly on guns and tanks and aircraft, America was winning markets in territories that for generations had bought British goods. These markets she would never entirely return to us. Meanwhile, Britain's overseas investments—railways, factories, traction systems built up over many years by British enterprise and energy—were being sold for little more than a week's supply of food.

For how long could all this go on? For how long could the people endure the nagging hopelessness of this grey twilit life?

If, against this picture of nightly raids and frayed nerves and poor food, rumour could hint that peace with Germany was offered by Hitler's Deputy, who felt so sincerely about the matter that he had personally flown to Britain to explain his terms, a substantial number of people would clamour to pursue this matter further.

Thus, if it became at all widely believed that Hess had arrived with power and authority to negotiate a genuine settlement, this news would run through Britain like flame through dry heather. Inevitably the speed of the factories would slow; the spirit of aggression would swiftly diminish. For what would be the point of waging war if peace could so easily be obtained? In these circumstances, it would be difficult, if not impossible, for Churchill to restore the national sense of urgency when this rumour proved false.

Although the Government might claim that Hess had arrived with no power whatsoever, and although he might also be discredited by his own country, the belief would still persist that 'there must have been something in it'. It would seem an act of incredible folly to fight on against an adversary so overwhelmingly strong, when the enemy themselves were willing for peace.

Churchill was well aware of these problems. If rumours of peace talks began, they would spread and multiply with an amoeba-like rapidity. Hess had to be quickly discredited in such a way that his visit would appear to be nonsense, the act of an unbalanced man, made on his own initiative and without authority. Once discredited in the public mind, nothing he claimed would be given serious attention; the newspaper leader-writers and cartoonists, the comics in music-halls and on the air would soon see to that.

Hess was thus placed in the care of psychiatrists. Coming so soon after Hitler's own claim that 'he lived in a state of hallucination', this discredited him completely in the public mind. He was dismissed by the many, if not by the few, as being a madman, a lunatic. In fact, of course, although a man of moody temperament and a strong believer in astrology, he was sane.

* * *

Meanwhile, knowing nothing of all this, for not until Hess had been in British hands for some months did he realize that the officers around him were psychiatrists—he had been told that they were 'camp doctors' sent to replace Colonel Graham who had returned to Drymen—Hess persisted in his request to see a Cabinet representative. Mr Churchill asked Sir John Simon, the Lord Chancellor, to interview him. The hope was that Hess might be induced to reveal secrets of Hitler's own intentions which could prove of value.

It was imperative that no one should know that a British Minister had seen Hess on behalf of the War Cabinet. Such news could cause immeasurable damage if made public either in this country or elsewhere, for the inference would immediately be that Britain, after much proud talk of fighting on to complete victory, was in fact preparing to conduct secret peace negotiations. This would be a blow to the entire war effort and to the country's prestige from which neither might fully recover.

In view of this, it was decided that Hess would be referred to throughout all arrangements for the meeting as 'Jay'; Ivone Kirkpatrick would be a distinguished psychiatrist, 'Dr McKenzie', and Sir John Simon would be another psychiatrist of equal note, 'Dr Guthrie'. Two British Intelligence officers who spoke fluent German were detailed to receive them at Mytchett Place, and they alone would know their real identity. No one else would be in the secret—not even the concealed stenographers who would record their conversation.

Accordingly Kirkpatrick set off from London and drove down through Staines and Virginia Water to Sunningdale, where he was joined by the Lord Chancellor. No one followed them and the roads, at such a time of strict petrol rationing, were almost deserted, apart from Service lorries and dispatch riders.

They drove on in silence through Aldershot to Mytchett Place. The guards had been instructed to expect two psychiatrists, and papers were produced to show that Dr McKenzie and Dr Guthrie were the gentlemen concerned; after due examination they were allowed in without question or comment.

Hess had asked to have a German witness present at this meeting, so some minor consular official, interned at the outbreak of war, was brought under guard to Mytchett Place to comply with this request.

For a few days beforehand Hess, knowing the date of the meeting and aware what could emerge if it were, from his point of view, successful, had been growing more and more nervous. Finally, he declared that he found it almost impossible to eat anything, and so meals were served in his room, and the officer of the guard ate with him. This served the dual purpose of proving that the food was not tampered with in any way, and also provided him with a companion.

In the morning of his interview with the Lord Chancellor, Hess did not eat anything, but he drank a considerable amount of milk. Then he put on his Air Force uniform and appeared, so his doctors noted, 'in a very confident and almost arrogant mood'.[1]

There was good reason for his arrogance. He considered that he was the most significant man in either Britain or Germany; he believed that he was one of the few who knew about Hitler's plan for attacking Russia—due to begin in twelve days. He did not realize, of course, that Britain was also well aware of this plan, and that Churchill had already warned Stalin to expect such an attack. That Stalin took no useful heed of this warning did not detract from its value or its accuracy.

The published account of this talk with Sir John Simon and Mr Kirkpatrick at Camp Z[2] reveals that Hess told Sir John Simon how the idea of flying to Britain had first occurred to him when he was with Hitler during the French campaign of 1940.

'Convinced as we all were that we would conquer England sooner or later—but in the end certainly—I expressed the opinion to the Führer that we must naturally demand from England the restitution of goods such as the value of the merchant fleet, and so on, which were taken from us by the Versailles Treaty.

'The Führer contradicted me immediately. He is of the opinion that the war could possibly lead finally to agreement with England, and he said that even if victorious, one should not impose any severe conditions on a country with which it is desired to come to an agreement.

'I thought that if England once knew of this fact it might be possible that England on its part was ready for agreement.'

---

[1] *Case of Rudolf Hess*, p. 39.
[2] First given in his defence on March 25, 1946, at Nuremberg.

He then spoke of his own thoughts of making this flight.

'I must confess that I faced a very critical decision—the most critical decision of my life. I believe it became possible for me through a thought. Not only on the German side, but also on the English side, I continually pictured an endless row of children's coffins with mothers crying behind them, and vice versa, coffins of mothers with children behind them.'

He repeated the familiar Nazi argument about the unfairness of the Versailles Treaty.

It seemed to his listeners that British air attacks, although small at that time, were having some effect, because Hess assured them that the Führer 'hesitated again and again to order counter-attacks . . . but gradually mothers who had lost their children, families who had lost their relatives reproached the Führer: "Why did he not finally retaliate?"'

'When the Führer had come to the conclusion that common sense could not prevail in England, he acted just according to the rule of conduct of Admiral Lord Fisher: "Moderation in war is folly. If you strike, strike hard and wherever you can." But I can conform that it was indeed always difficult for the Führer to give orders for these attacks. It pained him deeply. He was constantly in full sympathy with the English people who were victims of this method of waging war.'

Sir John Simon interrupted Hess at this moment.

'Herr Hess will, of course, understand that if I do not contradict or challenge what he says about the war it is not because I agree, but because the real purpose why I have come is to hear from him about his mission,' he announced blandly. 'Herr Hess must understand that the British people too, are a proud people—*Herrenvolk*—and will not easily accept such reproaches . . .'

'My flight was strongly influenced by the fact that the leaders of Germany are absolutely convinced that England's position is helpless,' replied Hess. 'In view of my personal relations with the flying world—Messerschmitt is a friend of mine, and I know all the factories and all the air chiefs—I have some idea of what will happen to England sooner or later. And that is one of the reasons why I have come here.'

'Your message is that you believe there will be in future a far more violent and terrific overwhelming attack on this country?' asked Sir John Simon.

'Yes,' replied Hess, and went on to give a gloomy account of the Germans' development and building of the U-boats.

'Nothing amuses the British people as much as German figures about sinking British tonnage,' Simon told him. 'It makes them laugh.'

'Maybe,' said Hess dourly, 'but I am convinced the day will come when the English people will no longer laugh about it.'

'The day may come, the day may come,' agreed Simon non-committally, 'but if German official figures are correct, you know it's a pity we are not all dead!'

If Germany managed to make Britain capitulate simply because food could not be brought into the island, Hess said, 'we would not consider occupying the Mother Country because we would have to feed the people there. In the event of a capitulation without occupation, we should only occupy a number of important air bases in the most extreme case, and we would shut them off from the population —so that our own soldiers would never see anything of it.'

'Do you come here with the Führer's knowledge or without his knowledge?' asked Lord Simon, breaking into this gloomy prophecy.

'Without his knowledge,' replied Hess. 'Absolutely.'

He laughed as he spoke this answer, and then he handed to his interviewers a sheet of paper which was headed 'Basis for Understanding'.

'This which I have written down here is what the Führer told me in several conversations,' he explained in rather stilted English.

The paper contained the familiar proposals that Germany should have a free hand in Europe and Britain in the Empire. There would be armistice and peace with Italy. Britain would leave Iraq and return the German colonies.

As the interview, which lasted for roughly three hours, came to its end, Hess assured his visitors that if Britain did not agree to these conditions, then 'sooner or later the day will come when you will be forced to accede them'.

'I do not think that that particular argument will be very good for the British Cabinet,' Simon told him, gathering up his papers. 'You know, there is a great deal of courage in this country, and we are not very fond of threats.'

After this discussion the doctors found Hess in his sitting-room virtually collapsed and exhausted. Three hours of question and answer with two interrogators as shrewd as Kirkpatrick and Simon had worn him out. Worse, he was beginning to realize that his belief that he could make peace between Britain and Germany was entirely false.

To try and restore his energy, a psychiatrist ordered tea, milk and cake for him, but Hess refused to touch any of them. The psychiatrist then mixed him a glucose drink and offered it to him. Hess looked at the doctor quizzically and then said grudgingly: 'I'll have it—if you'll have some first.'

The psychiatrist had already taken tea, but to humour Hess he ate a small piece of his cake and sipped some of the glucose to show that it was not poisoned. Only then would Hess consent to drink some himself.

Despite what Hitler might say, and Hess might think, the Deputy Führer was by no means forgotten in Germany, and a strange rescue operation was already being mounted. Whether it was the German intention to rescue Hess or to kill him to prevent him from revealing any secrets, after it became clear that his peace mission was a failure, may never be known.

On the Sunday afternoon after Hess arrived at Mytchett Place, Major John McCowen, a pre-war executive in a brewing concern, then serving as an Intelligence officer with the 1st Anti-Aircraft Corps, was having what he called 'a quiet cup of tea in sports clothes' in the RAF mess at Uxbridge. The telephone interrupted him; it was an urgent summons to report to the Air Officer commanding No. 11 Fighter Group, Air Vice Marshal Leigh Mallory.

McCowen found him in his underground office, surrounded by his RAF Intelligence staff. Leigh Mallory explained tersely that monitoring of the German radio had picked up 'by some unusual means' a message apparently intended for No. 11 Group. It warned that a bombing attack would be made at one o'clock on the following morning at Luton Hoo, in Bedfordshire. Its object was to provide cover for a simultaneous landing of German parachutists whose intention was to capture Rudolf Hess. Apparently the Germans believed that Hess was being held prisoner and being questioned at the RAF interrogation centre at Cockfosters, where most German prisoners were taken as soon as they landed.

The message had not said how heavy the attack would be, or how many parachutists would drop. It was thus decided to move all available anti-aircraft guns and searchlights immediately to Luton Hoo. Such was the urgency of the moment that orders were given for Bofors guns to be on the road within ten minutes. McCowen's task was to alert police and home guards in the area. He raced by car to Luton, saw a senior police officer, and as he recalls, 'apparently convinced him first of my sanity, and then of the urgency of the occasion'.

The local Home Guard Commander was bringing his men back from what appeared to be a week-end exercise. McCowen persuaded him to parade them again and deploy them in the area where the landings were expected. By that time guns and searchlights were already on the road, and 'with a supreme effort by all concerned the trap was set with minutes rather than hours to spare.

'After an hour's waiting on a very chilly early summer morning, enthusiasm waned,' he says. 'It was finally decided that we would stay put until first light and then move back to our normal positions.

'Another officer and I were dozing off in our Staff car when we heard the "alert" and the sound of planes. The bombing fell exactly as forecast on quite a small scale. The searchlights and guns had moved without their elaborate radar and predictor gear, and although the guns fired at the sound of the planes the searchlights were unable to illuminate them. We did, however, get a flick over of the search-light beams on one or more falling parachutes. A period of intense activity followed and around breakfast time this was suddenly called off.'

Officially that was the end of the incident, but McCowen heard later that Special Branch personnel had been the first to locate and apprehend two parachutists, who gave up without any struggle.

'I gathered, but could not of course confirm, that at least two ss men were captured in civilian clothing from which the German labels had not been effectively removed. They carried German rations and arms and bore the unmistakable harness weals from their recent parachute drop.'

McCowen believes that the parachutists were executed some time later.

The whole affair bore the same stamp of poor preparation that had characterized Hess's own flight.

CHAPTER TEN

Psychiatrists for Company

Now that it seemed clear that no successful results whatever would emerge from his visit, Hess decided to cut short his stay in Britain. He asked for a passage on a plane back to Germany. It would have been possible for a civil airliner to take him to Lisbon, which was neutral, because a regular service was maintained between London and Lisbon throughout the war. His request, however, was ignored.

Percival assured him that if he did Hitler would have him shot. He had flown away without the Führer's knowledge, so he maintained, and this Hitler would not be able to condone. Hess refused to believe Percival. He remained convinced that he would be well received, and that if he could not get an airliner to take him to Lisbon, he could easily parachute over Germany as he had parachuted over Scotland.

The argument ended when Hess heard a BBC news bulletin which said how the name of the Hess hospital in Germany had been changed. Thereafter Hess said no more to Percival about going home; he realized that, for the time being at least, he was out of favour.

Hess then asked to see the King, so that he could put his case before him. He received no answer to this proposal. Hess had arrived as an uninvited envoy, and now he was being pressed to stay. It seemed an unimaginable end to his mission: everything had gone wrong and he had achieved nothing at all. He sat hunched up in the big leather armchair, which the Ministry of Works had provided with other furniture for his use, and considered his future.

It did not seem either bright or hopeful. His journey, his plans, his dreams of making peace were a failure and a fiasco. Churchill had no intention of agreeing to peace on any terms but the complete surrender of Germany. There existed no hope of Britain negotiating peace on any other terms, and now he knew that there never had been; otherwise Hess would have been treated in a very different way from the hour of his arrival. Instead, he was a prisoner, guarded by doctors in case he came to any harm, and growing more convinced that they were adding drugs or poison to his food, either to make him go mad or to force him to reveal what he might know of Hitler's plans. No amount of denials from the doctors concerned would reassure him or convince him that he was mistaken.

Once he received a large box of chocolates from his wife through the Red Cross. He refused to eat them; he was certain that they had been poisoned. Percival did not share this view.

'Well, if you don't want them,' he said, 'can I have them for the Mess?'

Hess was reluctant to let them go in case all the officers of the Guards were killed.

'You can have them if you want,' he agreed finally. 'But you mustn't eat them. If you do, you'll die.' They did, and they didn't; Hess could not understand it.

Hess had first come under medical supervision on the night he landed. He was taken to the Military Hospital in Buchanan Castle to have his right ankle examined. While there, he complained to Lieutenant Colonel Gibson Graham that he was 'feeling confused, especially after talking for any length of time'.[1] This Hess put down to the strain of the flight. Later, Colonel Graham noted that 'he showed himself to be . . . very nervous and introspective about his health'.[2]

As time passed and no tangible results came from his mission, his nervousness increased. 'He was convinced he was surrounded by Secret Service agents who would accomplish his death either by driving him to commit suicide, committing a murder staged to look like suicide, or administering poison in his food . . .'[3] Colonel Graham reported that he was 'unable to convince him of the groundlessness of such assertions.' When Hess dined with Colonel Graham and their food was served from a common dish, Hess would carefully select whatever the meat might be—perhaps a chop—but never the one which happened to be nearest to him.

His conversations—about his early days in the Nazi Party, about his hopes for peace, the plans he had made for his journey 'with the mixture of grandiose background and flimsy woolly substance'— convinced Graham that Hess should be examined by a psychiatrist.

[1] *The Case of Rudolf Hess.*
[2] *Ibid.*
[3] *Ibid.*

Brigadier J. R. Rees, the Army's Chief Psychiatrist, was consulted; he interviewed Hess and agreed that the Deputy Führer needed psychiatric treatment. 'In my opinion Hess is a man of unstable mentality and has almost certainly been like that since adolescence,' he wrote later in *The Case of Rudolf Hess*. 'In technical language I should on my present acquaintanceship, diagnose him as a psychopathic personality of the schizophrenic type, i.e. a tendency to a splitting of his personality. He is, as many of these people are, suggestible and liable to hysterical symptom formation. Because of his constitutional make-up and the kind of life he has led of recent years, he is at present in some danger of a more marked depressive reaction now that he feels frustrated.'

Thus, Hess, the believer in herbs and homeopathic treatments and the influence of the stars, came under several of Britain's most senior and experienced psychiatrists. When he realized their close professional interest in him, he tended to dramatize his emotions. Then he pretended to lose his memory entirely, when, in fact, he had only lost his recollection of certain incidents. As he admitted later at Nuremberg, 'the reasons why I simulated loss of memory were tactical'.

He hoped that if he were declared of unsound mind then he might be considered for repatriation with other disabled prisoners of war; and latterly, if he were said to be insane, then he might be spared standing trial at Nuremberg. In the event, he achieved neither of these aims.

He wrote to his wife, giving her an account of his flight, and enclosing a sketch of his parachute landing for the benefit of his little son, Buz. His wife, and several friends, spent hours poring over this with magnifying glasses in the hope that it might contain a message in code or some concealed clue as to his whereabouts; but there was nothing. He wrote to Professor Haushofer in time for his birthday, sending the letter early 'as it transpires that my letters take months to reach their destination.

'Do not worry over me,' he wrote. 'You, less than anyone, need do this. That my present situation is not exactly agreeable goes without saying. But, in time of war, we have to put up with many things that are not agreeable.

> Let the waves like thunder break,
> Be your very life at stake;
> May you crash or may you land
> E'er as your own pilot stand!

'That I crashed is not to be denied, and it is equally certain that I was my own pilot! In this matter I have nothing with which to reproach myself. It was I who took the controls. You know as well as I do that the compass which guides our affairs is influenced by forces that are infallible—even when we know them not. May those forces be favourable to you in the years to come!'

Hess stayed at Mytchett Place for thirteen months—and with every month that passed his belief increased that his captors were administering truth drugs and poisons to him in his food and drink. The fact that an officer of the guard regularly ate with him did nothing to diminish this belief.

On two or three evenings a week, Hess and Percival would play L'Attaque, an old French game with a checker board, between opposing British and French armies. Each piece has a rank; this varies from the most senior, the Commander-in-Chief to the most junior, the Spy. At first Hess would not play because the German army was not involved. Percival persuaded him by suggesting that he should take the French side, since Germany had conquered France. Hess agreed. They played merrily, until one evening the humble British Spy moved by Percival captured the French Commander-in-Chief, manipulated by Hess.

Hess immediately swept the board and pieces onto the floor. 'It's not fair!' he cried. 'It's not fair!' He seemed very highly strung.

The frequent clatter of motor-cycle engines, revved up inexpertly by soldiers being taught to ride, the lights that burned continually in his room, the sudden entrance during the night of officers with torches to make sure he had not escaped—all these combined to produce in his mind the feeling that he was being systematically subjected to an experience calculated to irritate and annoy him. These incidents all had perfectly simple and straightforward explanations, but this he refused to accept. Hess believed that his guards were all members of a great conspiracy against him. Slowly there grew in his mind the certainty that somehow the Jews were behind this diabolical attempt to derange him.

One night he called the duty psychiatrist to his room. Then, fists clenched, obviously in a state of high emotional tension, he faced him across the table.

'I am being undone and you know it!' he shouted.

'What do you mean? In what way are you being undone?' asked the psychiatrist calmly.

'You know it! You know it!' roared Hess.

It was clear that his feelings were rapidly approaching a crisis; it was not impossible that he would attempt to take his own life; the watch on him was increased.

Shortly after this Hess asked for a copy of Goethe's poems. At the top of a sheet of writing-paper he copied out five lines from *Das Goettliche*:

> 'According to eternal, iron, great
> Laws
> Must we all
> Complete the cycles
> Of our being.'

Under these lines he wrote a personal letter to Hitler, in which he assured him of his continuing loyalty to National Socialism and of his personal devotion to him as a man. 'I die,' he wrote, 'in the conviction that my last mission, even if it ends in death, will somehow bear fruit. Perhaps my flight will bring, despite my death, or indeed partly because of my death, peace and reconciliation with England.'

Clearly Hess was becoming so depressed by the failure of his mission and so obsessed by his conviction that the British were slowly and systematically poisoning him that he was approaching a crisis in his mind. Either he would take his own life or at least do something dramatic that would give the impression of attempted suicide.

Thus those closest to Hess waited with some apprehension for events to unfold. The officer who was on duty throughout each night, sitting in one of the rooms at Hess's disposal, and inspecting his bedroom from time to time, was warned to be specially vigilant.

Late on the evening of June 15, five days after the interview with Sir John Simon and Ivone Kirkpatrick—and a week before Germany invaded Russia—the duty physician, Dr Henry V. Dicks, visited Hess in his room. He found him in bed and apparently preparing for sleep. Dr Dicks suggested that he should take some sleeping-pills that had been prescribed for his insomnia, but Hess, still maintaining that these were drugged, refused to do so. He could sleep quite well without them. Dr Dicks then wished him goodnight and went on to his own room across a landing from Hess's bedroom, and served by the same oak staircase in the centre of the house. The vigil of the night began. Outside the house guards walked silently in the dark garden; inside, troops waited, Tommy-guns at the ready, in case of any emergency. But the hours passed uneventfully until about two o'clock in the following morning.

Hess called out to his guard: 'I want to see the doctor. I can't sleep.' The guard told a messenger to relay this information to Dr Dicks.

The doctor put on his dressing-gown, picked up the carton of sleeping-pills he had earlier offered Hess, and walked towards the Deputy Führer's quarters—a bedroom, a sitting-room and a bathroom. They lay at the end of a passage that ran from the top of the stairs. In front of them a wire grille had been set up, with its own metal door. This was bolted from the outside whenever Hess was in his suite, and an armed Military Police sergeant sat on a chair outside it with the key.[1] As Dr Dicks approached, the sergeant stood up, undid the padlock and held open the door. At that moment Hess appeared at the door of his bedroom wearing his Air Force uniform. As soon as he saw that the wire door was open and that he could reach the landing, he began to race towards the doctor.

'The expression on his face was one of extreme despair, his eyes starting, his hair dishevelled,' wrote Dr Dicks later.[2] 'I felt sure that he was going to attack me physically. I was about to tackle him when he did a rapid side-step, and took a flying leap over the banister. A heavy thud occurred, after what seemed minutes later, on the floor of the hall, followed by agonized groans.'

At that precise moment, the second sergeant of the guard began to walk slowly up the stairs carrying a full cup of steaming tea in one hand for his colleague on duty. As Hess dived over the banisters to the floor beneath, the sergeant racing down the stairs to where Hess lay crumpled on the flagstones, dropped the cup with a crash of splintering china. He whipped his revolver out of his holster.

'Don't shoot!' shouted Dr Dicks. 'Don't shoot!'

The sergeant put away his .45 and, with his colleague from the wire door, joined the doctor.

'Give me morphia, give me morphia,' Hess gasped, writhing on the cold stones.

---

[1] Once Hess complained of this arrangement; he said that he was simply a prisoner in a cell. The officer of the guard disagreed; he explained that the wire gate was locked in case any attempt should be made from outside to harm Hess; it was therefore done for his own protection.

This satisfied Hess for a few days—until he suddenly realized that the lock and key were on the other side of the wire!

[2] *The Case of Rudolf Hess.*

The three men knelt by his side. The noise of his fall, the clatter of the breaking cup, the doctor's shout, had awakened everyone in the building. Doors were opening on all levels, and heads poking out in curiosity. 'What's happened? Who's hurt? Is he dying?' Someone brought pillows; someone else blankets; a third, the British panacea for all ills, a cup of hot tea.

Dr Dicks knelt down to examine Hess. So far as he could tell, he had not suffered any internal injury through his jump, but he had broken one leg. A surgeon was immediately sent for from a nearby military hospital.

Dr Dicks did not want to give Hess any morphia until he had been thoroughly examined, in case it should mask any signs or symptoms of internal injuries. To humour Hess, however, he injected him with distilled water. Hess waited for the injection to take effect. When it had no effect, he said coldly: 'That wasn't morphia at all. You have deceived me.'

At that moment the surgeon arrived. He diagnosed 'an uncomplicated fracture of the upper left part of the left femur.' It was set immediately. Hess bore this painful business stoically, but expressed regret and sadness that his magnificent breeches should have to be cut open with scissors so that his injured leg could be reached.

Somehow he was carried to his bed, and after all the fuss he seemed strangely quiet and peaceful. But this was not to last. Within a few hours he complained that he could not pass his water. Various methods were tried to help his condition but without success; finally Hess himself suggested that a catheter should be used, and that he should have a cocaine local anaesthetic.

No cocaine was available, and the doctor explained that from previous experience of similar cases he had not found it necessary to use this drug. Further, he was using a gum elastic catheter, which would be relatively painless. Hess disagreed, and began to shout: 'Help! Help!'

At this uproar, 'scenting further drama', Dr Dicks wrote later, 'the denizens of our house of mystery poured from all the doors, with myself torn between my duties to the patient and my wish to reassure a group of officers who had been already considerably upset by the day's incidents and their narrowly averted prospects of unpleasant courts of inquiry and displeasure in high places.'[1]

Somehow they were pacified, and the doctor turned his attention to Hess. He had been on duty for nearly twenty hours without

[1] *Ibid.*

proper rest, and he was very tired. Partly because of this weariness, and partly to shame Hess into silence, he addressed him shortly.

'Aren't you ashamed of yourself?' he asked. 'You, the second man in the German Reich, causing us all this trouble and then bellowing like a baby! I'll do nothing further to relieve your bladder.' This had the desired effect, and Hess lay silent and baleful while the procedure was carried out.

For most of his stay at Mytchett Hess was allowed to read *The Times* every day: he appeared pleased with the news that the German army was making such a tremendous and virtually unopposed advance into Russia. If their battle against the Russians proceeded at this pace with Germany fighting on her own, without allies, then his journey to Britain to seek British help against Russia had been needless. Also, his incarceration would not last much longer. But even so, Hess was conscious of personal failure in being unable to persuade Britain to accept the terms of peace he had brought to offer.

'From the psychological point of view his attempt at "making peace" had failed, as it had also from the political standpoint,' wrote one of the psychiatrists later. 'The bad impulses were not eliminated, for he found himself surrounded by a hostile prison regime.

'Instead of being hailed as the saviour of Britain and the world, he now became definitely persecuted, partly projecting his guilt over destructiveness into the notion of a hidden Jewish poisoner clique and partly increasing his hypochondriacal preoccupations with bad inside events in his stomach, and liver, etc.'

It was against this background, this awareness that while he personally had failed in his mission, the German army was still doing so well against their new enemy, that Hess prepared to receive another visitor, Lord Beaverbrook, then Minister of Supply.

CHAPTER ELEVEN

Hess is Disowned

On the Monday after Hess landed in Scotland, Lord Beaverbrook called to see Churchill at No. 10 Downing Street. The Prime Minister pushed a photograph across the desk towards him. It was of a man in middle life, with dark hair and bushy eyebrows, holding the hand of a little boy.

'Who's that?' asked the Prime Minister.

'Rudolf Hess,' replied Beaverbrook immediately. He recognized him from pre-war meetings in Berlin. 'Why do you ask?'

'He landed in Scotland on Saturday night,' explained Churchill simply.

This news seemed impossible, and beyond the limits of belief—as Hess himself agreed when Beaverbrook told him the story at Mytchett Place.

'I can quite understand your surprise,' he went on. 'But we were convinced in Germany that Britain hadn't got a chance, and so it seemed to me best to come and point this out personally.'

For security reasons, Beaverbrook visited Camp Z under the pseudonym of Dr Livingstone, following the cover plan adopted by Sir John Simon and Ivone Kirkpatrick, so that the guards would think that he was simply another visiting psychiatrist. He addressed Hess as Jonathan, so that the concealed stenographer who recorded their conversation would not know who was being interviewed.

When Hess and Beaverbrook had met in Germany before the war both had been men of power; now Hess was at the nadir of his fortunes, while Beaverbrook stood at the peak of his enormous war-time prestige. As Minister of Aircraft Production during the previous crucial year, his overwhelming and often ruthless determination had provided the RAF with the planes—and thus the opportunity—to win the Battle of Britain.

When Churchill became Minister in May 1940, almost a year to the day before Hess landed, Britain possessed exactly five aeroplanes in the storage units. She could have easily been overwhelmed by any concentrated aerial attack. Beaverbrook discovered that nearly two thousand fighter aircraft, either shot down or crashed, had arbitrarily been written off as being beyond repair. Also, many depots around the country contained vast stocks of aircraft spares. Immediately he ordered teams of mechanics to cannibalize these crashed aeroplanes and to construct one airworthy machine out of every two or three wrecks. At the same time the spares were assembled into fighter planes. Thus by September, five months later, when the Battle of Britain was at its height, Beaverbrook had increased these five reserve planes to 704 first-line fighters, with 289 in reserve.

The Battle of Britain was, in fact the Battle for Britain. Hitler, could not invade until Germany had aerial supremacy over this country. This, Goering and the Luftwaffe could not achieve. Thus Hitler, thwarted, turned his attention East. On December 12, 1940, he ordered plans to continue for a campaign against Russia.

Beaverbrook stood closer to Churchill than any other colleague in the War Cabinet. They had been friends for many years, and although they did not always agree, their differences never diminished the warmth of their relationship. Thus, in September 1941, Beaverbrook was the obvious choice to interview Hess, and to give Churchill his own personal opinion of the man and his mission.

The psychiatrists had already reported that Hess was unstable, neurotic, a hypochondriac, even a paranoid. But psychiatrists, working in their dim half-world of the human mind, sometimes have difficulty in marking the shadowy frontier between sanity and insanity. In simple language, Churchill wanted a straight answer to the question: is Hess mad or is he sane?

At their meeting, Hess repeated to Beaverbrook the steps that had persuaded him to fly to Britain. He even enlivened the conversation with a joke. He said that before he left Germany someone had told him how German pilots had bombed the Ministry of Information.

'That's all wrong,' he told them. 'You shouldn't bomb our ally!'

Before Brendan Bracken took over as Minister of Information, British propaganda had been rather less than successful.

Hess added that he had calculated on some of the British leaders having what he called 'the common sense' to reconsider fighting an unnecessary war. However, events had proved him wrong; he had been discredited and humiliated.

He complained that he could not understand why the real motive for his arrival had not been made public. Churchill's reasoning here was simple and direct. Should the British public—bombed, rationed, with shortages of every kind—learn that any possibility of peace existed, then this knowledge would drastically diminish their wish to continue fighting. If Hess's peace proposals were a ruse, and Germany intended to attack with redoubled vigour while Britain was anticipating an armistice, Britain would be at an enormous and perhaps fatal disadvantage.

Hess admitted the force of this argument, but persisted that he had arrived to negotiate peace with Britain, on any terms, providing Britain would join Germany in attacking her ally, Russia.

Eighteen years later, in a BBC television programme in 1959, Beaverbrook made public the conversation that followed.

'I repeat the arguments that Hess used to me,' he said, 'in the very words which he spoke at that time.'

'He said: "A victory for England will be a victory for the Bolsheviks. A bolshevik victory will sooner or later mean Russian occupation of Germany and the rest of Europe." England, he said, would be incapable of hindering it, as would any other nation.

' "England is wrong," said Hess, "if she believes that the German Bolshevik war will result in such a weakening of the Germans and Bolsheviks that danger to Europe and to the British Empire would cease to exist.

' "Not so," he said.

'Lastly, he declared: "I am convinced that world domination awaits the Soviet Union in the future if her power is not broken now. With the loss to Great Britain of her position as an Imperial Power." '

This was a prophecy of remarkable accuracy; certainly not the foolishness of an unsound mind.

Beaverbrook returned to London and reported on his visit to Churchill. The Prime Minister heard him out and then asked: 'Is he mad?'

'Certainly not,' replied Beaverbrook. 'Hess talks quite sanely and rationally. He may have unusual ideas on health matters, but he is not mad.'

Within a few days of this interview Beaverbrook led a British Government Mission to Stalin in Moscow, to report on the vast amount of war material Britain had already sent to Russia. Had Hess succeeded in his mission all this would naturally have been used against Russia with terrible and almost certainly conclusive results. Between that October and the following June, Britain was sending 1,800 fighter aircraft, plus 440 which had already been promised. There would also be 2,250 tanks, with a target of 250 additional tanks every month.

Naval assistance had already been agreed, but in addition to this a further 1,000,000 shells were on their way, with 1,000 twenty-five pounder guns; 2,250 two-pounder high velocity guns for use in the tanks were being sent separately, with a further 500 in reserve for use against German tanks, and 7,000 Bren guns. Britain was also giving 23,000 American Tommy guns to Russia which she had already ordered for her own troops; and 2,000 British-made Sten guns.

To keep Russia's own war factories supplied, gigantic quantities of tin from Malaya and rubber from Burma were on their way, although Britain had already pledged this tin and rubber for British factories.

Seventy-two thousand tons of rubber would be sent immediately, with 25,000 tons of electrolytic copper, 5,000 tons of aluminium, with a further 2,000 tons every month until the contract ended. Britain would also give Russia 3,000,000 pairs of boots and 250,000 greatcoats for her soldiers.

In addition to this direct aid, which was to the limit of British ability at that time, there were plans to occupy Persia and run a railway route from the south to Teheran in the north and beyond to the Russian border. Thus constant convoys of supplies could be ferried into Russia.

Churchill had even empowered Beaverbrook to tell Stalin that British troops could be sent—to be under his command—in the Caucasus.

'There's no war in the Caucasus,' Stalin pointed out.

'Well, we'll send the troops to Archangel,' said Beaverbrook.

'That proposal at least has the advantage that Churchill knows the way there—and the way back,' replied Stalin dryly; the last time British troops had been in Archangel was 1918, during their unsuccessful intervention against the Bolsheviks.

During Beaverbrook's talks with Stalin, the Russian leader frequently turned the conversation to Hess and his mission. Why had he flown to England? Why had he not already been shot as a Nazi war criminal?

'You just don't shoot a person in England,' Lord Beaverbrook explained. 'He was to have a trial before a jury, but I can tell you why he is in Britain.'[1]

He then showed Stalin a transcript of his interview with Hitler's Deputy, in which Hess suggested that Britain and Germany should join together against Russia.

'That really knocked old Stalin for six,' said Lord Beaverbrook afterwards.[2] And well it might, for ungrateful though Stalin appeared for the prodigious quantities of goods being supplied by Britain without thought of gain or reward, he realized quite well that had Hess's mission succeeded then this cataract of weapons would have been turned against him. Worse, from the Russian point of view, Germany would not be fighting at sea, in the North African desert, and in the air as well as in Russia. She would be fighting on one front only; the Russian front. And aiding her efforts would be the growing might of the British war machine.

Even with Germany weakened by fighting on two fronts, she came nearer to defeating Russia than any previous invader. And finally it was the Russian weather—Generals January and February —that finally halted the German armies. Had Germany and Britain been allies in this invasion, their combined forces would have reached Moscow and beyond before the winter. The outcome would never have been in doubt.

It was thus no wonder that the question of Hess continued to fascinate Stalin throughout the war. He feared a plot; Britain would give Germany the same freedom to attack Russia that Russia had given Germany to attack Poland and the West. And afterwards, at Nuremberg, Stalin took his revenge on Hess.

In the year following Beaverbrook's visit, on October 20, 1942, John Fisher, an Australian commentator in Moscow, broadcast extracts from an article in *Pravda* on the subject of Hess.

'*Pravda* calls in an outspoken manner for the trial of Rudolf Hess, Hitler's former Deputy, who dropped onto the soil of Scotland seventeen months ago.

'The Soviet Government has issued an unusually picturesque writ of Habeas Corpus calling on the British Authorities to produce the body of Hess so that the whole world can see exactly what he represents . . .

---

[1] In a report in the *Evening Standard*, the newspaper owned by Lord Beaverbrook, September 15, 1959.

[2] *Ibid.*

'It is time to make clear exactly what Hess is. Is he a criminal, subject to punishment, or is he the authorized representative of Hitler's Government in England, enjoying immunity?

'Many Russians feel that Hess's flight to Britain is in some obscure way linked up with the absence of the second Front in Europe.'

When Churchill met Stalin in Moscow two years later, in 1944, the British Prime Minister noted how the Russian dictator still kept returning to Rudolf Hess.

'He asked at the dinner table what was the truth about the Hess mission. I had the feeling that he believed there had been some deep negotiation or plot for Germany and Britain to act together in the invasion of Russia which had miscarried.

'Remembering what a wise man he is, I was surprised to find him silly on this point. When the interpreter made it plain that he did not believe what I said, I replied through my interpreter, "When I make a statement of facts within my knowledge I expect it to be accepted."

'Stalin received this somewhat abrupt response with a genial grin.

' "There are lots of things that happen even here in Russia which our Secret Service do not necessarily tell me about!"

'I let it go at that.'[1]

Had the counsels of Rudolf Hess prevailed, and had Churchill been a man of lesser breed and calibre and agreed to compromise, victory in the East would almost certainly have gone to Germany; Russia would have been defeated for the first time in her history.

With the conquest of Russia, the heart of the great Communist octopus would have been mortally wounded, its legend of impregnability and invulnerability shattered for a generation if not for ever. As a result, the bitter East-West conflict that has burned on unceasingly since the war, erupting in different countries, different continents, but always fed by Communist envious hatred for any individualistic way of life, would never have begun.

The face of history, the map of the world, would not be as it is today. The fever of post-war nationalism in the East, in Africa, in Cuba, with its explosive hatred against the Western powers which colonized and civilized these frequently backward peoples, would never have arisen. Communist sympathizers in high places in so many outwardly non-Communistic countries would have found it expedient to follow the National Socialist line.

What would have happened to Britain had Churchill been per-

[1] *The Second World War*, vol. III: *The Grand Alliance.*

suaded to take what could have seemed an easy way of securing peace? For one thing, Churchill would have been forced to resign. Hess insisted that Hitler could never begin to negotiate peace terms with Churchill. Thus a new Prime Minister would have been installed, naturally a man of Nazi leanings, and close sympathies with Germany.

At first many people in Britain might be persuaded—or even persuade themselves—that their country would lose little except her honour in agreeing to such proposals. She would still be in apparent control of an enormous Empire, untouched by the ravages of war or nationalism. Her income from India, from the Argentine, her vast investments in other countries, might stay virtually as they had been for generations. Rationing could cease, and the blackout be lifted; within a few weeks everyday life in Britain in that summer of 1941 might have seemed to be back on a peacetime basis.

But such a pleasant illusion could only exist while British aid in arms and armies was of use to Germany in her mortal struggle against Russia. With Russia defeated what then would have been Britain's position? Who could oppose any wish or whim of a Führer who controlled two-thirds of the world—whose area of influence far exceeded those of such past conquerors as Tamburlaine, Gengis Khan, Caesar and Hannibal put together?

Even assuming that Hitler, weary of blood and slaughter, decided against taking Britain or her possessions by force, he could control them just as easily. He could say: 'We want to be friends with you. But to prove that *you* want to be friends, you should *give* us these countries, these peoples for our own. If you do not, then we must treat this as an unfriendly action and deal with it accordingly.'

As Hess had already admitted to Ivone Kirkpatrick and the Duke of Hamilton, Britain could be starved into submission. Across the world, Australia and New Zealand, with their vast territories of sparsely populated land, would have stood alone and at the mercy of the Japanese.

Had the Japanese still decided to attack Pearl Harbour, then America, with her regular army of barely 75,000 men, an air force one third of this size and a one-ocean Navy, would have fared even worse than when Japan did attack, in December, seven months after Hess landed.

By Christmas 1941 the Nazi flag would have flown above Moscow. By early 1942 the Germans would have controlled the greater part of Russia; Italians would rule the Mediterranean, and Japan would be the dominating power east of Suez, with Fascists in South America and elsewhere preparing to seize power. The spring of that year would have seen a world in eclipse; nations, continents, peoples, brought to the edge of darkness.

Had any British voice then spoken against this rising flood of Nazi tyranny, it would have been met with derision and contempt. For Britain, throughout the centuries the voice and land of freedom, had compromised with honour. Britain had talked, but had not equated brave words with brave deeds.

That all this remains no more than a nightmare of what-might-have-been stands to the credit of Winston Churchill. On April 17, a fortnight before Hess landed, he gave a speech in London in which he said:

'I have thought in this difficult period, when so much fighting and so many critical and complicated manœuvres are going on, that it is above all things important that our policy and conduct should be on the highest level, and that honour should be our guide.'

That this was indeed Churchill's unswerving principle was shown by his refusal to entertain the proposals Hess brought so hopefully with him.

* * *

Meanwhile, what was happening in Germany? What speculations and rumours had Hess's sudden disappearance aroused—and how did Hitler deal with them?

Hitler's interpreter, Dr Paul Schmidt wrote later that it was 'as though a bomb had struck the Berghof'.[1]

General Keitel saw Hitler walking up and down his study, one hand held to his head as he tried to 'figure out'—the General's own words—what he should do and say.[2] Finally, the Führer decided what to say—but he took five days to make up his mind. Then, on May 15th—the Thursday after Hess's departure—Hitler called the heads of the army to a special meeting, and informed them that he had been 'completely taken by surprise' by Hess's flight. Hess, he declared, had suffered 'inner conflicts' by the thought of 'two Germanic peoples destroying each other'.

In addition Hitler said that Hess was 'inwardly disturbed because he was not on active service'; he was also 'inclined to mysticism,

[1] *Hitler's Interpreter*, P. Schmidt, New York, 1951.
[2] 'Keitel Interrogation' (Nazi Conspiracy and Aggression), part of Nuremberg Document, Supplement B, pp. 127–73.

visions and prophesies and so addicted to utterly reckless flying that the Führer had forbidden him to go up'.[1]

The generals received this information in silence. Clearly, they wondered why, if the second most important man in Germany was so unbalanced, this fact had only so recently been discovered. Certain selected journalists were then informed that Hess had suffered from 'stomach ailments' and that, in fact, his work had been done for him 'for some time' by Bormann. Now it was the turn of German newspaper readers to become sceptical; the more Hitler excused, the more he accused.

Hitler did not seem to realize this; he was as anxious to prevent any rumours of a possible peace negotiation as Churchill—and for exactly the same reasons. On his instructions, Nazi headquarters issued a special statement to the German press.

'As far as it is possible to tell from papers left behind by Party Member Hess, it seemed that he lived in a state of hallucination as a result of which he felt he could bring about an understanding between England and Germany.

'It is a fact that Hess, according to a report from London, jumped from his aeroplane near the town to which he was trying to go and was found there injured. The National Socialist Party regrets that this idealist fell as a victim to his hallucinations.

'This, however, will have no effect on the continuation of the war which has been forced upon Germany. Dr Karl Haushofer, head of the Geopolitical Institute, Willi Messerschmitt, Frau Hess and others were arrested.'

Apart from the basic news that Hess had jumped from his plane and that 'others'—his adjutant, and later, his driver and detective— had been arrested, this statement was not true. Hess left no papers behind except the letter to Hitler with a copy addressed to his wife, and a memorandum to the 'effect that I would say to the English that Italy must be included, as an essential condition'.[2]

Neither Karl Haushofer, Messerschmitt or Frau Hess were arrested. Haushofer and Messerschmitt were questioned; Albrecht Haushofer was arrested and ordered to explain his part in the earlier attempts to contact British representatives in Lisbon.

Haushofer realized that Hess was psychologically as unable to

[1] See General Halder's Diary for May 15, 1941.
[2] Note by Hess to his wife from Nuremberg, May 8, 1947, enclosing extracts from Halder's Diary.

wait for results from the more subtle moves he had made as he was to criticize Hitler or to question any of his decisions. But as he told his brother, 'Hess is the most honourable among the Nazis—and therefore the weakest in the chain from their point of view.' Thus, both as a friend and an adviser to the German Foreign Office on matters concerning Britain, Haushofer had deliberately cultivated Hess.

According to his brother, Albrecht Haushofer was furious when he heard that Hess had flown off on his mission without informing him of his intention to fly on that particular day. 'And to think that one is forced to conduct politics with such fools,' he exclaimed bitterly. Thereafter, he referred to Hess as 'the motorized Parsifal'—taking the name of the fool in Wagner's opera.

His bitterness at Hess's impetuosity was increased by the fact that on the evening of May 10—when Hess was actually on his way to Scotland and beyond all hope of contact or recall—Haushofer received a telegram from Herr Stahmer, Secretary of the German Embassy in Madrid.

'The pre-arranged wording . . . indicated that Stahmer in Madrid had been able to contact the British Ambassador, then Sir Samuel Hoare, and that Haushofer's venture, to which Hess had eventually agreed, was apparently a success. But it was too late.'[1]

It was all far too late.

On May 12, the Monday following Hess's departure, the Gestapo flew Albrecht Haushofer to Bad Godesberg in a special aeroplane. There he was interrogated, and despite the lateness of the hour at which he had arrived, he was forced to write a full account of 'the kind and extent of his English connections, destined for Hitler'. As Haushofer was already the principal adviser to Hitler's Foreign Office on British affairs, and since Hitler already knew of the previous attempts to reach some form of compromise armistice with Britain, it is not likely that the Führer discovered much that he did not know. This exercise was purely a means to cloak and cover Hitler's own prior knowledge of these attempts.

After the interrogation, an enemy of the Haushofer family, envious of their standing, their estate and their intellectual capabilities, remarked to Himmler: 'This is the right moment to finish off *all* the Haushofers.'

Himmler disagreed, possibly not for any motives of humanity but

[1] Translation from *Vierteljahrshefte fuer Zeitgesichte*, 8 Jahrgang, 1960. Walter Stubbe: *In Memoriam Albrecht Haushofer*, pp. 236 *et seq.*

more likely because he either knew or guessed the real reasons behind Albrecht Haushofer's arrest. Haushofer was kept in custody for three months, and then released and allowed to return home and to resume his career.

His brother, Dr Heinz Haushofer, recalls that after Mr Eden had announced in parliament that Hess had arrived with visiting cards from both Karl and Albrecht Haushofer, their telephone line was tapped, but no further action was taken against the family until July 1944. Then Albrecht was arrested on a charge of complicity in the attempt on Hitler's life, and what was known as 'the 20th of July Movement'. He was imprisoned in Moabit Gaol, Berlin. He occupied the months in captivity by writing sonnets. Altogether he composed eighty, which became known as the 'Moabit Sonnets' by his friends.

Haushofer never faced trial. At the end of April 1945, just before the Russians entered the city, the Nazis shot him. A year later his father took his own life. He was seventy-six.

Hitler's statement that Ilse Hess had been arrested was quite without foundation. In fact, he issued specific instructions that her husband's possessions should not be touched or moved or interfered with in any way. Further, Frau Hess was to receive the pension of a Cabinet Minister who was a prisoner of war. But before these orders filtered down the echelons of the Party, Martin Bormann, Hess's Deputy, and anxious to assume his master's authority, did his best to discredit his old chief and to humiliate his wife.

First, he ordered her to Berlin to the flat which her husband maintained on the third storey of Wilhelmstrasse 64. Then, under the eyes of a Party official, Frau Hess had to list all the furniture and fittings in the flat as either 'private or official'. Since this flat was only used when Hess was in Berlin on government affairs, the furniture and most of the other contents—even the spoons—were Government property. But the carpets were their own, and Bormann told Ilse Hess condescendingly that she could have the bedroom furniture cheap 'as a remembrance'.

Elsewhere in Germany, hospitals and streets named after her husband were having their nameplates removed as ostentatiously as possible—and Hess's membership card was also removed from the Party Index. Clearly, Hitler did not wish the slightest suspicion to remain that he had known of Hess's intention or that he condoned it in any way.

Bewildered and bemused, Ilse Hess was grateful for the friendship of two people at this time. One was Eva Braun, who sent her a personal letter saying that if ever Ilse was in serious trouble she must contact her immediately through a certain tradesman they both knew. 'I liked you and your husband best of all,' she wrote. 'Please tell me if things become unbearable, for I can speak to the Führer without Bormann knowing anything about it.'

Ilse Hess's other friend in need was a retired banker, who assured her that although everyone knew why Bormann hated Hess, Bormann had no authority to sell Hess's house in Harthauser Strasse without Hitler's knowledge and permission. This old friend stayed with her until Bormann's men arrived to interview her in this house, led by Dr Hansen, who had come to see her as soon as news of her husband's flight had been released. But to Frau Hess's surprise, instead of being rude and boorish, they were now quite pleasant. As Dr Hansen said smilingly: 'Everything has changed, our orders are different. They have been issued from the highest level!'

'What has changed?' asked Frau Hess.

'It is the Führer's strict instruction that nothing belonging to Rudolf Hess shall be confiscated or moved, and that you will not be embarrassed in any way.'

Ilse Hess suggested that since her house was really too large for her and her son to occupy alone, it might be used as a hospital, but Bormann, mindful of Hitler's new orders, could not agree. Although she received the full income due to a Cabinet Minister held as a prisoner of war, Ilse Hess still felt that the house was too large for her, and so she closed it.

All her books she sent to Hindelang, where she and her husband rented a small wooden chalet in the hills, about 100 miles south-west of Munich. Then Ilse and her son moved out into their chauffeur's flat. As they were packing up their belongings, the little boy kept asking his mother where his father had put one of his toys; a khaki metal tank. It was a toy of which he was extremely fond. Finally, the tin tank was discovered in his toy cupboard. Tied to it was the key of Hess's private safe.

Wondering what she might find in the safe, Ilse Hess opened the door. Inside she saw a letter addressed to her. It was from her husband, and explained why he had gone to England. With this was a copy of the letter he had left for Hitler, which he concluded by saying that if his mission was unsuccessful the Führer could escape all incriminations by simply saying that he was mad—advice which Hitler had quickly and gratefully accepted.

Ilse realized that her husband had hidden this particular toy, knowing that it would eventually be discovered, and, with it, the key to his safe. But he had calculated that she would not find the letter in time to try and persuade him not to go. Both these letters and nearly all her possessions were destroyed when the house was bombed and burned out in the last year of the war.

Some time after interest in the whole episode had died down, Hitler hinted what his public denunciation of his oldest friend had meant to him. He was visiting Frau Elsa Bruckmann, shortly after the death of her husband, Hugo, a Munich publisher who had helped and advised Hitler in his early days as a politician. Frau Bruckmann, a Roumanian Princess before her marriage, and a clever, shrewd woman, had known Hitler since his hungry days. She was thus not afraid to speak to him frankly and so risk his momentary displeasure.

Hitler came to visit her when she was designing a headstone for her husband's grave.

'We all have our graves and grow more and more lonely, but we have to overcome our feelings and go on living, my dear gracious lady,' he said gently, trying to comfort her. 'I, too, am now deprived of the only two human beings among all those around me to whom I have been truly and inwardly attached: Dr Todt[1] is dead, and Hess has flown away from me!'

'That is what you say now and to me, but what does your official Press say?' retorted Frau Bruckmann. 'Year after year we all go to Bayreuth and are deeply moved, but who understands the *real* meaning? When our unhappy age at last produces a man, who, like the Valkyrie, fulfils the deeper meaning of Wotan's command and seeks to carry out *your* most sacred wish with heroism and self-sacrifice—then he's described as insane!'

She paused. Had she gone too far, even for an old friend? Would the Führer fly into one of his rages? To her relief, he answered her quietly. 'Isn't it enough, what I have said to you—and to you alone—about my *real* feelings?' he asked. 'Is that not enough for you?'[2]

[1] He was killed in an aeroplane accident.
[2] This is a reference to Wagner's opera *The Valkyrie*, in which Siegmund and Sieglind, brother and sister, are parted when very young. Years later Siegmund returns and falls in love with his sister, not knowing her identity, and disregarding the fact that she is already married to someone else.

A son, Siegfried, is born to them. Wotan, the head of the Gods, knows the great destiny that awaits Siegfried, but Wotan's wife, knowing nothing of this, feels that the two guilty lovers should be punished.

The girl's husband fights a duel with Siegmund. Wotan officially tells the Valkyrie—the handmaids of Odin—to help the husband. Privately, he wills them to help Siegmund, which they do. Siegmund wins.

At about this time one of the British psychiatrists concerned with Hess, interviewed a German POW who had been employed by Berlin Radio. He had dealt with incoming wireless messages in the Central Information Bureau.

'A few days before Hess's flight to England Hitler and Hess were seen leaving the Brown House at Munich together, arm in arm, smiling and extremely friendly. The above-mentioned Information Bureau seemed to have had advance notice (off the record) of Hess's flight, so much so that the men on duty on the day of the flight would come in excitedly saying: "Any news yet?" or "Has he landed yet?"

'The informant thought it quite impossible for anybody to be able to fly a military plane out to sea without at least the cognisance of the German Air Force. He ventured the opinion that Hitler knew about Hess's project and encouraged it with typical crooked motives: (a) if Hess were successful in obtaining peace from Great Britain he would permit the mission to be acknowledged and Hess to be a hero, but (b) should it fail, he would be rid of a somewhat difficult and cranky personality who had incurred the displeasure of the SS and he could then publish a disavowal of Hess as a psychopath and traitor. This latter course was in fact followed when the world knew that Hess had landed in Britain.'[1]

Later in the war, Hitler told Colonel Otto Skorzeny, who rescued Mussolini from captivity on Hitler's orders after Italy sued for peace in September 1943, that he would disown him if his rescue bid failed, in the same way that he had disowned Hess when his mission failed.[2]

Looking back now, there seems little doubt that Hitler knew about Hess's attempts to be a go-between. Albrecht Haushofer was sure that his discussions with Hess were made with the Führer's consent.[3] His father, Karl Haushofer, was convinced that Hitler had 'dispatched' Hess, or, as he put it 'sacrificed him'.[4]

Bodenschatz thought that 'Hitler's consternation and surprise'— at the news of Hess's flight 'were superbly played . . .' It was clear to all that Hitler, faithful to his wartime practice of discussing top

---

This reference to one of his own favourite operas was Hitler's way of admitting that while he had officially to condemn Hess's mission, privately he had been in favour of it.
[1] *The Case of Rudolf Hess.*
[2] Serial of his life story, by Charles Foley, *Daily Express*, April 15, 1952.
[3] Letter No. 3 in Appendix I.
[4] Frau Ilse Hess.

secrets only with the people immediately concerned, had hatched a plot with Rudolf Hess, his closest associate.[1]

Further, Hess actually asked Hitler's pilot, Hans Baur, to provide him with maps of the 'forbidden zones' in Germany which he would have to cross on his flight; Baur already knew that Hess was flying despite the Führer's strict ban. He says that Messerschmitt 'of course, knew all about the prohibition'.[2] But despite this knowledge, Messerschmitt obligingly provided a plane, and modified it extensively with extra fuel tanks, compasses and radio so that the Deputy Führer could fly for nearly 900 miles without refuelling! His chief test pilot, Flight Captain Stöhr, also knew about Hess's activities, and so did Theo Croneiss, one of his chief executives; so, obviously, did the mechanics who did the work.

It is unbelievable that in a dictatorship riddled with Gestapo agents and others eager to report unusual happenings, word of all this did not reach either Bormann, who hated Hess, or Hitler who had publicly forbidden him to fly.

Without Hitler's knowledge and consent Hess could never have made twenty trial flights from Augsburg, far less the two attempts to reach Scotland that failed before his third and successful flight on May 10th. In addition, there were the arrangements Hess made for radio location signals to help him on his way, and also the various weather reports his adjutant received which, as Frau Hess remembers, were frequently telephoned direct to his home and not to the airfield he might be using.

Had all these complicated preparations and rehearsals not been made with Hitler's general acquiescence, then how would all those who helped Hess have fared when Hess finally flew away? There seems little doubt that their punishment would have been severe; the Third Reich had no mercy for those who disagreed with its policies or its leader. Hitler claimed that Hess would be shot if he returned—but these words are at variance with the way he treated the people who helped him go.

True, Pintsch was gaoled, but he was later released; he had the misfortune to be on the spot when Hitler needed a scapegoat urgently. Had Hess sent another officer to Berchtesgaden with the letter for the Führer, then Hitler's wrath would have fallen on him. Messerschmitt was not punished at all. His part in the events was treated with laughter; Goering thought him 'incorrigible'. He even

[1] *The Rise and Fall of Hermann Goering.*
[2] *Hitler's Pilot.*

promised, in his own words, to 'help you out of the mess, if the Führer shall seek to make trouble for you'.[1] Lastly, Frau Hess was not arrested or questioned by the Gestapo. She was indeed questioned by one of Bormann's aides, but Bormann wanted her husband's job and so acted out of greed and envy. Hitler soon came to her aid, and she received the full pay and allowances of a Minister who was a prisoner of war.

Thus, by all the available evidence, it seems certain that the only important fact about Hess's mission with which Hitler was not cognisant was the actual date of his departure. This would account for Hess's letter which reported that at last he had flown beyond recall; it would also help to explain the Führer's remark to Pintsch that 'at this particular point in the war' Hess's flight 'could be a very hazardous escapade'. Hess had already failed with two other serious attempts to reach Britain months earlier; by May 10, Hitler's invasion of Russia was barely five weeks away. Better than anyone, he knew how little time was left for any negotiations before 'Barbarossa' began.

But whether Hitler knew of Hess's flight, or whether he did not; whether Hess was mad as Hitler claimed, or sane, as those closest to him believe, Churchill had no intention of negotiating any peace treaty with Germany which he was convinced would leave Britain in a position of accepting German suzerainty.

It was therefore essential that no so-called 'peace party' should appear in Britain in opposition to Churchill's policy of all-out-war. Thus Churchill necessarily deprecated the Hess mission, and made as much propaganda as he could against taking it seriously.

[1] Interview with Professor Willi Messerschmitt, quoted in *Frankfurter Neue Presse,* May, 1947.

CHAPTER TWELVE

The Deceptions and Delusions
of a Failure

After Hess's interview with Lord Beaverbrook Hess remained at Mytchett for several months, until June 1942, when he was moved to Abergavenny in South Wales, where he stayed for the rest of the war.

During his stay at Mytchett Place Hess would frequently remark with pleasure to Percival that all his cutlery and crockery bore the Royal cipher, G.R.VI. He felt sure this was a personal tribute by the King to his importance. He did not realize that all War Department property is stamped with this cipher. He also felt that the presence of the Guards, the elite of the British Army, was another real, if obscure compliment to his rank.

When Hess moved to Abergavenny, Percival said goodbye to him; he had received another posting. He explained to Hess that the Guards would also be saying farewell. In future, at Abergavenny, Hess would be in the care of the Pioneer Corps.

'The Pioneer Corps?' repeated Hess. 'I've not heard of them. What are their usual duties?'

'Digging latrines,' replied Percival laconically.

It was thought inadvisable for Hess to be kept in a military prisoner-of-war camp, and clearly he could not remain indefinitely at Mytchett. He had only remained there so long because it was near London while he was being interviewed. Although he persisted in his belief that he was being poisoned, it was not feasible to remove him to hospital where his delusions could be treated more easily. Once in hospital, Hess might become a case for repatriation. This Churchill had no intention of allowing.

After some discussion a compromise was reached. Outside Abergavenny stood a great house, Maindiff Court, which before the war had been the admission hospital of the County Mental Hospital, about one and a half miles away. During the war it was turned over to Service patients. Here Hess could be adequately guarded and treated should he fall ill or should his depression at the failure of his mission grow worse. Here, in a small suite of rooms overlooking the gardens, he spent the next four years, until October 1945, when he flew to Nuremberg to stand trial with the handful of other Nazi leaders who had not by then been killed or taken their own lives.

Although Hess enjoyed conversations with his doctors and an occasional call from the Swiss envoy who, as the representative of the Protecting Power, made routine visits to him, as to ordinary POW camps, to make sure that the terms of the International Red Cross and the Geneva Convention were being met, Hess had no one of his own nationality near him. He was thus in virtual solitary confinement. His guards treated with correctness, but always he was on his own, with his thoughts and the memory of the dream that had failed.

It was understandably a time of worry and gloom for him, when fears of persecution and poison plots darkened his mind. Already a person of unstable outlook and attitude, the strain he endured during his four years in Britain did nothing to help the traits which the psychiatrists had already noted. Sometimes his worries and fears produced real physical pain. On such occasions Hess would lie on the ground and cry out in agony, begging an orderly to bring him a hot-water bottle to ease the violent cramps in his stomach. Later in the war, when his rubber hot-water bottle perished, and it became impossible to buy a replacement, Hess appeared content to lie with a medicine bottle filled with warm water clasped to his stomach.

Hess was grateful for any company; he would frequently walk to limit of his wire 'cage' in the garden and talk to the young daughter of one of the psychiatrists, Dr Ellis Jones. She kept her pony in a field adjoining the hospital. He would also have long talks with Dr Jones himself. They would discuss such diverse subjects as the possibility of Communism sweeping the world after the war, the future of gypsies, the power of hypnotists over their patients.

The Swiss envoy usually presented Hess with a cigar each time he came to see him. Hess did not smoke, but he would accept this gift with a grave courtesy, smell the leaf like a connoisseur, and carefully put the cigar into his breast pocket. When the envoy left, Hess would wrap up the cigar and wait for Dr Jones' routine visit later in the day. 'A present for you, doctor,' he would say with a smile—and give him the cigar.

Time and again, during their talks, Hess would discuss what he felt was the greatest danger facing Europe and the world should Nazi Germany be destroyed; the creeping tide of Communism, which he was sure would emerge from the war as the world's most potent political force.

'You live in an island, doctor,' he would say, 'so to some extent you feel insulated from it, as you feel insulated from other Continental problems. But the danger is very great, whether you realize it or not.'

Although he was frequently morose and withdrawn, he bore his imprisonment with dignity. He wrote regularly to his wife and received her letters in reply.

On May 20, 1942, he also wrote to Professor Haushofer. 'Do not worry over me!' he announced cheerfully. 'You, less than any one, need do this. That my present situation is not exactly agreeable goes without saying. But, in time of war, we have to put up with many things that are not agreeable. That is not important. You know best what counts in the long run. . . . You know as well as I do that the compass which guides our affairs is influenced by forces that are infallible—even when we know them not.'

On September 9 of the same year he wrote to his wife about his son, Wolf Rüdiger, born on November 18, 1937, and known in the family as Buz.

'How closely my life is bound up with mountains! Isn't it extraordinary? I estimate that roughly one half of my life has been spent somewhere near a high mountain range. And I am more than glad that the little chap will become a regular mountain boy now that he's going to Ostrachtal. The language certainly won't bother him. I can see him quickly picking up the genuine dialect. Though it's almost impossible to think of him as a schoolboy, confronted for the first time with the serious side of life; but it will be next year!

'In my eyes he is still the tiny wide-eyed child who was sitting on his chamber in the nursery at Harlaching when I last saw him! But one must remember that, even if he were never to go to school, we still could not make him stay put at the age when children are most fascinating.

'It gives me great delight to hear about every little thing that happens to you and around you—go on writing this sort of letter! It means more to me than anything else you could write. What you think, I know already! And you know what I think on the same lines, without having to write about it. . . .

In the following year (February 14, 1943) he wrote:

'Oh! how I rejoiced to know that the little chap still remembers his dad; that he still knew where all the splendid toys were put away—the puffing trains, wheels rattling on the rails, with which we secretly amused ourselves in my study during those days before I left. I often think of the things I intended to tell him and show him, following up the bent of the "technical, geographical and scientific" Buz.

'I certainly never dreamed at one time how vitally important my technical and mathematical gifts would some day become in my life. Without this knowledge I could not have achieved the "flight of my life", nor could I ever have mastered the complicated mechanism of the ME machine or navigated it. Everything in our lives has its purpose, seen in the long view—even if half a century may elapse before we really know what it is. Many never know what it is! . . .

Never during these years of captivity did his natural shrewdness desert him. He realized that his regular letters to his wife were censored, so he made a copy of every letter he wrote. He would send a copy of the first with the second; a copy of the second with the third; and so on. The censor apparently did not bother to read the duplicates. In this way Hess smuggled out to his wife certain details regarding his whereabouts.

For instance, on July 16, 1943, when he was at Maindiff Court outside Abergavenny, in Wales, he remarked:

'I have broken off my habit of resting after the chief meal. Sometimes I have the opportunity of taking a walk in the neighbourhood, which is beautiful. When the weather is good I enjoy little rests on the way, selecting spots where there is as enjoyable view as possible. The colours of this landscape are unusual and attractive. An essential part is the red earth, lying between meadows and fields of green turning to yellowish tinges when ripe, and matching the autumn trees. Every cloud shadow at once changes the effect of the colours and with it the whole impression. It can happen that a distant mountain, dominating the background, changes within a few minutes, under the influence of the light, from darkest violet through dark blue to olive and emerald green, with reddish brown and yellow turning to bluish grey. Further, I found that the colours are more beautiful in autumn and winter than other seasons. On the other hand, this has something to do with the softer light and, on the other, with the ploughed up fields which look even redder against the green of those left unploughed in the winter. I am quite ready to believe, as I am told, that artists are especially attracted to this district.

'But the more beautiful it is, the more one realizes the truth of Goethe's words:

> 'When lovers hear the nightingale,
> He sets their joyous hearts a-winging,
> But when the captive hears his tale,
> He finds but sadness in their singing.'

The original letter had the information about the red earth deleted; in the carbon copy this passage was not even touched.

Ilse Hess asked Professor Haushofer in what part of Britain he thought her husband was being guarded. With Haushofer's great knowledge of soils and their location, he found this an easy question to answer.

'There are two main areas in England that have this colour earth,' he told her. 'One is near Windermere and the other is centred around Abergavenny, in South Wales. Since there are no fields with such crops near Windermere, then I think that your husband must be somewhere near Abergavenny.' In fact, Hess was about two miles out of that town.

Oddly enough, while missing such items which could be important if Hitler had wished to discover the whereabouts of his Deputy, for a rescue attempt could be made, the British censors regularly struck out what Hess called a 'laughter-line' in his letters. This was a wavy line if written in pen and ink, or a string of 'V's in a type-written note. It was simply a harmless family way of showing surprise or amusement. The censor thought that it must have some far more sinister significance.

On September 3, 1943, Hess wrote:

'It makes me very happy to see, again and again, from your letters that nothing has changed in your inward relationship to the man[1] whose destiny we have been so closely linked in joy and in suffering, for more than twenty years. You have changed no more than I myself have changed. One must never forget that these times have placed him under a nervous strain, hard to imagine—a strain responsible for states of excitement, in which decisions have been made which would not have been made in more normal times. Writing

[1] Hitler.

179

thus, I am not thinking of myself—not in the least—but of my lads. As regards myself, I was prepared for anything.

'Taking any such excitement into account didn't alter the fact that thinking of my lads and their fate, I was overcome with anger from the start, although your latest news puts things in a different light from the way I saw them in my ignorance. The result was that, for several days running, I stamped up and down my room with rage, expressing and explaining my views—all in a regrettably one-sided manner. My explanations were certainly not directed to the man responsible for certain points of detail, who assuredly could not plead that he had to make quick decisions for his "executive measures" under strain of excitement. In this relationship there is nothing but a complete vacuum, which will always remain a vacuum.'[1]

Then, in January 1944, his letters struck a different note; he was pretending to lose his memory in the hope he would be repatriated. The psychiatrists were puzzled; they felt that he was fooling them, but against this they had to set his temperamental instability. Hess was a most determined man—but on this occasion he did not get his way; he was not sent home.

The psychiatrists at Abergavenny considered that 'the condition was psychogenetic and not organic and . . . of an hysterical nature. Memory,' they said rightly, 'was not far beyond the scope of voluntary recall.'[2]

On January 15, knowing that his letters would all be closely read for any clues as to his condition, he wrote to his wife:

'I have been sitting here for, literally, several hours wondering what I can write to you about. But I get no further; and that I regret to say is for a very special reason. Since, sooner or later, you will notice it or find out about it, I may as well tell you: I have completely lost my memory. The whole of the past swims in front of my mind enveloped in a grey mist. I cannot recollect even the most ordinary things. The reason for it I do not know. The doctor gave me a lengthy explanation, but I have already forgotten what it was. He assured me, however, that all would be well again. I trust he is right.

'Moreover, that is the reason why I can't actually write a sensible letter; for that, memory is needed—more than one might think. It

[1] This remark referred to Martin Bormann.
[2] *The Case of Rudolf Hess.*

is different though, if one has a letter in front of one to answer, providing subject matter and stimulus. Your last letter reached me on 13th September of last year!'

On February 26, 1944, he wrote:

'Please write again! Since September last year I have had nothing from you.

'When you do not write, I can't write either, for I need stimulus. Without a letter of yours I truly do not know what I can say to you. For, as I said in my last letter, I have completely lost my memory—even if this be only a temporary state of things, as the doctor assures me.

'At the very least, tell me how the boy likes going to school.'

Ilse Hess had to wait for three years to hear the reason for this 'loss of memory' which, at the time, naturally worried and perplexed her. Then, from the gaol at Nuremberg on March 10, 1947, her husband felt able to reveal his motives.

'That my letters from England, for a time, came so infrequently had to do with an assumed loss of memory. For it is very difficult to write letters when one is supposed to have no memory! There is the danger of making a mistake that will reveal the truth. It was my contention that I had a family, that I could just recollect that and nothing more. The address of my family had slipped my mind. It was there on one or other of your letters; but I had "forgotten" that I had any letters VVVVV.

'Your new letters always contained something or other that gave me a starting point, apparently, for my letters; thus I would not have to use my memory in any way to arouse suspicion. In short, I was forced to wait for a letter from you before I could write. However, owing to the unfathomable wisdom of unknown forces, there was always a gap of four, or even six months, between yours; so now you will understand why I was often silent for long periods . . .

'Towards the end, this farce went so far that I allowed myself to be given injections against loss of memory. At first I made some resistance, but I saw there was nothing else for it if I did want to strengthen the suspicion they had that at the very least I exaggerated my trouble. Luckily, it was admitted beforehand that it was not certain the treatment would recall lost ideas. The worst of it was that as part of the treatment I was given a narcotic, and under its influence had to answer questions supposed to "re-unite the conscious and subconscious". So I was faced with a double danger: I might reveal things that, as a German, I should hold secret (very likely the intention of the instigator of the injections!) or I might let the cat out of the bag concerning my loss of memory!

'In the long run, as I have said, I had to give way. But, by calling up every scrap of will-power, I managed not to lose consciousness whilst pretending to be unconscious—and they gave me more than the normal dose. To every question I simply said: "I do not know", with a pause between each word speaking softly in a flat, absent-minded voice VVVVV. After a long time, I was able to recall my own name, which I breathed in the same flat manner. Finally, I thought it time to return to consciousness and woke up, eyes full of astonishment, to return slowly to life. It was a real drama. Add: a complete success! They were now utterly convinced that my memory was quite gone.

'I now began to hope that I would at last be exchanged and sent home; but it came to nothing. Yet every now and then a hint was given me that I might be allowed to go back on the next voyage of the Drottningholm as I think the Swedish hospital ship was called. You can imagine what that meant to me! But the ship sailed without me, and the next time, and the next time . . . and every next time.

'How completely the experiment with the narcotic convinced my doctors that my loss of memory was genuine is shown by the fact that when at a later date, for special reasons of my own, I thought it best to reveal my trickery, the medical gentlemen at first refused to believe that they had been taken in. Only when I repeated to them all the questions that had been put to me when I was "unconscious" and when I played over again the comedy of "awakening", using the same mode of speech and flat voice, were they forced to admit that I had brought off a terrific "leg pull" VVVVV. So there can be little doubt that I did really do all that lay within my power to bring about the intervention of the gods—but the gods thought otherwise, and they must have known!'

The failure of his mission helped to convince him that he was the victim of a Jewish plot. He claimed that the Jews had 'some power' to hypnotize people without them realizing it. Then, in this strange hypnotic state, they could conduct 'their misdeeds'. Towards the end of the war—on February 5, 1945—Hess made a list of people whom he was sure had been hypnotized in this way. It included Winston Churchill, Anthony Eden, the King of Italy, General Von

Paulus—even Hess himself. Hypnosis, according to him, changed Churchill from being an anti-Bolshevik into a person who was pro-Russian. Once, so he said, he remembered that Anthony Eden had been rude to Goering at some forgotten State occasion; clearly the British Foreign Secretary had been under the same evil hypnosis. Nor would the King of Italy and Marshal Badoglio have concluded an armistice with the allies, after solemnly assuring Hitler that they would never do this, unless they had been hypnotized.

Hess then declared that he was sure that he also had been hypnotized in this way; otherwise *he* would never have been rude to German collaborators in Italy at a banquet long ago when clearly he should have been pleasant to them!

After drawing up this list, Hess asked an orderly if he would be kind enough to bring him a bread-knife; he wanted to make himself some toast. This explanation was believed; a knife was produced. Hess carried it into his bedroom, shut the door, changed into his Air Force uniform—and deliberately stabbed himself in the chest.

It was not a very serious gash, and only two stitches were required; but half an inch either way and the wound could have been fatal.

Why did he attempt suicide again, however half-heartedly, when he had endured nearly four years of imprisonment with patience and dignity? Hess explained readily that he was sure he would never be allowed to leave Britain. Secondly, it was clear that Germany had lost the war. This meant that the Communists would overrun his country and eventually France and then Britain. Thereafter, however, he appeared calm and composed; he had made his last protest. Now, philosophically, he awaited the outcome of events he could neither control or influence.

The Swiss envoy had brought him several German books which he read avidly in search of comfort and consolation. Hess wrote to his wife on June 21, 1945, that in Konrad Günther's book *Naturlebem*, he had found one passage that he felt applied to him: 'The work of a great man does not achieve its full effect until after the death of its creator, for the present cannot grasp it . . .'

'Can there be anything more heroic,' he asked, 'than a development that follows an undeviating course in the pursuit of a great task, imposed from the earliest beginnings even when the chosen path appears again and again to become confused and lost and becomes a pilgrimage of suffering?'

Also in this book was a quotation from Schopenhauer which impressed him equally: 'The highest that can be achieved is an heroic passage through life. Such a life is led by the man who, pursuing a purpose for the benefit of all, struggles against all-too-great difficulties, receives yet a poor reward or *no* reward at all!'

During his stay at Abergavenny, he prepared a statement about his treatment since his arrival, which showed how the strain of his confinement added to his feeling of failure caused the ever-deepening image of persecution to darken his mind.

'In Mytchett I was constantly awakened from sleep, partly by the officers who came into my room with a lot of noise and who flashed a strong light on my face, allegedly to make sure that I was still alive. Partly, also, by the many air-raid alarms and all clears which sometimes went up to four a night and which were repeated by sirens and horns that were mounted on the house. I could hear neither the noise of motors nor anti-aircraft fire. If I tried to catch up on my sleep during the day, this was prevented by constant slamming of doors; people running up and down stairs on a stairway which was apparently right over my room . . .

'They offered me food and drinks constantly which the others would not accept. Once, when I was careless and drank a little bit of milk by myself, a short time later I got dizzy, had a terrific headache and could not see straight any more. Soon thereafter I got into an hilarious mood, and increased nervous energy became apparent. A few hours later, this gave way to the deepest depression and weakness. From then on I had milk and cheese brought into my room every day, but merely to deceive the people that I was eating that stuff.

'The people around me put more and more peculiar questions to me, touching upon my past. My correct answers evidently caused disappointment. However, loss of memory, which I simulated, gradually caused satisfaction. Finally, I got to such a state that apparently I could not remember anything any more that was further back than a few weeks. Then a conference with Lord Chancellor Simon, of which I had been informed before, was planned for the 9th of June. I was convinced that the obvious endeavour to weaken my memory had some connection with that conference.

'I suspected that I was to be prevented in this manner from making any proposals for an understanding and that moreover Lord Simon was to receive the impression that I was mentally not normal because I was not capable of answering the simplest questions that were to be put to me.

'Thus, in order to be safe, I did not eat anything the last three days before the conference except for drinking some water. When he came I had some wine brought up to my room, but instead of drinking it I poured it away. Major F. a German-speaking officer who was with me, was informed by me that the wine had caused a miracle, my memory had suddenly returned completely.

'I shall never forget his horrified and confused face.

'However, the conference could not be called off any more since Lord Simon was already in the adjoining room. I was well enough for a conference lasting two and a half hours, even though I was still under the influence of a small amount of brain poison . . .

'A doctor who was detailed to be with me, gave me what were supposed to be pills against pain and that were supposed to make me sleep. They did not have any such effect. Instead of that my bladder became closed and for twenty-four hours I could not pass any water. The doctor recommended me to drink lots of water but the only result was a further increase of my suffering. Then I tried to deceive him by merely making it appear like I was taking the tablets and then my bladder could not close any more.

'If I took only a small part of the pills the cramps which would close my bladder would start again. Repeated experiment always had the same result.

'When I refused to take any more pills they then apparently put the same thing in my food, which I noticed by making further experiments when, in order to alleviate my pain, I drank only a very little water, they put an excessive amount of salt in my food so that thirst would force me to drink . . .

'Of course, the aim of all this was to cause my nerves to collapse. The same goes for the extreme restriction in reading material. It was said that any edition of Goethe could not be obtained in the whole of England. It could not even be borrowed, it was said. This same goes for a German history of the world. I could not even get a German text-book of higher mathematics or medicine. I only received a few English books from time to time. However, I was given an English novel which told of a little boy of the age of my own boy.

'Every page was to remind me of my child and I was to be reminded that there was hardly any hope of ever seeing him again and, if I was to see him again, his father would be crazy without knowing it . . .

'In November 1941, I got in touch with the Swiss Envoy in London, and asked him to visit me as the representative of the Protecting Power.

'I had hardly mailed the letter when, again, huge quantities of brain poison were put in my food to destroy my memory, after I had not been given any of this poison for a long while, nor any of the poison which closed my bladder. Again I deceived them into believing that I had lost my memory. After I appeared to have lost my memory completely, the Envoy appeared.

'After the visit of the Envoy, I was given a daily dose of brain poison for eight weeks. After the second failure they apparently wished to find out whether I was immune. When it was found out unmistakably that I was not losing my memory, they gave it up . . .

'Daily they caused my bladder to close and only let it open once for a short time in twenty-four hours. Apart from the salt, the hottest Indian pepper—curry—was put in my food to make me thirsty. I suffered indescribably during this period.

'Finally, however, the medicine did not have the desired effect any more. Once, when the doctor tried to ask me in a very affable manner whether I had had any previous illnesses, I was careful enough to tell him that one of my kidneys was slightly out of order, and therefore I had recently eaten only slightly salted foods or foods without any spice at all. Then they put so much salt in my food that even the nurses, after I had made them taste some of the food, admitted that the food could not be eaten although they themselves were used to eating strongly spiced food. All of my complaints were without success . . .

'For three years, they caused my intestines to close by a medicine that they put in my food, and it could only be opened by a special antidote. At the same time, they put the strongest laxatives in my food which caused me terrible stomach and abdominal cramps several times daily. Only at intervals of several days did they make it possible for me to empty my bowels, and after the next meals they would close again.

'They refused to give me any pills against pain, but rather they gave me pills which did not have any effect. Heat had some effect against pain—hot-water bottles which were given me on the other hand increased the cramps by their weight. They claimed that an electric heating pad could not be obtained in the whole of England . . .

'The ill-baked bread which I received regularly and the meat that was so tough that I could hardly chew it, peas that were as hard as stones, beans which the cook again and again forgot to soak before he cooked them, vegetables with mildew and margarine that was more than rancid, evidently were used to cause pain in the stomach and an illness of the bowels.

'The food tasted interchangeably of soap, dishwater, manure, fish-odour, petrol and carbolic acid. The worst was the secretion from camel and pigs' glands from which even the starchy foods were not safe.

'I choked the food down with the greatest willpower as the necessary evil to prevent starvation. The doctor, though, brought me cartoons from the English Press, in which I was feasting at a table that was straining under the weight of delicacies.

'As long as a doctor or an officer shared a meal with me during the day, the meal would be slightly better. By the way, though, he would be very moderate when taking food and I suspected that he stilled his hunger later from other dishes. The baker put bits of plum into the cake by mistake. Meat dishes were crammed with bone splinters, and thousands of small gravel splinters were put into the vegetables. Probably I was to break my teeth on them . . .

'One hot summer day the air was suddenly filled with the smell of corpses which increased continuously during the next few days. Allegedly it was impossible to find the origin. Finally I went on reconnaissance myself and found that a car load of big fish heads had been thrown into a cesspool which was at a little distance from my quarters and they were decaying in the sun.[1]

'On the 26th of November, 1944, I asked the Swiss Envoy to request leave of absence for me in Switzerland to restore my health, and I wished to be put under the treatment of specialists there.

'According to a report by (a psychiatrist) either new environment or a shock like seeing my family again would restore my memory to me.

'I would undertake on my word of honour to return to England any time it was desired. The Envoy, who was the successor of the previous one, came to see me on the 20th of December and told me that my leave of absence unfortunately was impossible because of some fundamental considerations . . .

'After the one-and-a-half year long pretence of having lost my memory I had to tell myself that the further continuation of this would be futile. Thus, I decided to talk quite frankly to (the psychiatrist) if only to see how the doctor would react. He could not hide his surprise that I had suddenly regained my memory to its full extent.'

[1] This smell apparently came from a nearby farm.

On the afternoon of October 10, 1945, Hess took his first aeroplane flight since he landed in Scotland. He flew back to Germany, making the journey which he had hoped to make within hours of his arrival in 1941. He flew to Nuremberg, with Dr Ellis Jones as his companion.

A military officer armed with a revolver, a sergeant and Dr Jones entered the plane with Hess. At the last moment some civilian official decided to come too, and there was no seat available for the sergeant; he sat on the floor. The plane was small and cold, and the passage bumpy. The sergeant was sick first, then the officer, then Hess. When they landed at Brussels to refuel, Dr Jones was the only one fit enough to eat any lunch.

'What's wrong with you, old boy?' he asked Hess jocularly, because Hess had told him many times of his ability as a pilot.

'Excitement,' replied Hess simply.

He thought that now his time of imprisonment in British hands was over he would be released after his trial; or indeed it might be that in view of his medical history and his attempts to prove that he had lost his memory, he would be declared unfit to stand for trial, and immediately released.

As the plane circled over the airfield, Hess looked through the small perspex window beside his seat and recognized Nuremberg. He turned to Dr Jones.

'Well, Jones,' he said. 'I don't know what will happen to me, but I'll make this prophecy to you, and time will prove it right. Within ten years from now, Britain will agree with everything I've said against Communism. That will be the enemy then!'

CHAPTER THIRTEEN

The Nuremberg Trial

Nuremberg in 1945 was a city of ruins, a tombstone marking the death of the Third Reich, a monument to the futility of war. It had been one of Europe's few remaining walled mediaeval cities, with gabled houses and lovely historic buildings. But Hitler had set up factories there for his war machine, and the RAF had bombed Nuremberg ruthlessly.

The gabled houses were hollow, empty shells, blackened with flame; the cobbled streets were no more than alleys through heaps of rubble and twisted, rusting metal. Under the mounds of bricks and girders thousands found their only grave; the smell of unnumbered dead hung sourly on the air. Elsewhere among the ruins the living dwelt like rats in home-made caves.

The massive Palace of Justice, pillared with marble, had been largely rebuilt for the trial of such Nazi leaders as had not fled or taken their own lives. During the months in which their trial dragged on, this Palace became a town within a city. Inside its doors the charred reality of Nuremberg could temporarily be forgotten, for the Palace of Justice had its own cafeteria, a tailor's shop, a barber, a post office, even novelty shops selling souvenirs of the trial. A honeycomb of offices and partitioned rooms housed 5,000 people—guards, stenographers, cooks, waiters, signallers, journalists and the lawyers of many nations. The United States prosecuting team numbered 600; the British mustered 160.

The courtroom where the prisoners were to stand trial was a panelled, oblong room, entirely unlike any English assize court; huge arc lights blazed down from its roof; green velvet curtains covered the windows through which no daylight came; others were draped across the marble doorways. At one end of this long room a stage had been built with benches for the prisoners; incongruously, they resembled choir stalls in a church. The prisoners wore earphones for interpretations.

Elsewhere, little glass cages had been set up for interpreters and for newsreel camera men. Newspaper photographers worked in the well of the court, near the American guards in their distinctive white helmets and white belts, and the Russian prosecutors, all solid, bulky men in green uniforms. Beyond them again was a visitors' gallery to hold 150 spectators, with places for 250 journalists underneath. Their chairs were upholstered like theatre seats and fitted with earphones. On the right arm of each chair was a black dial that could be set in four positions for a running translation in Russian, French, English or German.

The scene was as theatrical as any of Hitler's pre-war rallies, and its strangeness was matched by the events played out against it.

Hess's counsel, a German lawyer, Dr von Rohrscheidt, asked for what he called 'an expert designated by the Medical Faculty of the University of Zurich or of Lausanne' to pronounce whether Hess was fit to stand trial or not. This request was refused. But certainly Hess did not lack examination by doctors of distinction.

Lord Moran, Churchill's own physician, Dr Rees, Consulting Psychiatrist to the British army, and Medical Director of the Tavistock Clinic in London; and Dr George Riddoch, Consulting Neurologist to the Army, and Director of Neurology at the London Hospital, telephoned from London on November 19 that they had reached the following conclusions about Hess.

'1. There are no relevant physical abnormalities.

'2. His mental state is of a mixed type. He is an unstable man, and what is technically called a psychopathic personality. The evidence of his illness in the past four years, as presented by one of us who has had him under his care in England, indicates that he has had a delusion of poisoning, and other similar paranoid ideas.

'Partly as a reaction to the failure of his mission, these abnormalities got worse, and led to suicidal attempts.

'In addition, he has a marked hysterical tendency, which has led to the development of various symptoms, notably a loss of memory, which lasted from November, 1943 to June, 1944, and which resisted all efforts at treatment. A second loss of memory began in February, 1945, and lasted till the present. This amnesic symptom will eventually clear, when circumstances change.

'3. At the moment he is not insane in the strict sense. His loss of memory will not entirely interfere with his comprehension of the proceedings, but it will interfere with his ability to make his defence, and to understand details of the past, which arise in evidence.

'4. We recommend that further evidence should be obtained by narco-analysis and that if the Court decides to proceed with the Trial, the question should afterwards be reviewed on psychiatric grounds.'[1]

The American psychiatrists declared that:

'Rudolf Hess is suffering from hysteria characterized in part by loss of memory. The nature of this loss of memory is such that it will not interfere with his comprehension of the proceedings, but it will interfere with his response to questions relating to his past and will interfere with his understanding his defence.

'In addition there is a conscious exaggeration of his loss of memory and a tendency to exploit it to protect himself against examination.

'We consider that the existing hysterical behaviour which the defendant reveals was initiated as a defence against the circumstances in which he found himself while in England; that it has now become in part habitual and that it will continue as long as he remains under the threat of imminent punishment, even though it may interfere with his undertaking a more normal form of defence.

'It is the unanimous conclusion of the undersigned that Rudolf Hess is not insane at the present time in the strict sense of the word.'

The Russian medical men announced more bluntly:

'Rudolf Hess, prior to his flight to England, did not suffer from any kind of insanity, nor is he now suffering from it. At the present time he exhibits hysterical behaviour with signs of a conscious-intentional (simulated) character, which does not exonerate him from his responsibility under the indictment.'[2]

So all doubt as to his ability to stand trial was dispelled. The trial of Rudolf Hess and nineteen other Nazi leaders, including Goering, Von Ribbentrop and Admiral Doenitz, opened before the International Tribunal at Nuremberg on Tuesday morning, November 20, 1945.

It was to be the longest trial in history, lasting for 217 days. Three million documents were produced at 403 sessions; 80,000 feet of film were shown in evidence; 88,000 affidavits had been signed by 150,000 people submitted for the defence, plus 158,000 on behalf of organizations. Sixty-one witnesses were called for the defence, and thirty-three for the prosecution.

[1] Quoted in *The Case of Rudolf Hess.*
[2] *Ibid.*

The main charges on which twenty-one prisoners stood trial were:

1. Conspiring or participating as leaders or accomplices to commit crimes against peace; committing specific crimes against peace by planning, preparing, initiating and waging wars of aggression against a number of states.
2. War crimes—which included murder, deportation for slave labour, killing of hostages and ill-treatment of prisoners of war.
3. Crimes against humanity, which included murder, extermination, enslavement, deportation and political, racial and religious persecutions.

As early as October, 1943, the Allies had set up a War Crimes Commission to collect evidence to prepare an indictment against the Nazi leaders. After the German surrender, legal experts from Britain, America, Russia and France met in London and set up an 'International Military Tribunal' to try the major war criminals according to international law. Their charter laid it down that no war criminal could challenge the Tribunal or question the criminality of what had been declared criminal. Further, it was a principle of the Tribunal's charter that although a crime might have been committed on the orders of a superior, this would not remove responsibility for the crime, although it might provide mitigation.

The indictment of the Nazis ran to forty-three pages of 30,000 words, and traced the growth of the Nazi party through the years, and the steady subjection of the German nation to Hitler's regime. Its horror increased with every page. Of 228,000 French political and racial deportees, barely one in ten had survived. In Leningrad, 172,000 were shot or tortured; in Stalingrad, 40,000. At Maidanek camp alone, half a million people had been exterminated; at Auschwitz, four million died.

Four of the twenty-four Nazi leaders escaped the official executioners to become their own; Hitler, Goebbels, Ley and Himmler. Hitler and his mistress Eva Braun died together in his bunker in the Reich Chancellery in Berlin on April 30, 1945, and their bodies had been burned with petrol. Two days later, Goebbels, the 47-year-old master mind of the Nazi propaganda machine, poisoned his children, shot his wife, and then killed himself just before Berlin fell. Heinrich Himmler, the 44-year-old Gestapo leader and ss chief, poisoned himself during interrogation at Luneberg on May 21, 1945. Martin Bormann, who succeeded Hess, and who had been in the Chancellery with Hitler in April 1945, when the Russians entered Berlin, was said to have been killed when trying to escape in a tank.

On October 25, a month before the trial opened, Robert Ley, Hitler's former labour leader, hanged himself in his cell. He passed into eternity on the end of a chain from the lavatory cistern, with a towel stuffed into his mouth to silence his cries. After this, prisoners were not allowed to use towels except under supervision.

Of the twenty-one who actually stood trial—Goering, Ribbentrop, Keitel (the Chief of the German High Command), Rosenberg (the intellectual high priest of Nazism), Streicher (the ruthless prosecutor of the Jews), von Papen and Hess were probably the most important.

The Germans who had come so close to conquering the world, now lived with less privacy than beasts in cages. Each had a single cell on the ground floor with his name painted above the door; he might have been a horse in a stable. Every cell contained an iron bed bolted to the wall, and a plain table bolted to the floor. A wooden chair, which each prisoner was allowed during the day, was removed at dusk. The lights in the cells never went out, although they dimmed slightly at night.

Throughout the hours of darkness, the prisoners had to sleep facing the door, their hands outside the blankets. At intervals of thirty seconds, a guard would peer at each of them through a peephole in the door. They were not allowed spectacles, ties, braces or shoe laces in case of suicide attempts. For the same reason, they could not use a needle to sew on a button. Every day they were shaved by a German prisoner with a safety razor under the scrutiny of an American guard.

Each had one suit or his uniform (with medals and rank badges removed) for appearance in Court. Every day, after the hearing, these clothes were taken away to be pressed and searched in case somehow a weapon or a poison phial could have been passed to one of them. Laundry was done in the prison wash-house.

The men who had dined for years on the finest foods in Europe now ate their meals from mess tins with metal spoons. For breakfast, they might have oatmeal and biscuits. For lunch, soup, a hash of potatoes and cabbage, and coffee; for supper, scrambled eggs, carrots and bread.

Every morning, as they passed through the bare, bleak connecting corridors of the gaol to take their places in the courtroom, they

193

were screened from the view of other prisoners. For the first few weeks of the trial they had to pass an open space. One day an ss prisoner threw a knife at them; thereafter, this space was boarded up. At the end of the corridor from the cells the prisoners stepped into a steel lift to go up to the courtroom on the second floor. The lift was divided into separate compartments to minimize the chances of their passing anything to each other on their brief journey.

Whenever the gaol commander, an American colonel, Burton C. Andrus, or any Allied officer or civilian entered a cell, the prisoner inside had to rise and remain standing at attention until ordered to do otherwise. Every morning each prisoner swept out his own cell. Their routine job was cleaning dustbins. As they shambled around the exercise yard outside, they had to maintain a space of at least ten yards between them. They were forbidden to pick up anything from the ground.

Punishment for disobeying these orders was a loss of privileges, which included the most precious right of all: the chance to exchange the gloom of a cell each day for a walk under guard around the dingy courtyard; the chance to breathe fresh air under a square of open autumn sky.

Partly to prevent the onset of melancholia and also to keep them alert, each prisoner faced a number of regular appointments every day; visits from the padre, the doctor, the barber. They were allowed selected books to read, pencils and paper if they wanted to write, even a small monthly ration of tobacco. A Lutheran Evangelic parson and a Roman Catholic priest ministered to their spiritual needs in a small chapel with an improvised altar. Most prisoners attended a service at one time or another. Hess did not. He claimed that he was a Christian but not a churchgoer; he said he refused to go in case people might say he was afraid of death.

The four-and-a-half years that Hess had spent under guard in Britain had left their mark on his appearance. His face was cadaverous; his once thick hair was thinning, and the dark, intense eyes looked dull under their bushy brows. Hess weighed less than ten stone, and in a sports coat bought in Abergavenny and not too good a fit, he looked little like the spruce, commanding figure who had parachuted down to Eaglesham in 1941. Indeed, all the defendants looked like caricatures of the men they had once been. Goering, much thinner, and pasty, with puffy eyes, sat in the blue-grey uniform he had once filled so well, now stripped of all the medal ribbons. Hess's face was the colour of clay and his eyes more deepset and sunken than ever. Ribbentrop, in a brown suit, a light brown tie and a khaki shirt, seemed unrecognisable as the former German Ambassador who had given the Nazi salute in London on so many occasions. The aristocratic von Papen, in a dark pin-striped blue suit, with a clean white handkerchief in his breast pocket, was easily the best dressed prisoner; von Schirach, the Nazi youth leader, possibly the best looking.

On the morning of November 21, Goering, who had prepared notes of a political statement he wished to deliver through the medium of the Court, stood up.

'Before I answer the question of whether or not I am guilty', he began. The President, Lord Justice Lawrence, son of a Lord Chief Justice, interrupted him. Goering was reminded that he was entitled to make no statement, only to plead Guilty or Not Guilty. For a moment Goering hesitated, then he said: 'Not Guilty.'

The trial had begun and the Lord Justice Lawrence had exerted his authority. From then on this short, thick-set man dominated proceedings from the bench he shared with Sir Norman Birkett—now Lord Birkett—and the other Allied members of the Tribunal. Lord Lawrence handled witnesses with patience and dignity, but he could challenge counsel with a firm rasping voice when the occasion arose.

The British dominated the prosecution. Sir Hartley Shawcross—now Lord Shawcross—led the British team, but as Attorney-General in the Socialist Government, he also had political and other commitments in Britain. Sir David Maxwell Fyfe—now Lord Kilmuir—conducted his cross-examination brilliantly and soon became the counsel most feared by the prisoners.

Hess appeared curiously remote from the proceedings, and detached, as though he had no part of them. Whereas the other Nazi leaders seemed tense and nervous, as though clearly aware of their fate, Hess gazed around him with the bland imperviousness of a man not quite certain why he was there at all, and what all this array of judges and lawyers had to do with him.

He still kept up the pretence that he had lost his memory. To Allied interrogators who showed Hess photographs of Hitler, Goering and others of his Nazi colleagues, he simply repeated: 'I remember nothing. I cannot remember.' Even when brought face to face with Goering and Von Papen, he insisted that he did not recognize them. He still claimed that he was being poisoned, and refused to eat food which was not first tasted by someone else in his presence.

His counsel, Dr von Rohrscheidt, resolutely maintained that his client was not fit to stand trial. 'He doesn't seem to remember very much about his wife and son,' he explained. 'He hasn't even asked to see them.'

This was quite true, but it did not arise through any question of insanity. Hess refused to see them then—and has still not seen them since—because, as he explains in letters to his wife, he has conditioned himself to life as a prisoner. Should he see his wife and son again for the brief period that is all visitors are allowed to spend with prisoners, then the protective shell he had so carefully and painfully built around himself would be destroyed for ever. The cocoon of isolation would be ruined, and so would his spirit: the prospect of further imprisonment would be unbearable.

As the trial progressed, the ex-Deputy Führer behaved in a way intensely annoying to Goering and the other Nazi leaders, who thought that their trial should be conducted in an atmosphere of dignity that befitted their position as world figures. On the first day, Hess entirely ignored his surroundings and the people around— judges, counsel, even his companions in the dock. He sat back on his bench, earphones switched off, eyes closed, apparently asleep. He showed a small flicker of interest for a few moments on the second day when a diagram explaining the organization of the Nazi Party was exhibited with his own name prominent; then he lapsed once more into apathy. He did not recognize the authority of the court; this was his way of demonstrating his contempt for it.

On the morning of the third day, Hess underlined this by bringing a novel into the dock with him. For much of the trial he sat reading, despite a rebuke from Goering, who told him: 'You are disgracing us.' Even when his own name was under discussion, Hess showed no interest; he simply read on, laying his book aside from time to time, either to close his eyes or to stare vacantly into the public galleries.

His counsel had a different explanation of his client's deliberate indifference. 'He is paying no attention to the proceedings because he is convinced that there will be a death sentence for all the Nazi Party Leaders,' von Rohrscheidt explained. 'He has reconciled himself to it, preferring to amuse himself by reading.'

On November 30th, Hess found himself alone in the limelight. The early part of the day had been taken up with a special showing of a film that revealed the horrors of Nazi concentration camps. Even the defendants seemed moved by this fearful evidence; only Hess continued to absorb himself in his reading, never once glancing at the screen.

Then his counsel rose to speak. 'I am of the opinion that the defendant is not capable of pleading,' he said. 'I therefore consider it my duty and I feel forced to make the following application:

'Firstly, I should ask that the proceedings against Hess be temporarily quashed; secondly, in case his inability to plead should be admitted by the Tribunal, I should request the Tribunal not to carry out the proceedings if the defendant is not there. But in case the Tribunal should consider Hess fit to plead, I should ask for an arbitral expert opinion in order to decide the question.

'Before I come to the reasons for my application, I should like to say on behalf of the defendant that he, Hess himself, thinks he is fit to plead and would like to tell the court so himself . . .

'If my defendant—my client, rather—should not be fit to plead, I should like the proceedings against Hess to be temporarily quashed.

'I should like to refer to the opinions already submitted to the Tribunal. In this opinion it is said that the capacity of the defendant Hess is reduced. That is to say, his capacity to defend himself and to face a witness and to understand the evidence. I have cited this formulation because it is closest to the question put to the experts by the Tribunal.

'The opinion says that even if Hess's amnesia does not prevent the defendant from understanding what is going on about him and to follow the proceedings in court . . . the capability of the defendant Hess is reduced in respect of being able to defend himself, to face a witness, and to understand the details of the evidence given . . .

'I am of the opinion that this statement made by the medical experts shows, as was stated in the question to the experts, that on account of this mental defect, the amnesia, proper defence for the defendant Hess is not possible. The opinions also assume that the defendant is not actually insane. That is not the important point at the moment because according to the medical opinion it is affirmatively stated, in my opinion, that the defendant is not in a condition to follow everything in consequence of the reduction of his mental capacity.

'I consider that the defendant—I am basing this on my own experience with him—is not capable of understanding what the Tribunal says to him in such a manner as is necessary for his defence, because his memory is very unreliable.

'Through his loss of memory he knows neither events which have happened in the past nor the persons who were associated with him in the past. I therefore am of the opinion that the opposite opinion of the defendant himself, namely, that he is fit to plead, is irrelevant.

'As the reduction of the defendant's capacity, according to medical opinion, will not soon be improved, I am therefore of the opinion that the proceedings against defendant Hess should be quashed . . .

'If the defendant is not capable of pleading, incapable of defending himself, as medical opinion says, and if this state is likely to last for a long time, this would be a condition for temporary suspension of the proceedings against him.'

The President: 'I want to ask you one question: Is it not consistent with all the medical opinions that the defendant is capable of understanding the course of the proceedings, and that the only illness from which he is suffering is his forgetfulness about what happened before he flew to England?'

Dr von Rohrscheidt: 'Mr President, it is true that the experts say that the defendant Hess is capable of following the proceedings. But they emphasize, on the other hand, that the defendant is not capable of defending himself. In the manner in which the questions were put to the experts, the Tribunal asked the experts to state their views on the follownig: Is the defendant mentally sound or not?

'This question is answered by all experts in the affirmative, that he is mentally sound. But that does not exclude the fact that the defendant might at the moment be incapable of pleading and in this respect the experts again, referring to the questions put to them—the Tribunal would like to know whether the defendant is capable of following the course of the proceedings?'

General Roman Rudenko, the chief Russian Prosecutor: 'In connection with the statement made by the defence, and as a result of the doctor's opinion, I am inclined to say the following: the condition of Hess was examined by experts. These experts appointed by the Tribunal have agreed that Hess is sane and can answer for his actions. The Chief Prosecutors have discussed the results of this according to the orders of the Tribunal . . . We have no questions and doubts about the Commission's report. We are of opinion that Hess can be tried . . .'

Sir David Maxwell-Fyfe, the British Deputy Chief Prosecutor: 'May it please the Tribunal: it has been suggested that I might say just a word, and as shortly as the Tribunal desire, as to the legal conceptions which govern the position with which the Tribunal and this defendant are placed at the present time.

'The question before the Tribunal is whether this defendant is able to plead to the Indictment and should be tried at the present time.

'If I might very briefly refer the Tribunal to the short passages in the report, which I submit are relevant, it might be useful at the present time. The first report is that signed by the British doctors on November 19th, 1945.

'And in that report the signatories say: "At the moment he is not insane in the strict sense. His loss of memory will not entirely interfere with his comprehension of the proceedings, but it will interfere with his ability to make his defence, and to understand details of the past, which arise in evidence."

'The next report is that signed by the American and French doctors, "We find, as a result of our examinations and investigations, that Rudolf Hess is suffering from hysteria characterized in part by loss of memory. The nature of this loss of memory is such that it will not interfere with his comprehension of the proceedings, but it will interfere with his response to questions relating to his past and will interfere with his undertaking his defence."

'If the Tribunal will proceed to the third report, signed by the Soviet doctors, there is a paragraph beginning "Psychologically"— which I submit is of importance—"Psychologically, Hess is in a state of clear consciousness; knows that he is imprisoned at Nurnberg under indictment as a war criminal; has read and, according to his own words, is acquainted with the charges against him.

' "He answers questions rapidly and to the point. His speech is coherent, his thoughts formed with precision and correctness and they are accompanied by sufficient emotionally expressive movements. Also, there is no kind of evidence of paranoia.

' "It should also be noted here that the present psychological examinations, which were conducted by Lt. Gilbert, Doctor of Medicine, and of the testimony, is that the intelligence of Hess is normal and in some instances above average. His movements are natural and not forced."

'Now, if I may come to the report which is signed by the three Soviet doctors and Professor Delay of Paris, dated the 16th, which is the last in my bundle, that says in Paragraph 3:

' "At present he is not insane in the strict sense of the word. His amnesia does not prevent him completely from understanding what is going on around him, but it will interfere with his ability to conduct his defence and to understand details of the past which would appear as factual data . . ."

'In these circumstances, the question in English law, and I respectfully submit that to the consideration of the Tribunal as being representative of natural justice in this regard, is, in deciding whether the defendant be insane or not, and the time which is relevant for the deciding of that issue is at the date of the arrangement and not at any prior time.

'Different views have been expressed as to the party on whom the onus of proof lies in that issue, but the latter, and logically the better view, is that the onus is on the defendant, because it is always presumed that a person is sane until the contrary is proved . . .

'I submit he should be tried.'

The long and convoluted argument went on, to the obvious amusement of Hess, who sat grinning at the various theories put forward. Finally, the President of the Court addressed his counsel.

'Dr Rohrscheidt,' he said, 'the Tribunal would like, if you consider it proper, that the Defendant Hess should state what his views on this question are.'

Dr. Rohrscheidt:

'As his defence counsel, I have certainly nothing to say against it, and I think it would be the defendant's own wish, and the Tribunal would then be in a position to judge what mental state the defendant is in. He can speak as to whether he considers himself fit to plead from where he is.'

At these words a startling change occurred in Hess's attitude. With something of the old confidence he had displayed at Nazi party rallies, he rose from his seat and strode purposefully to the microphone placed in the well of the court. Plucking an old envelope from his jacket pocket, he began to read from some notes he had scribbled on it.

'Mr President, I would like to say this: at the beginning of the trial of this afternoon's proceedings I gave my defence counsel a note that I am of the opinion that these proceedings could be shortened if one would allow me to speak myself. What I say is as follows:

'In order to anticipate any possibility of my being declared incapable of pleading, although I am willing to take part in the rest of the proceedings with the rest of them, I would like to give the Tribunal the following declaration, although I originally intended not to make this declaration until a later point in the proceedings:

'My memory is again in order. The reasons why I simulated loss of memory were tactical. In fact, it is only that my capacity for concentration is slightly reduced. But in consequence of that, my capacity to follow the trial, my capacity to defend myself, to put questions to witnesses or even to answer questions—these, my capacities, are not influenced by that.

'I emphasize the fact that I bear the full responsibility for everything that I have done or signed as signatory or co-signatory. My attitude in principle, is that the Tribunal is not competent—is not affected by the statement I have just made.

'Hitherto in conversation with my official defence counsel I have maintained my loss of memory. He was, therefore, in good faith when he asserted I lost my memory.'

There was only one answer for the President to give. 'The trial is adjourned,' he said.

Crumpling the envelope back into his pocket. Hess returned to his seat near the corner of the dock and sat there, smiling ironically as tumult and uproar broke out around him. He was easily the most composed man in the entire courtroom.

Later and privately, von Rohrscheidt insisted that his client was not entirely sane. 'I still claim that Hess isn't fit to defend himself,' he said. 'This one statement, which caught everyone by surprise, doesn't suddenly restore him to normality.'

This was not in accordance with his client's own opinion. After declaring that he had made 'the psychiatrists of five nations look ridiculous', Hess added modestly that it was all really of no importance, as he expected to be executed, anyway.

That night Major Douglas Kelley, the American psychiatrist in Nuremberg, saw Hess. Later, in the course of a report, he noted that

'He was elated over the impression he had created in the courtroom and stated that his memory was now in good shape. He claimed that his memory now extended throughout his entire life, but on persistent questioning indicated that there were still a number of things on which he was not quite clear and for which his memory was still faulty.

'The reaction of his fellow prisoners was not so enthusiastic. Goering was amazed and upset, and while he enjoyed the frustration of the Court, demonstrated considerable resentment that he had been so completely fooled.

'Von Schirach felt that such behaviour was not the action of a normal man, and while he enjoyed Hess's jest upon the world, felt that it was not a gesture expected of a good German whose position was as important as that of Hess.

'Ribbentrop, upon learning the news, was dumbfounded, and was hardly able to speak when told Hess's statement, and merely kept repeating: "Hess, you mean Hess? The Hess we have here? He said that?" Ribbentrop became quite agitated and seemed to feel such action was not possible. He stated: "But Hess did not know me. I looked at him. I talked to him. Obviously he did not know me. It is just not possible. Nobody could fool me like that."

'Streicher's comment, as usual, was direct and blunt: "If you ask me, I think Hess's behaviour was a shame. It reflects on the dignity of the German people . . ." [1]

Hess was also interviewed by Dr G. M. Gilbert, the British psychiatrist, who wrote: 'Two days after his dramatic "recovery" I broached the subject of Hitler's attitude towards his mental state and flight to England, merely asking him if he knew what Hitler had said and done about it at the time.

'Hess bristled and retorted: "I don't know what he said and I don't want to know! It doesn't interest me!" [2]

Four days after Hess's dramatic avowal the Tribunal announced its decision on the question of his sanity.

Lord Justice Lawrence, the President, said:

'The Tribunal has considered the very full medical reports, which have been made on the condition of the defendant Hess, and has come to the conclusion that no ground whatever exists for a further examination to be ordered . . .

'The Tribunal is of the opinion that the defendant Hess is capable of standing his trial at the present time, and the motion of the counsel for the defence is therefore denied.'

So the legend of Hess's insanity, started by Hitler at Hess's own suggestion, followed up by Churchill to try and undermine the importance of his mission, was finally killed.

On February 7, 1946, the Allies began their case against the former Deputy Führer.

Mr Mervyn Griffith Jones, opening the British case, said that originally he had intended to prove Hess's guilt by means of captured documents showing his individual responsibility, but the crimes were organized on such a scale that 'everyone in authority must have known of them'.

[1] *The Case of Rudolf Hess.*
[2] *Ibid.*

He declared that Hess was 'deeply involved' in the preparation of aggression upon Austria and Czechoslovakia, and he had been concerned in sending the Waffen ss to Poland, where they destroyed the Warsaw ghetto. Mr Griffith Jones said that among the many documents bearing Hess's signature which had been discovered in Germany were several providing penalties for offences against the State (Third Reich), the Nuremberg decrees against the Jews, and the law extending these decrees to Austria. Also, Hess was supreme head of the Organization of Germans Abroad, which formed the basis of the Nazi Fifth Column.

Mr Griffith Jones said that he had in his hand a copy of the statement Mr Anthony Eden made to Parliament on September 22, 1943, when the Foreign Secretary said that Hess claimed to have come 'on a mission of humanity'. Hess had 'authoritatively' put forward six proposals which had all the appearance of coming direct from the Führer, and he had added a 'savage threat' that if, after a successful invasion of Britain, the Churchill Government carried out its plan to continue the fight from Canada, the people of Britain would be deliberately starved to death. Mr Griffith Jones alleged that at the time Hess put forward these proposals he already knew of the planned 'Action Barbarossa'—the pending German invasion of Russia.

The first document referred to in detail was the Duke of Hamilton's report of his interview with Hess.

Mr Griffith Jones also produced an official record of a conversation between von Ribbentrop and Mussolini in Rome on May 13, 1941, three days after Hess's flight to Britain. It stated that Ribbentrop said the Führer had sent him to the Duce to inform him about the Hess affair. The Führer had been taken completely aback by Hess's action. Von Ribbentrop described it as 'the action of a lunatic', and said that Hitler had been 'deeply shaken'. The Führer had stripped Hess of his rank and had said that he would have him shot if he returned to Germany. Mr Griffith Jones added how von Ribbentrop had told Mussolini that Hess had been suffering for a long time from bilious complaints and had fallen into the hands of 'magnetists and nature cure doctors'. Von Ribbentrop said Hess had not acted from any lack of faithfulness to the Führer and with this Mussolini agreed.

Referring to Hess's flight to Britain, Griffith Jones said: 'It is difficult to see how he could plan it, practise it for months, and make three unsuccessful attempts without anybody knowing. But at any rate we can see what von Ribbentrop was saying to his Italian ally three days later.' Then, turning to face Ribbentrop, he said with quiet but deadly effect: 'Of course, we all know that von Ribbentrop is a liar.'

Dr Gilbert, studying Hess's mental relapse, watched him in court while Mr Griffith Jones was speaking.

Later he wrote: 'The prosecutor's scorn was shared by even the defendants, who felt partly amused and partly disgraced by the naïve and presumptuous gesture by Hess in offering the British peace on his terms. During the presentation. Goering repeatedly turned to Hess and asked him if he had really said that. Hess nodded that he had. 'At the end of the session, Goering, hardly able to control his own scorn at Hess's attempt to meddle in diplomacy, slapped him on the back in mock congratulation and encouragement for a good try.'

Hess's continued apparent lack of interest in the proceedings did not necessarily mean a relapse to the condition he had simulated at the opening of the trial, but as the time drew near for his defence, speculation was intense as to whether he would actually take the stand.

Shortly before the day his counsel, Dr Rohrscheidt, was due to speak in Hess's defence, he broke his leg. As a result, he was unable to appear in court, and another lawyer now enters this strange story: Dr Alfred Seidl. For five years during the war Seidl had been a private soldier (First Class) with the infantry stationed in Bavaria. After the war he joined the office of a successful Munich lawyer, Dr Sauter. In October 1945 the American authorities offered Sauter the opportunity of defending some of the Nazi leaders at Nuremberg. At first Sauter declined the assignment. Then, having reconsidered the matter, he changed his mind and sent Seidl to Nuremberg to discover whether the briefs could still be obtained. Seidl was thus the first defence counsel to see the prisoners, and to take their statements and generally prepare the way for his senior colleagues.

One of the first defendants he met was Dr Hans Frank, formerly Governor-General of German-occupied concentration camps and sending labourers back to Germany. Before the war Frank had been a lawyer practising in Munich, and he appeared pleased to meet Seidl, and asked him to take over his defence.

It was thus agreed that while Sauter would defend Baldur von Schirach, the Hitler Youth leader and Gauleiter of Vienna from 1940 to 1945, and Walther Funk, Hitler's Minister of Economics and President of the Reichbank, Seidl would defend Dr Frank. When

Dr Rohrscheidt broke his leg, leaving Hess without a lawyer, the former Deputy Führer asked Seidl to take over his defence as well. Seidl agreed.

Physically the two men were the antithesis of each other. Hess was tall and gaunt, and moody; Seidl was a plump, short, bouncing man with irrepressible good humour and vivacity. They got on well together. Looking back on those days, Seidl insists that Hess was completely sane in the normally accepted sense of the word, but agrees that he was a strange man, given to long and brooding silences. But then the reception accorded to his peace proposals in Britain, and the four years he had spent in Mytchett and Abergavenny had not done anything to improve this side of his character.

When Seidl opened the defence for him on March 22, Hess was still facing the original four charges: War Crimes, Crimes against Humanity, Conspiracy, and Crimes against Peace. Seidl felt confident that his client would be acquitted of War Crimes and Crimes against Humanity, if only for the fact that Hess had not been in Germany while the wartime barbarities against Jews and occupied countries had been carried out.

The charges that worried him were those of Conspiracy and Crimes against Peace, for clearly, as one of the inner caucus of the Nazi Party, Hess had obviously discussed with Hitler the events that led to war, and until May 1941 had been privy to the Führer's decisions. There thus seemed little chance that Hess would be acquitted on these charges, but Seidl, a most resourceful lawyer, was not a man to surrender easily. He believed that if he could find some way of discrediting the Court; if he could somehow show that there had also been any conspiracy against peace on the part of one or more of the Four Powers—Britain, America, France or Russia—who were judging the German defendants, then, on a point of law—Hess might yet go free.

For days he puzzled over this problem. Then, quite unexpectedly, he found the loophole he was seeking. One afternoon, as he was leaving for home after a long and unrewarding discussion with his client, he heard Goering and Ribbentrop discussing their chances and the probable outcome of the trials. Ribbentrop was explaining that when he had been in Moscow in August 1939 to arrange the German-Soviet treaty, he and Molotov, the Soviet Foreign Minister, had also signed a secret treaty, word of which had never been made public.

In brief, this secret agreement defined 'spheres of interest' in the event of any war. On a map of Europe the Foreign Minister had drawn a line along the Vistula and the Bug, two rivers which divide Poland. Then they had agreed that, should war come, the territories to the West of these rivers would become a German 'sphere of interest', and those to the East would be under Russian control. The Soviet sphere included Finland, Estonia, Latvia, the eastern parts of Poland and certain areas of Roumania. Ribbentrop added conversationally to Goering that the Russians had told him since his arrest that it would be—so he said—'easier' for him if he did not mention the matter of this secret agreement in Court. Certainly if he did not, no one else would, for it was not in the German interests to bring it up—if anyone else even knew of it.

At once Seidl realized the fearful significance of this conversation, and how it might be turned to his client's advantage. After the military action of Germany and Russia against Lithuania, Latvia and Estonia in June 1940, the German Reichsregierung and the Soviet Government had vehemently denied that they had concluded any other political agreement apart from the treaty concerning boundaries, on August 23, 1939, and one of mutual friendship signed on September 20. Despite this, rumours had nevertheless persisted that another secret agreement had also been reached. Now, these suspicions seemed justified.

If Seidl could verify and substantiate this conversation, then, in his view, Stalin was equally as guilty of crimes against peace and conspiracy as any of the Nazis in the dock. In Seidl's argument the Russian leader, or his representatives, could not be a judge as well as a defendant.

Seidl began an immediate search for anyone who had accompanied Ribbentrop to this meeting in Moscow seven years earlier to discuss whether there had been an additional and secret agreement.

It seemed a difficult, almost hopeless task. Germany was a ruined country, laid waste by war, on the brink of famine. Hundreds of thousands were homeless; postal communications were chaotic, railway journeys almost impossible. In these circumstances, it seemed unlikely that he would be successful, but Seidl, as well as being diligent, was also fortunate.

He located a brother lawyer, Dr Friedrich Gaus, who had been Under-Secretary of State and Ambassador in the Foreign Office and who, in this capacity, had accompanied Ribbentrop on his journey to Moscow in 1939. Was there such a secret pact? Seidl asked him. Yes, replied Gaus; he remembered it clearly. Where could a copy of it be found now? Gaus had no idea, but he told Seidl that to the best of his knowledge, all important files of the German Foreign Office had been micro-filmed at the end of the war and surrendered to officials of the United States.

Seidl was thus still some way from his objective; having found the man he sought, he now had to unearth the papers that were essential to his case. This seemed a task at least as difficult, but he persevered. He mentioned his search to everyone he met, and brought up the subject deliberately when in the presence of American officers.

As the days passed without bringing any result, his cheerful round face concealed the worry he felt about the apparent hopelessness of this search. And then one evening as he was leaving the Court, his endeavours were unexpectedly and mysteriously rewarded.

An American in officer's uniform approached him. 'Are you Alfred Seidl?' he asked in German. Seidl nodded.

The American introduced himself, and handed him a plain sealed envelope that bore no name or address. 'I think there is something here that you've been looking for,' he said.

Seidl was puzzled, but ripped open the envelope. It contained a typed copy of an agreement apparently reached between Molotov and Ribbentrop in Moscow, 1939. Seidl looked up in amazement to ask the American where he had found this, but the man had disappeared. He could be any one of a score of other Americans in uniform strolling through the late sunshine.

That night Seidl read the document through a number of times. It was not a photostat, and it bore no seals or other marks of authenticity. Was it possible that the paper was a fake, a forgery?

Seidl again sought out Dr Gaus and showed it to him. So far as Dr Gaus could recollect, it seemed a true copy of the same pact. He willingly signed an affidavit[1] explaining what had happened in Moscow in 1939, and the terms and the implications of this pact.

Looking back now, Seidl thinks that the document was made available to him so expeditiously because the American authorities were genuinely astonished at the discovery of this secret document. They wanted to make known the perfidy of the Germans and Russians to as wide an audience as possible. Seidl was a useful person to perform this function, because he could easily introduce the paper at the trial; there would thus be no need for the Americans to make a special issue of the matter.

[1] See Appendix for full translation.

Meanwhile, the case went on. Throughout the hearing Hess kept repeating to Seidl that he did not acknowledge the authority of the Court to try him. Seidl advised his client that he should not go into the witness stand. Also, he should behave in such a way that no one would have any doubt as to his feelings about the Court's authority.

Hess should continue to sit and read a novel and look bored with the proceedings, and yawn and even laugh out loud if he reached an amusing passage in his book. Seidl reasoned that this behaviour would underline his own plea to show that the Court was not fit to try Hess.

When the defence opened on March 22, Dr Seidl declared: 'The defendant Hess contests the jurisdiction of the Tribunal in so far as other than war crimes proper are the subject of the trial. However, he specifically assumes full responsibility for all laws or decrees which he has signed. Furthermore, he assumes responsibility for all orders and directives which he, in his capacity as Deputy Führer and Minister of the Reich, has issued. For these reasons he does not desire to be defended against any charges which refer to the internal affairs of Germany as a Sovereign State.'

Here Hess, who for once had shown some interest in the proceedings, jumped to his feet and shouted angrily: 'I don't want to be defended—I accept responsibility for what I have done!'

Unperturbed by this interruption, Dr Seidl continued: 'This applies, among other things, to the motives which caused Rudolf Hess to fly to England and to the purposes for which he was doing it . . . I shall today only read the affidavit of the witness Hildegard Fath.[1] The affidavit reads as follows:

'Having been advised of the consequences of a false affidavit, I declare the following which is to be submitted to the International Military Tribunal in Nuremberg under oath.

'I was employed as private secretary of the Führer's Deputy, Rudolf Hess, in Munich, from October 17, 1933, until his flight to England on May 10, 1941.

'Beginning in the summer of 1940—I cannot remember the exact time—I had, by order of Hess, to obtain secret weather reports about weather conditions over the British Isles and the North Sea, and to forward them to Hess. I received the reports from a Captain Busch. In part I also received reports from Fraulein Sperr, the Secretary of Hess, with his liaison staff in Berlin.

'Hess left a letter behind on his departure by air for England,

[1] Secretary to Rudolf Hess for many years.

which was handed to the Führer at a time when Hess had already landed in England. I read a copy of this letter. The letter began with the words like this: "My Führer, when you receive this letter, I shall be in England."

'I do not remember the exact wording of the letter . . .

'I can, however, state definitely that no word was mentioned about the Soviet Union or about the idea that a peace treaty should be concluded with England in order to have the rear free on another front. If this had been discussed in the letter, it certainly would have been impressed upon my memory.

'From the content of the letter the definite impression was to be gained that Hess undertook this extraordinary flight in order to prevent further bloodshed, and in order to create favourable conditions for the conclusion of a peace . . .'

March 24—the ninetieth day on which the defendants had trooped in and sat down like docile schoolboys upon the hard wooden benches, was taken up by Dr Seidl in reading out Hess's own account of his interview with Lord Simon.

The trial dragged on. Hess went back to reading his novel, sometimes grinning widely from the dock, at other times occupying his time by sending a stream of scribbled messages to Dr Seidl.

On March 30 Ribbentrop was questioned about the secret agreement. He grudgingly admitted its existence. 'If war broke out,' he said, 'occupation of those zones was to be undertaken by Germany and Russia. At that time I heard expressions both from Stalin and Hitler that Polish and other territories thus delineated were regions which both sides had lost in an unfortunate war.' No more details were allowed, but even so the significance of this pact did not seem to be realized until Dr Seidl rose to speak.

Dr Seidl said that if the court would not allow full details of the pact to be known he would demand that Molotov, Russia's Foreign Minister, should be called as a witness. He declared that this would bring 'at least one of the prosecuting nations into the conspiracy that led to the war'.

Later Baron von Weizäcker, formerly Secretary of State in the German Foreign Office, was put in the box, and Seidl pursued the matter by putting a copy of the pact to him. He explained that it had been handed to him by 'an Allied officer whose name could not be divulged'.

This move instantly brought General Roman Rudenko, the Soviet prosecutor, to his feet. He clearly had no idea that a copy of the secret agreement was in existence; perhaps he did not know that there had been a secret agreement, but, as an experienced lawyer, he immediately recognized the political dynamite in Seidl's hands. He objected most strongly to any mention of the document. The court was investigating the case of the major German war criminals, he said, and not the foreign policy of the Allies, and 'this anonymous document', already rejected by the Tribunal, 'could have no probative value'.

Despite this, after some discussion among the Judges, Weizäcker was allowed to speak of the affair from his memory, which provided the most informative summary of the pact so far heard. This secret protocol of extensive scope, he confirmed, drew a line of demarcation between areas which in given circumstances would be 'of interest' to the Soviet Union, and those which would belong to the German sphere of interest. In the Soviet sphere were included Finland, Estonia, Latvia, the eastern parts of Poland, and certain areas of Roumania; everything west of that line was left to Germany.

Later, in September or October, he continued, amendments were agreed upon by which Lithuania or the greater part of it was transferred to the Soviet sphere, and the line of demarcation in Poland was moved considerably to the west. Explicitly or implicitly, the secret agreement was to create a completely new order in Poland, and when it came into operation this line of demarcation was followed closely.

In answer to Lord Justice Lawrence, the witness stated that he had kept a photostat copy of the pact in his personal safe, and that he would have no hesitation in recognizing it if it were put to him. This again seemed a chance for Seidl but again he was refused permission to state his unique defence.

After a long adjournment the President declared that the contents of the secret pact had been confirmed 'from several sources', but since the origin of the present document was unknown it would not be put to the witness. Seidl had made his point—but he had not won his case.

On July 5 he opened the final defence speech for Hess. Seven times Lord Justice Lawrence rebuked him for trying to claim that the Treaty of Versailles had been illegal and unjust. Finally, the Tribunal adjourned for two hours and asked him to submit a new pleading. Seidl did so.

'I come now to the event which was to conclude the political career of the defendant Rudolf Hess, his flight to England on May 10, 1941,' he began. 'For several reasons this undertaking is of considerable importance in this trial as evidence. As is shown by the presentation of the evidence, the defendant Rudolf Hess had made the decision for this flight as early as June 1940—that is, immediately after the surrender of France . . .

'When the defendant Hess was led before the Duke of Hamilton on the day after his landing, he declared to the latter, "I come on a mission of humanity." During the conversation which the defendant had with Mr Kirkpatrick of the Foreign Office on the 13th, 14th, 15th of May, he explained to him in detail the motives which had induced him to take this extraordinary step. At the same time he informed him of the conditions under which Hitler would be prepared to make peace.

'On July 9th a conversation took place between Rudolf Hess and Lord Simon, who interviewed him on behalf of the British Government . . . It is shown by this document that the motive for this extraordinary flight was the intention to avoid further bloodshed and to create favourable conditions for the opening of peace negotiations.

'During the course of this conversation, the defendant Hess handed a document to Lord Simon which stated the four conditions under which Hitler would have been prepared at that time to conclude peace with England. The conditions were:

'1. In order to prevent future wars between the Axis and England, a delimitation of sphere of interests is proposed. The sphere of interest of the Axis Powers is to be Europe, and that of England its colonial Empire.

'2. Return of German colonies;

'3. Indemnification of German nationals who were domiciled prior to or during the war in the British Empire, and who suffered damage to life or property because of measures taken by a government in the Empire or through incidents such as pillage, riots, etc. Indemnification to British nationals on the same basis in Germany.

'4. Conclusion of an armistice and peace treaty with Italy at the same time.

'Rudolf Hess explained to Mr Kirkpatrick, as well as to Lord Simon, that such were the terms on which Hitler was prepared to make peace with Great Britain. Hitler had undergone no further change since completion of the campaign against France.

'There are no indications of any kind why this account of the

211

defendant should not appear plausible. On the contrary, it is fully in harmony with many statements which Hitler himself had made concerning relations between Germany and England.

'In addition to that, the defendants Goering and von Ribbentrop likewise confirmed while in the witness box that the terms which Hess disclosed to Lord Simon corresponded completely with Hitler's views.

'The defendant Hess himself does not wish to have any favourable conclusions drawn for him on the course of this trial from this flight and from the intentions connected with it. His influence on the course of events within the development of the war as a whole ceased, at the latest, with his flight to England.

'That it was his intention thus to protect Germany's rear in its planned campaign against the Soviet Union . . . is contradicted by the fact that the defendant Hess had already decided on the flight as early as June 1940, in other words, at a time when no one in Germany thought of a campaign against the Soviet Union . . .

'Had the defendant Rudolf Hess been successful in establishing the necessary conditions for an armistice and peace negotiations in England, the political and military situation in Europe would have been so fundamentally changed that under these modified conditions an attack by the Soviet Union on Germany would have appeared most unlikely, and the apprehensions entertained by Hitler would have become untenable.

'The conclusion must be drawn that the criminal responsibility of the defendant Hess will in any case be confined to acts which were committed prior to the flight to England.'

On August 31st, the two hundred and sixteenth day of the trial, more than nine months after he had first been led into the court-room, Rudolf Hess was called to make a last speech in his own defence before the Judges pronounced sentence.

President: 'I call on the defendant Rudolf Hess.'

Hess: 'First of all, I should like to make a request to the High Tribunal that I may remain seated because of my state of health.'

President: 'Certainly.'

Hess: 'Some of my comrades here can confirm the fact that at the beginning of the proceedings I predicted the following:

'1. Witnesses would appear who, under oath, would make untrue statements and, at the same time, would be able to create an impression of absolute reliability, and would be highly thought of.

'2. It was to be reckoned with that the Tribunal would receive affidavits containing untrue statements.

'3. The defendants would be astonished and surprised by some German witnesses.

'4. Some of the defendants would act rather strangely. They would make shameless utterances about the Führer, they would incriminate each other, and wrongly. Perhaps they would even incriminate themselves, and also wrongly.

'All of these predictions have come true, and as far as the witnesses and affidavits are concerned, in dozens of cases; cases in which statements under the equivocal oath of the defendants stand in opposition to statements formerly sworn by them . . .

'In the years 1936 to 1938 political trials were taking place in one country. These were characterized by the fact that the defendants accused themselves in an astonishing way. For example, they cited a great number of crimes which they had committed or which they claimed to have committed. At the end, when death sentences were passed upon them, they clapped in frenzied approval, to the astonishment of the world . . .

'These incidents were recalled to my mind by a certain happening in England. While looking through some numbers of the *Völkische Beobachter* I came across . . . a report from Paris . . . about the means which were apparently used in these trials . . . These means make it possible for the selected victim to be made to act and speak according to the orders given them.'

Hess rambled on, taking in such diverse subjects as the number of casualties in the Boer War and his own spiritual relationship with the Church, until the President of the court interrupted him. 'I must draw the attention of the defendant Hess to the fact that he has already spoken for twenty minutes,' he pointed out. 'The Tribunal has indicated to the defendants that it cannot allow them to continue to make statements of great length at this stage of the proceedings. We have to hear all the defendants. The Tribunal therefore hopes that the defendant Hess will conclude his speech.'

Hess began to end his long peroration.

'I was permitted to work for many years of my life under the greatest son whom my country has brought forth in its thousand-year history,' he said proudly.

'Even if I could, I would not want to erase this period of time from my existence. I am happy to know that I have done my duty to my people, my duty as a German, as a National Socialist, as a loyal follower of my Führer. I do not regret anything.

'If I were to begin all over again, I would act just as I have acted, even if I knew that in the end I should meet a fiery death at the stake. No matter what human beings may do, I shall some day stand before the judgment seat of the Eternal. I shall answer to Him, and I know He will judge me innocent.'

Hess sat down. He had said his last words in public.

On October 1, 1946, Rudolf Hess was found Not Guilty of War Crimes and Crimes against Humanity, but, despite Seidl's ingenuity, guilty of Conspiracy and Crimes against Peace.

Delivering judgment, Lord Justice Lawrence said:

'Hess was an active supporter of the preparations for war . . . His signature established military service . . . He supported Hitler's policy of vigorous rearmament . . . He expressed a desire for peace and advocated international economic co-operation . . . but of all the defendants none knew better than Hess how determined Hitler was to realize his ambitions, how fanatical and violent a man he was.

'With him on his flight to England Hess carried certain peace proposals which he alleged Hitler was prepared to accept. It is significant to note that this flight took place only ten days after the date on which Hitler determined 22nd June, 1941, as that for attacking the Soviet Union.

'That Hess acts in an abnormal manner, suffers from loss of memory and has mentally deteriorated during this trial, may be true. There is nothing to show that he does not realize the nature of the charges against him, or is incapable of defending himself. There is no suggestion that Hess was not completely sane when the acts charged against him were committed.

'Defendant Rudolf Hess, on the counts of the Indictment on which you have been convicted, the Tribunal sentences you to imprisonment for life.'

Seidl had not saved his client, but his discovery of the secret German-Soviet agreement produced some unexpected results. First, it showed how hopeless had been the bargaining position of the British Government Mission which was sent to Moscow in 1939 to reach agreement with Russia. Nazi Germany could offer Russia a partition of Poland plus control of the Baltic States and Bessarabia, which Russia wanted. Britain, however, as the proclaimed champion of the independence of small nations, could not acquiesce to such proposals, and had no alternative propositions to offer.

At the time the failure of this British Mission was blamed on the fact that it had not been led by a Senior Minister, but by Mr William Strang, afterwards Lord Strang, whom Churchill later described as 'an able official but without any special standing outside the Foreign Office'.[1] In fact, Germany succeeded with Russia where Britain failed simply because Germany could offer Stalin what he wanted; Britain could not.

The next point to emerge from Seidl's ingenious defence was the astonishment it caused in the Russian prosecution. Rudenko was obviously amazed at the disclosure. No doubt their superiors felt that the news of this secret agreement should have been prevented from reaching the public. One Russian prosecuting lawyer, slightly junior to General Rudenko, died a violent death almost immediately afterwards; it was said that he had been killed while cleaning his pistol.

The American in uniform who handed Seidl the letter outside the Court was also dead within a matter of months. He was killed in Berlin while driving his car. Apparently it had been in a serious collision with another vehicle. But no other damaged vehicle was ever found, nor was one reported.

Lastly, Ribbentrop, despite the assurance he claimed the Russians had given him that his sentence would be 'easier' if he did not go into details of this pact, found that the promise vastly exceeded the performance; he was hanged.

When Hess came up for sentence the Russian judge, clearly acting on instructions from above, vociferously demanded the death penalty in a dissenting opinion. Stalin had obviously not forgotten what Beaverbrook had told him of Hess's mission in 1942.

* * *

Since 1947 Hess has been Prisoner No. 7 in Spandau Gaol. Ironically, the Nazis used this prison from 1933 until the end of the war as a collecting place for political prisoners on their way to concentration camps.

At first Hess's companions were Walther Funk, Erich Raeder, Albert Speer, Baldur von Schirach, Baron Constantin von Neurath and Karl Doenitz. One by one they were released, until now only

[1] *The Second World War*, vol. I: *The Gathering Storm*, Sir Winston S. Churchill.

Albert Speer, Hitler's Armaments Minister; von Schirach, the former Youth Leader; and Hess remain. Speer and von Schirach are serving twenty-year sentences; they can hope to end their days in freedom. Hess is there until he dies—or until the four Powers agree to remit his sentence. Spandau is the last organization that they control together. It is said that Britain, America and France have no wish to perpetuate this costly farce which ties up large numbers of troops and officials, plus an annual cost of £30,000 to the West Berlin Government. They would be willing to 'reconsider' the sentences. But the Russians will not agree.

Hess has consistently refused to see either his wife or his son, and this had been held against him. He will not see them because he has conditioned his mind and resigned himself to an acceptance of his situation. As he admits in letters to his wife, if he sees either her or the young man he last saw as a child of four, this protective cocoon of isolation would be broken; and the future would become even more unbearable than it is.

He is allowed to write and receive one letter a week. In his letters he shows no evidence of insanity. Once, when Ilse Hess offered to send him a shirt as a Christmas present, Hess replied that he had no use for such a thing. If the Four Powers kept him a prisoner, the least they could do was to see that he was clothed. In his letters home he gives his son good advice on the choice of a career (engineering), on the problems of a young man, on his aims and ambitions.

Ilse Hess has not had an easy life since the war. She left Munich in 1945 and travelled to Hindelang with her son. There the French arrested her; she was a prisoner for eighteen months. Her mother looked after the little boy. When she was released she had no work and no money. At one time her main source of income was to sell the puppies of her dachshund bitch.

Then a friend asked her to manage a small guest house, Die Bergherberg, in the Hindelang mountains. The owner has given her a special room there for her husband, should he ever be released; she remains confident that one day he will be freed and will come home to her.

The room is lined with pale unstained wood, and commands a magnificent view across the pine-covered mountains over which Hess flew on that Saturday evening, so long ago. Here are gathered such small possessions of her husband as she has been able to preserve through the war, the occupation and her own imprisonment. His books and his papers await him; his Siemens radio is still tuned to Kalundborg; even the toys he and his son played with together during the days before his flight are now stacked neatly in this empty room awaiting his return.

When her son Wolf Rüdiger was twenty-one and called up for national service in July 1959, he applied for exemption. In a letter to the Conscription Appeals Tribunal, he pointed out that the Nuremberg Trial in 1946, which had sentenced his father to life imprisonment, included representatives of the NATO powers. His conscience forbade him to do military service for the former judges of his father. He added that one of the reasons the court had given for their sentence on his father was the part he had played in building up the German Army. In these circumstances, it would be impossible for him to serve in this same army.

His appeal was rejected in February 1960. An official of the recruiting office explained: 'We exempt only those whose conscience forbids them to do military service on religious or philosophic grounds.' For all that, young Hess has heard no more of the matter; nor are there any indications that he will.

In Britain, three mementoes remain of his father's unsuccessful mission. First, in Lennoxlove, the home of the Duke of Hamilton, there is still preserved the creased and faded map by which Hess steered his course towards Eaglesham. The house is open to the public, who always show much interest in this relic.

Next, Douglas Percival still keeps a small leather wallet, embossed with a swastika, that Hess gave him when they parted in 1942. It is in a glass case in his home next to the ancient ruined abbey in Shaftesbury, Dorset. It was the wallet that held the photographs of his wife and son which Hess brought to prove his identity.

In Eaglesham, too, the arrival of Rudolf Hess is still vividly remembered. On the night he landed, Basil Baird, who lives in Floors Farm, went out when he heard the commotion in David McLean's house and marked the spot at which the parachutist descended with a large flat stone. This stone marks more than the arrival of an uninvited envoy from the night sky. It marks the hour and the place when Britain was presented with what seemed an easy road to peace; when Churchill chose instead the harder path of honour. It marks the time—possibly the only time—when Russia could have been defeated, and when the Communist shadows that now darken two-thirds of the world might have been dispelled for ever. The stone is weathered, mellowed and changed by twenty summers and winters. So are the other actors in this drama, those who still survive.

Only Hess seems curiously untouched by these passing twenty years that so quickly saw the crumbling of the Third Reich which Hitler boasted would last for a thousand years. By stepping out of time, Hess has been rendered almost timeless, forgotten by many of his contemporaries, unknown to a new generation. Yet surely the greatest ironies of this strange story are that the prophet of *lebensraum* —of room to live—should have lived for so long in a prison cell; and the Nazi who sought to end the war was sentenced for crimes against peace.

'Reflecting upon the whole of this story,' wrote Churchill in his memoirs, 'I am glad not to be responsible for the way in which Hess has been and is being treated.

'Whatever may be the moral guilt of a German who stood near to Hitler, Hess had, in my view, atoned for this by his completely devoted and fanatic deed of lunatic benevolence.

'He came to us of his own free will and, though without authority, had something of the quality of an envoy. He was a medical and not a criminal case, and should be so regarded.'

APPENDIX I

(The following letters are reprinted by courtesy of Her Majesty's Stationery Office. They are taken from *Documents in German Foreign Policy* (1918–1945), Series D, vol. XI; *The War Years*, September 1, 1940–January 31, 1941, published by H.M.S.O.)

C109/C002185–87 (1)

Dr Karl Haushofer to Dr Albrecht Haushofer

Munich, September 3, 1940.

Dearest Albrecht: Cordial thanks for your letter of the 29th[1] from the Hotel Imperial in Vienna. I had almost a vague premonition that you might be there.

If you composed your birthday letter to me in the air raid cellar, I could have reciprocated this kind service on the night of the 1st and 2nd because I promised your mother when I left the mountain cabin to go down when the alarm sounded and consequently spent $1\frac{1}{2}$ hours in exercise and gymnastics.

For, as with you, everything has changed with us too. Through Lisa's sudden departure, which you witnessed, mother's trip to the Hart became unnecessary. Because her stomach and knee both took a turn for the worse, she remained at the Alpine cabin and, only because everything was so arranged, let me go down to the valley alone from the 31st to the 3rd. But I was rewarded, for it brought me a meeting with Tomo[2] from 5:00 o'clock in the afternoon until 2:00 o'clock in the morning, which included a 3-hour walk in the Grünwalder Forest, at which we conversed a good deal about serious matters. I have really got to tell you about a part of it now.

As you know, everything is so prepared for a very hard and severe attack on the island in question that the highest ranking person only has to press a button to set it off. But before this decision, which is perhaps inevitable, the thought once more occurs as to whether there is really no way of stopping something which would have such infinitely momentous consequences. There is a line of reasoning in connection with this which I must absolutely pass on to you because it was obviously communicated to me with this intention. Do you, too, see no way in which such possibilities could be discussed at a third place with a middle man, possibly the old Ian Hamilton[3] or the other Hamilton?[4]

[1] Not found.
[2] The name given to Rudolf Hess in this correspondence.
[3] Sir Ian S. M. Hamilton (1853–1947), British general and author.
[4] On the basis of references later in this correspondence the reference here is to Douglas Douglas-Hamilton, Duke of Hamilton.

I replied to these suggestions that there would perhaps have been an excellent opportunity for this in Lisbon at the Centennial,[1] if, instead of harmless figureheads, it had been possible to send well-disguised political persons there. In this connection it seems to me a stroke of fate that our old friends, Missis (*sic*) V.R., evidently, though after long delay, finally found a way of sending a note with cordial and gracious words of good wishes not only for your mother, but also for Heinz[2] and me, and added the address.

Address your reply to: Miss V. Roberts, c/o Postbox 506, Lisbon, Portugal.[3] I have the feeling that no good possibility should be overlooked; at least it should be well considered.

C109/C002188–89.   (2)

Rudolf Hess to Dr Karl Haushofer at present at Gallspach

September 10, 1940.

Dear Friend: Albrecht brought me your letter,[4] which, at the beginning, besides containing official information, alluded to our walk together on the last day of August, which I, too, recall with so much pleasure.

Albrecht will have told you about our conversation, which beside volksdeutch matters, above all touched upon the other matter, which is so close to the hearts of us both. I reconsidered the latter carefully once more and have arrived at the following conclusion:

Under no condition must we disregard the contact or allow it to die aborning. I consider it best that you or Albrecht write to the old lady, who is a friend of your family, suggesting that she try to ask Albrecht's friend whether he would be prepared if necessary to come to the neutral territory in which she resides, or at any rate has an address through which she can be reached, just to talk with Albrecht.

If he could not do this just now, he might, in any case, send word through her where he expected to be in the near future. Possibly a neutral acquaintance, who had some business to attend to over there anyway, might look him up and make some communication to him, using you or Albrecht as reference.

This person probably would not care to have to inquire as to his whereabouts only after he got there or to make futile trips. You thought that knowing about his whereabouts had no military significance at all; if necessary, you would also pledge yourselves not to make use of it with regard to any quarter which might profit from it. What the neutral would

[1] On June 2, 1940, Portugal had begun a series of celebrations commemorating the 800th anniversary of the foundation of the state and 300th anniversary of the restoration of national independence.

[2] Dr Heinz Haushofer, brother of Albrecht.

[3] This sentence is in English in the original.

[4] See letter No. 1.

have to transmit would be of such great importance that his having made known his whereabouts would be by comparison insignificant.

The prerequisite naturally was that the inquiry in question and the reply would not go through official channels, for you would not in any case want to cause your friends over there any trouble.

It would be best to have the letter to the old lady with whom you are acquainted delivered through a confidential agent of the AO to the address that is known to you. For this purpose Albrecht would have to speak either with Bohle or my brother. At the same time the lady would have to be given the address of this agent in L.—or if the latter does not live there permanently, of another agent of the AO who does live there permanently, to which the reply can in turn be delivered.

As for the neutral I have in mind, I would like to speak to you orally about it some time. There is no hurry about that since, in any case, there would first have to be a reply received here from over there.

Meanwhile let's both keep our fingers crossed. Should success be the fate of the enterprise, the oracle given to you with regard to the month of August would yet be fulfilled, since the name of the young friend and the old lady friend of your family occurred to you during our quiet walk on the last day of that month.

With best regards to you and to Martha,

Yours, as ever,

R(UDOLF) H(ESS)

Can be reached by telephone through: Linz-Gallspach A.

C109/C002190–94 (3)

Memorandum by Dr Albrecht Haushofer

Berlin, September 15, 1940

TOP SECRET

ARE THERE STILL POSSIBILITIES OF A GERMAN-ENGLISH PEACE?

On September 8, I was summoned to Bad G. to report to the Deputy of the Führer[1] on the subject discussed in this memorandum. The conversation which the two of us had alone lasted 2 hours. I had the opportunity to speak in all frankness.

I was immediately asked about the possibilities of making known to persons of importance in England Hitler's serious desire for peace. It was quite clear that the continuance of the war was suicidal for the white race. Even with complete success in Europe, Germany was not in a position to take over inheritance of the Empire. The Führer had not wanted to see the Empire destroyed and did not want it even today. Was there not somebody in England who was ready for peace?

First I asked for permission to discuss fundamental things. It was neces-

---

[1] Rudolf Hess.

sary to realize that not only Jews and Freemasons, but practically all Englishmen who mattered, regarded a treaty signed by the Führer as a worthless scrap of paper. To the question as to why this was so, I referred to the 10-year term of our Polish Treaty,[1] to the Non-Aggression Pact with Denmark signed only a year ago,[2] to the 'final' frontier demarcation of Munich.[3] What guarantee did England have that a new treaty would not be broken again at once if it suited us? It must be realized that, even in the Anglo-Saxon world, the Führer was regarded as Satan's representative on earth and had to be fought.

If the worst came to the worst, the English would rather transfer their whole Empire bit by bit to the Americans than sign a peace that left to National Socialist Germany the mastery of Europe. The present war, I am convinced, shows that Europe has become too small for its previous anarchic form of existence; it is only through close German-English co-operation that it can achieve a true federative order (based by no means merely on the police rule of a single power), while maintaining a part of its world position and having security against Soviet Russian Eurasia. France was smashed, probably for a long time to come, and we had opportunity currently to observe what Italy is capable of accomplishing. As long, however, as German-English rivalry existed, and in so far as both sides thought in terms of security, the lesson of this war was this: Every German had to tell himself: we have no security as long as provision is not made that the Atlantic gateways of Europe from Gibraltar to Narvik are free of any possible blockade. That is: there must be no English fleet. Every Englishman, must, however, under the same conditions, argue: we have no security as long as anywhere within a radius of 2,000 kilometres from London there is a plane that we do not control. That is: there must be no German air force.

There is only one way out of this dilemma: friendship intensified to fusion, with a joint fleet, a joint air force, and joint defence of possessions in the world—just what the English are now about to conclude with the United States.

Here I was interrupted and asked why, indeed, the English were prepared to seek such a relationship with America and not with us. My reply was: because Roosevelt is a man, and represents a Weltanschauung and a way of life, that the Englishman thinks he understands, to which he can become accustomed, even where it does not seem to be to his liking. Perhaps he fools himself—but, at any rate, that is what he believes.

A man like Churchill—himself half-American—is convinced of it. Hitler, however, seems to the Englishman the incarnation of what he hates, that he has fought against for centuries—this feeling grips the workers no less than the plutocrats.

---

[1] See series C, vol. II, document No. 219.
[2] See vol. VI of the H.M.S.O. series, document No. 461.
[3] See vol. II of the H.M.S.O. series, document No. 675.

In fact, I am of the opinion that those Englishmen who have property to lose, that is, precisely the portions of the so-called plutocracy that count, are those who would be readiest to talk peace.

But even they regard a peace only as an armistice. I was compelled to express these things so strongly because I ought not—precisely because of my long experience in attempting to effect a settlement with England in the past and my numerous English friendships—to make it appear that I seriously believe in the possibility of a settlement between Adolf Hitler and England in the present stage of development. I was thereupon asked whether I was not of the opinion that feelers had perhaps not been successful because the right language had not been used. I replied that, to be sure—if certain persons, whom we both knew well, were meant by this statement—then certainly the wrong language had been used. But at the present stage this had little significance. I was then asked directly why all Englishmen were so opposed to Herr v. R(ibbentrop). I conceded, that, in the eyes of the English, Herr v. R., like some other personages, played, to be sure, the same role as did Duff Cooper, Eden, and Churchill in the eyes of the Germans. In the case of Herr v. R., there was also the conviction, precisely in the view of Englishmen who were formerly friendly to Germany that—from completely biased motives—he had informed the Führer wrongly about England and that he personally bore an unusually large share of the responsibility for the outbreak of the war.

But I again stressed the fact that the rejection of peace feelers by England was today due not so much to persons as to the fundamental outlook mentioned above.

Nevertheless, I was asked to name those whom I thought might be reached as possible contacts.

I mentioned among diplomats, Minister O'Malley in Budapest,[1] the former head of the Southeastern Department of the Foreign Office, a clever person in the higher echelons of officialdom, but perhaps without influence precisely because of his former friendliness toward Germany; Sir Samuel Hoare, who is half-shelved and half on the watch in Madrid, whom I do not know well personally, but to whom I can at any time open a personal path; as the most promising, the Washington Ambassador Lothian, with whom I have had close personal connections for years, who as a member of the highest aristocracy and at the same time as a person of very independent mind, is perhaps best in a position to undertake a bold step—provided that he could be convinced that even a bad and uncertain peace would be better than the continuance of the war—a conviction at which he will only arrive if he convinces himself in Washington that English hopes of America are not realizable.

Whether or not this is so could only be judged in Washington itself; from Germany not at all. As the final possibility I then mentioned that of a personal meeting on neutral soil with the closest of my English friends:

[1] Owen St. Clair O'Malley, British Minister in Hungary since 1939.

the young Duke of Hamilton, who has access at all times to all important persons in London, even to Churchill and the King. I stressed in this case the inevitable difficulty of making a contact and again repeated my conviction of the improbability of its succeeding—whatever approach we took.

The upshot of the conversation was H.'s statement that he would consider the whole matter thoroughly once more and send me word in case I was to take steps. For this extremely ticklish case, and in the event that I might possibly have to make a trip alone—I asked for very precise directives from the highest authority. From the whole conversation I had the strong impression that it was not conducted without the prior knowledge of the Führer, and that I probably would not hear any more about the matter unless a new understanding had been reached between him and his Deputy.

On the personal side of the conversation I must say that—despite the fact that I felt bound to say unusually hard things—it ended in great friendliness, even cordiality. I spent the night in Bad G, and the next morning still had the opportunity, on a walk together in the presence of the Chief Adjutant, to bring up all the volksdeutsch questions from the resettlement in all parts of Europe to the difficulties as to personnel in the central offices in Berlin—which resulted in H.'s direct intervention.

A(LBRECHT H(AUSHOFER)

C109/C002197–202 (4)

Dr Albrecht Haushofer to his Parents

Berlin, September 19, 1940

Dear Parents: I am sending you enclosed herewith some important documents:

First, T.'s letter to Father;[1]

Secondly, my answer to T.,[2] which has already been sent and, I hope, has your subsequent approval.

Thirdly, the draft of a letter to D.,[3] which I will keep to myself and not show to anyone else. I request that you examine it to see whether it might involve any danger for the woman who may transmit it. I really believe that it sounds harmless enough. I have inserted the reference to the 'authorities' over there purposely as a safeguard for the transmitter and recipient. So I should like to have your honest opinion and any corrections.

Fourthly a report of what I said on the 8th in G.,[4]—as an accounting before history (save till the last).

[1] Letter No. 2.
[2] Enclosure 1.
[3] Enclosure 2.
[4] Letter No. 3.

APPENDIX I

The whole thing is a fool's errand,[1] but we cannot do anything about that. According to our latest reports the treaties of union between the Empire and the United States are about to be signed.

Best wishes,

ALBRECHT.

Enclosure 1

September 19, 1940

TOP SECRET

My Dear Herr Hess: Your letter of the 10th[2] reached me yesterday after a delay caused by the antiquated postal service of Partnach-Alm. I again gave a thorough study to the possibilities discussed therein and request—before taking the steps proposed—that you yourself examine once more the thoughts set forth below.

I have in the meantime been thinking of the technical route by which a message from me must travel before it can reach the Duke of H(amilton). With your help, delivery to Lisbon can of course be assured without difficulty. About the rest of the route we do not know. Foreign control must be taken into account; the letter must therefore in no case be composed in such a way that it will simply be seized and destroyed or that it will directly endanger the woman transmitting it or the ultimate recipient.

In view of my close personal relations and intimate acquaintance with Douglas H(amilton) I can write a few lines to him (which should be enclosed with the letter to Mrs R., without any indication of place and without a full name—an A. would suffice for signature) in such a way that he alone will recognize that behind my wish to see him in Lisbon there is something more serious than a personal whim. All the rest, however, seems to be extremely hazardous and detrimental to the success of the letter.

Let us suppose that the case were reversed: an old lady in Germany receives a letter from an unknown source abroad, with a request to forward a message whose recipient is asked to disclose to an unknown foreigner where he will be staying for a certain period—and this recipient were a high officer in the air force (of course I do not know exactly what position H. holds at the moment; judging from his past I can conceive of only three things: he is an active air force general, or he directs the air defence of an important part of Scotland, or he has a responsible position in the Air Ministry.)

I do not think that you need much imagination to picture to yourself the faces that Canaris or Heydrich would make and the smirk with which they would consider any offer of 'security' or 'confidence' in such a letter if a subordinate should submit such a case to them. They would not

[1] The preceding part of this sentence is in English in the original.
[2] See letter No. 2.

merely make faces, you may be certain! The measures would come quite automatically—and neither the old lady nor the air force officer would have an easy time of it! In England it is no different.

Now another thing. Here too I would ask you to picture the situation in reverse. Let us assume that I received such a letter from one of my English friends. I would quite naturally report the matter to the highest German authorities I could contact, as soon as I had realized the import it might have, and would ask for instructions on what I should do myself (at that, I am a civilian and H. is an officer).

If it should be decided that I was to comply with the wish for a meeting with my friend, I would then be most anxious to get my instructions if not from the Führer himself, at least from a person who receives them directly and at the same time has the gift of transmitting the finest and lightest nuances—an art which has been mastered by you yourself but not by all Reich Ministers. In addition, I should very urgently request that my action be fully covered—vis-à-vis other high authorities of my own country—uninformed or unfavourable.

It is not any different with H. He cannot fly to Lisbon—any more than I can!—unless he is given leave, that is unless at least Air Minister Sinclair and Foreign Minister Halifax know about it. If, however, he receives permission to reply or to go, there is no need of indicating any place in England; if he does not receive it, then any attempt through a neutral mediator would also have little success.

In this case the technical problem of contacting H. is the least of the difficulties. A neutral who knows England and can move about in England —presumably there would be little sense in entrusting anyone else with such a mission—will be able to find the first peer of Scotland very quickly as long as conditions in the Isle are still halfway in order. (At the time of a successful invasion all the possibilities we are discussing here would be pointless anyway.)

My proposal is therefore as follows:

Through the old friend I will write a letter to H.—in a form that will incriminate no one but will be understandable to the recipient—with the proposal for a meeting in Lisbon. If nothing comes of that, it will be possible (if the military situation leaves enough time for it), assuming that a suitable intermediary is available, to make a second attempt through a neutral going to England, who might be given a personal message to take along. With respect to this possibility, I must add, however, that H. is extremely reserved—as many English are toward anyone they do not know personally. Since the entire Anglo-German problem after all springs from a most profound crisis in mutual confidence, this would not be immaterial.

Please excuse the length of this letter; I merely wished to explain the situation to you fully.

I already tried to explain to you not long ago that, for the reasons I gave, the possibilities of successful efforts at a settlement between the Führer and the British upper class seem to me—to my extreme regret—infinitesimally small.

Nevertheless I should not want to close this letter without pointing out once more that I still think there would be a somewhat greater chance of success in going through Ambassador Lothian in Washington or Sir Samuel Hoare in Madrid rather than through my friend H. To be sure, they are—politically speaking—more inaccessible.

Would you send me a line or give me a telephone call with final instructions? If necessary, will you also inform your brother in advance? Presumably I will then have to discuss with him the forwarding of the letter to Lisbon and the arrangement for a cover address for the reply in L(isbon).

With cordial greetings and best wishes for your health.

Yours, etc.

A(LBRECHT H(AUSHOFER)

Enclosure 2

Draft Letter to D.H.[1]

My dear D. . . Even if this letter has only a slight chance of reaching you —there is a chance and I want to make use of it.

First of all to give you a sign of unaltered and unalterable personal attachment. I do hope you have been spared in all this ordeal, and I hope the same is true of your brothers. I heard of your father's deliverance from long suffering; and I heard that your brother-in-law Northumberland lost his life near Dunkerque. I need hardly tell you, how I feel about all that. . . .

Now there is one thing more. If you remember some of my last communications before the war started you will realize that there is a certain significance in the fact that I am, at present, able to ask you whether there is the slightest chance of our meeting and having a talk somewhere on the outskirts of Europe, perhaps in Portugal. There are some things I could tell you, that might make it worth while for you to try a short trip to Lisbon—if you could make your authorities understand so much that they would give you leave. As to myself—I could reach Lisbon any time (without any kind of difficulty) within a few days after receiving news from you. If there is an answer to this letter, please address it to . . .

---

[1] The draft letter is in English in the original. The Duke of Hamilton's report of his interview with Hess on May 11, 1941, is printed in Trial of the Major War Criminals Before the International Military Tribunal (Nuremberg, 1948), vol. xxxviii, document No. 116-M. This refers to a letter dated September 23, 1940, from Albrecht Haushofer. This excerpt is evidently a draft of that letter. See also Rainer Hildebrandt Wir sind die Letzten: Aus dem Leben des Widerstandskampfers Albrecht Haushofer und seiner Freunde (Neuwied-Berlin, n.d.), p. 110.

C109/C002203 (5)

Dr Albrecht Haushofer to Rudolph Hess

September 23, 1940

My dear Herr Hess: In accordance with your last telephone call I got in touch with your brother immediately. Everything went off well, and I can now report that the mission has been accomplished to the extent that the letter you desired was written and dispatched this morning.[1] It is to be hoped that it will be more efficacious than sober judgment would indicate.

Yours, etc.

H(AUSHOFER)

C109/C002204–05 (6)

Dr Albrecht Haushofer to Dr Karl Haushofer

Berlin, September 23, 1940

Dear Father: I am enclosing the copy of a short letter[2] of serious contents, which perhaps had better be kept by you than by me. I have now made it clear enough that in the action involved I did not take the initiative . . .

Now to the English matters. I am convinced, as before, that there is not the slightest prospect of peace; and so I don't have the least faith in the possibility about which you know. However, I also believe that I could not have refused my services any longer. You know that for myself I do not see any possibility of any satisfying activity in the future . . .

Best regards to both of you.

ALBRECHT

[1] See letter No. 4,
[2] See letter No. 5. enclosures 1 and 2, and footnote 1 on previous page.

APPENDIX II

Translation of Affidavit of Dr Friedrich Gaus, dated March 15, 1946[1]

About noon on August 23 [1939] the plane in which I was travelling with the Reichsaussenminister, landed at Moscow. I was acting as his legal adviser in regard to certain negotiations with the Government of the Soviet Union.

Later in the afternoon the discussion started between von Ribbentrop and Stalin. I was not present, but the Reichsaussenminister took part and also a Councillor from the Embassy Hilger, who acted as an interpreter. Also present was Ambassador Count Schulenburg.

The outcome seemed to be a happy one for the Reichsaussenminister, who expressed the opinion that Germany would be successful in her proposals.

In the evening a second discussion took place for the purpose of completing and signing the necessary documents. I had prepared the draft for Herr von Ribbentrop, and I took part in the discussion. Ambassador Count Schulenburg and the Councillor from the Embassy Hilger were also there. Stalin and Molotov carried on the negotiations for the Russian side aided by Pawlow as interpreter.

An agreement was quickly reached regarding the Non-Aggression-Pact between Germany and Soviet Russia, but a phrase regarding the friendly shaping of German-Russian relations was objected to by Stalin, who said that the Soviet Government could not suddenly publicize a German-Russian friendship after the National Socialist Reichsregierung had poured 'buckets of putrid ditch water' over them for six years, and it was necessary for it to be reworded.

Besides the Non-Aggression-Pact there were negotiations at some length about a special secret document, which in my recollection, was called 'Secret Protocol' or 'Secret Additional Protocol'. This aimed at the delimitation of the mutual spheres of influence in the European territories situated between the two countries. I cannot remember whether the expression 'spheres of influence' was used or not.

In this document Germany said she was disinterested in Latvia, Estonia and Finland, but regarded Lithuania as part of her 'sphere of interest'. At the same time, Germany wanted to have an interest, but not political, in the Baltic ports which were free from ice. This of course was not acceptable to the Russians. Obviously the Reichsaussenminister was acting on instructions, as he had booked a telephone call to Hitler which came through at this time. He was told to accept the Soviet point of view.

[1] Affidavit of Dr Friedrich Gaus, from 'Die Beziehungen zwischen Deutschland und der Sowjetunion 1939–1941. Dokumente des Auswaertigen Amtes.' Herausgegeben von Dr Alfred Seidl, Rechtsanwalt in Muenchen 1949. H. Laupp'sche Buchhandlung/ Tuebingen.

For the Polish territory a demarcation line was fixed. Whether it was marked exactly on a map or described in words in the document, I cannot remember. The agreement reached about Poland was to the effect that both powers should settle all questions concerning that country at a final meeting. Regarding the Balkans, it was established that Germany should have only economic interests.

The Non-Aggression-Pact and the secret document were signed at a rather late hour of the same night.

Approximately one month later at discussions about the second German-Soviet Political Treaty, the document mentioned above was altered—following a suggestion communicated by the Soviet Government to Berlin earlier—to the effect that Lithuania was to be taken out of the German 'sphere of interest' except for a 'lappet' adjacent to East Prussia. In return, however, the demarcation line in Poland was moved further to the East.

At subsequent negotiations, through diplomatic channels, either at the end of 1940 or the beginning of 1941, this Lithuanian 'lappet' was given up by the Germans.

INDEX

Abergavenny, Haushofer locates Hess at, 179; Hess at, 175, 176, 178, 184, 205
Ageing Parachutist, The (Stephen Watts), 32
Aircraft Production, Minister of, 159, 160
Air Ministry (German), 14, 94, 95
Air raids, on Britain, 11, 95, 105, 109 143; affect of, 144; Hess view of, 147
Alexandria, Hess brought up in, 37, 40
Alfieri, 127, 128
Alias used by Hess, 26, 30, 38, 132
American who gave document to Seidl, 207, 215
Amnesia, *see under* Hess, memory
Andrus, Burton C., 194.
Associated Press, 119, 120
Augsburg, Hess flight from, arrival for, 91, 92; leaves, 18, 92 93, 123 practice flights from, 71, 73, 173; unsuccessful flights from, 81
Auschwitz, 41, 192
Auslandorganisation, Hess works with, 43, 203; and peace moves, 50, 221.
Avon, Lord Anthony, *see* Eden

Bad Godesberg, Hess and A. Haushofer at, 51, 221
Badoglio, Marshal Pietro, 183
Baird, Basil, 217
Balmoral 'offered' by Hess, 142
'Barbarossa', *see under* Germany and Russia, invasion
Battle of Britain, 159, 160
Baur, Lt. Gen. Hans, on Hess flight, 71 72, 173; Hitler's pilot, 16
Bavarian Reserve Infantry, 40
Beaverbrook, Lord William Maxwell Aitken, and Churchill: discuss Hess, 161; relations with, 160
and French surrender, 113
and Hess, interviews, 158, 159, 175; peace moves discussed with, 160, 161
as Minister of Aircraft Production, 159, 160
and Stalin, discuss Hess, 162, 163, 215; mission to, 161, 162
Bechstein family, 66
Berchtesgaden, Hitler's home at, 66, 67
Berlin Radio, *see* Radio
Birkett, Sir (Lord) Norman, 195
Bismarck, sinking of, 101
Bodenschatz, General Karl, reaction to Hess flight, 124, 125, 172; 103
Bohle, Ernst Wilhelm, 51, 221
Books, Hess requests, 185; reads at trial, 196
Bormann, Albert, Hitler's adjutant, 98; marriage of, 131; and Pintsch, 98, 99; 102

Bormann, Martin, death of, surmised, 192, 193; and Ilse Hess, 131, 169, 170; and Hess, attitude to, 169, 170, 174; and Hess flight, attitude to, 68, 102, 103, 126; at Hitler's luncheon, 67, 68; position in Nazi party, 43, 67; 167
Bracken, Brendan, 109, 160
Braun, Eva, as friend of Ilse Hess, 169, 170; at Hitler's luncheon, 67, 68, 102; death of, 192
Britain: conditions in, May 1941, 143, 144 after fall of France, 48, 101 and Hess: landing of, silence about, affect on Germany, 122–4; and his peace moves, possible effect, if publicized, 143–5—if successful, 164, 165; release of, wish, 216 invasion of, German needs for, 160 peace with, *see* Peace moves and Russia, aid to, 162, 163 and USA, victory forseen by Hess, 75, 76
war with, Haushofer against, 45, 46
BBC, *see* Radio
British Government: Mission to, Moscow, 1939, 215; Stalin, 1941, 161
Navy, bombard French, 48 prosecutors at Nuremberg, 189
Broadcasting, *see* Radio
Bruckmann, Elsa, 171; Hugo, 171
Buchanan Castle, Military Hospital, Hess at, 39, 61, 104, 107, 114, 118, 134, 136, 138, 152; possible rescue from, 139
Buchenwald, 41
Busby, Home Guard hut at, 32
Busch, Captain, 208

Cabinet Council (secret) of Germany, Hess member of, 12, 41
Cadogan, Sir Alexander, and Hamilton, 107, 109, 112
Canaris, Admiral W. W., 54, 225
Carol, King of Rumania, 101
Casement, Sir Roger, 140
Case of Rudolf Hess (ed. Dr J. R. Rees), 38, 146, 152, 153, 156, 157, 191, 202
Censorship: and *Daily Record*, 116, 117; function of in wartime, 117; and Hess landing story, 64, 65, 115
Chamberlain, Neville, 66, 101
Cherwell, Lord, 109
Churchill, (Sir) Winston, and French surrender, 48, 113
German view of, 52, 222, 223 and Hess: discusses with, Beaverbrook, 159, 160; Hamilton, 108, 110, 111; Roosevelt, 140, 141; Stalin, 164